How Children Think and Learn

Understanding Children's Worlds

General Editor Judy Dunn

The study of children's development can have a profound influence on how children are brought up, cared for and educated. The central aim of this series is to encourage developmental psychologists to set out the findings and the implications of their research for others – teachers, doctors, social workers, students – who are responsible for caring for and teaching children and their families. It aims not to offer simple prescriptive advice to other professionals, but to make important innovative research accessible to them.

How Children Think and Learn

The Social Contexts of
Cognitive Development

DAVID WOOD

Basil Blackwell

First published 1988
Reprinted 1988, 1989

Basil Blackwell Ltd
108 Cowley Road, Oxford OX4 1JF, UK

Basil Blackwell, Inc.
3 Cambridge Center
Cambridge, Massachusetts 02142, USA

British Library Cataloguing in Publication Data

Wood, David
  How children think and learn
  1. Cognition in children
  I. Title
  155.4′13   BF723.C5
  ISBN 0–631–16138–4
  ISBN 0–631–16139–2 Pbk

Library of Congress Cataloging in Publication Data

Wood, David, 1944–
  How children think and learn.
  Bibliography: p.
  Includes index.
  1. Cognition in children.   2. Learning, Psychology of.
I. Title.
BF723.C5W66   1988   155.4′13   87–35531
ISBN 0–631–16138–4
ISBN 0–631–16139–2 (pbk.)

Typeset in 10 on 12pt Palatino
by Columns of Reading
Printed in Great Britain by Page Bros (Norwich) Ltd.

I dedicate this book, with greetings and gratitude, to Jerome S. Bruner

Contents

Acknowledgements

I would like to express my thanks to three colleagues in the Psychology Department at Nottingham, Heather Wood, Amanda Griffiths and Marian Kingsmill, each of whom read and commented upon draft chapters of this book. I am also in debt to Maureen Copley and Margaret Tait, who read my penultimate draft through 'teachers' eyes' and made many useful criticisms and observations. Peter Robinson dedicated a good deal of his time to reading draft chapters and has exerted an important influence on the final product. Needless to say, any deficiencies or inaccuracies remain my responsibility. I would also like to thank David Dingwall and Howard Martin for maintaining a sometimes temperamental computing system which, despite its foibles, makes a writer's task so much easier.

Acknowledgement is given for permission to reproduce the following figures: 2.4: from Margaret Donaldson (1978) *Children's Minds*, William Collin & Co. Ltd, and W. W. Norton & Company, Inc.; 3.1, 3.2 and 3.5: from E. Vurpillot (1976) *The Visual World of the Child*, Allen & Unwin and International Universities Press; 4.1: from J. Bruner and A. Garton (eds) (1978) *Human Growth and Development*, Oxford University Press, based on Clark and Garnica (1974) *Journal of Verbal Learning and Verbal Behavior*, no. 13; 4.2: from A. Karmiloff-Smith (1979) *A Functional Approach to Child Language*, Cambridge University Press; and 7.4: from K. M. Hart (1981) *Children's Understanding of Mathematics: 11-16*, John Murray Ltd.

Introduction

From Pavlov to Piaget

Theories about how children think and learn have been put forward and debated by philosophers, educators and psychologists for centuries. E. B. Castle in his book The Teacher, *for example, explores the historical influences that have helped to shape modern views about children and their growth into adults and citizens. He traces back to Ancient Greece, Rome and Judea competing views on the nature of learning and education that are still debated today. He also discusses the way in which ideas about the nature of infancy and childhood dictate the ways in which we think about teaching and education. Our images of children-as-learners are reflected, inevitably, in our definition of what it means to teach.*

In this book, I will be describing and discussing theories about learning and thinking that have been formulated and explored over the past twenty-five years or so. However, it is important to recognize the fact that contemporary thinking about education, learning and teaching is not 'brand new' or untouched by the work of previous generations of scholars and teachers. Their ideas and insights have been absorbed and transformed over time and translated into modern terms, not eradicated. Although I have chosen to focus on recent developments, mainly for reasons of space, I will try in this chapter to give a brief overview of how and why certain theories of human development, particularly that of Jean Piaget, became prominent and influential in the mid-1960s. I begin with what seem to me to be some of the more important 'landmark' discoveries and observations that have helped to shape contemporary theories of human nature.

Changing perspectives on learning and development

For the past twenty years or so, our thinking about the nature of children's thinking and learning has been dominated by the ideas of Jean Piaget. It should come as no surprise to find frequent references to his theory in this book. Although not an educationalist, nor primarily a psychologist, Piaget's astute observations of children and his extensive theorizing about what these have to tell us about the growth of mind can hardly be ignored in a book about children's learning and thinking. And yet, and this is perhaps surprising, Piaget's theory was neglected for many years, at least by English-speaking psychologists. Although his first works were translated into English in the 1940s, it was not until the mid-1960s that they were given serious consideration by the majority of American and British psychologists.

The rise of learning theory

In a book that he edited in 1964, *Theories of Learning and Instruction*, the American psychologist E. Hilgard predicted that Piaget's views, neglected for twenty years or so, were destined to achieve prominence thereafter. How right he was. But why was the theory neglected for so long, and what was happening in the 1960s that brought it onto centre stage? Well, the major theories and debates that figured in Hilgard's book and had dominated the psychology of learning for several decades were of such a nature that they effectively ruled out any serious consideration of the ideas that Piaget was putting forward. For example, a great deal of thought, time and study had been given to analysing the nature of 'reinforcement' and its role in learning and instruction. Ivan Pavlov, a Russian physiologist and psychologist, had demonstrated in 1927 that it was possible, using quite simple experimental techniques, to teach an animal to make novel 'responses' to new 'stimuli'. For example, given sight of food, a hungry dog will, naturally, salivate. Normally, a 'neutral' stimulus, say the sound of a bell ringing, will have no such effect on the beast. However, if on a number of occasions the bell is made to ring just *before* food is presented to an animal, its sound alone will come, eventually, to evoke the salivation response. From this apparently simple observation grew several different theories of learning.

Psychologists in many parts of the world attempted to discover general *laws* that would lead eventually to a scientific theory of learning. Such theories, and there are several, are usually referred to as 'S–R' or 'learning theory'. Pavlov's experimental demonstrations of animal learning were replicated many thousands of times with different species, focusing on a wide variety of behavioural responses that were conditioned to many types of stimuli and 'reinforced' in a multitude of different ways. Although several alternatives to Pavlov's theory arose out of this research, most shared the same quest: to formulate laws whereby, irrespective of the species, the stimuli, responses or reinforcer used, the relations between the *conditions* of learning (e.g. when and how often a response to a given stimulus was reinforced) and the learning *outcomes* could be predicted. To give but one example, one of the most influential American psychologists, B. F. Skinner (e.g. 1938) demonstrated in many experiments that the best way to guarantee that an animal learns how to make a particular response to a stimulus is *not* to give it reinforcement every time it performs the response. The secret to rapid and enduring learning is what Skinner termed an *intermittent schedule* of reinforcement. His experiments showed that the key to effective teaching (a process that he refers to as 'shaping behaviour') involves only the occasional reinforcement of the desired response. So, for instance, if a hungry rat is being taught to press a lever, only some of the presses should deliver a pellet of food. The experimenter's aim should also be to withdraw reinforcement as quickly as possible.

Basically, what Skinner has shown is that shaping an animal's behaviour to ensure that it maintains the response (that is, it continues to make the response whenever it meets the appropriate stimulus), involves a specific and rather complex relationship between response and reinforcement. It is not simply a case of rewarding behaviour every time it occurs. When Skinner applied his findings on animal learning to the teaching of children, it led him to criticize teachers for not employing effective 'schedules of reinforcement' in the classroom. In 'Why teachers fail', a chapter of his 1968 book, he argued that formal education is usually based on 'aversive control'. Teaching rests on punishment and ridicule for inappropriate behaviour rather than showing a concern for the shaping and reinforcement of responses to be learned. He also claimed that lessons and examinations are designed to reveal what pupils do not know and cannot do, rather than to expose and build upon what they do know and are able to learn. Thus, he argued, teachers fail to 'shape' their children's behaviour effectively, leading to inappropriate learning or to learned responses that are quickly forgotton. Skinner went on to design the first 'learning programs' for use on teaching machines in an attempt to apply his theory to education.

Skinner's observations led to a vast technology of experimental studies of learning. Many different reinforcement schedules were designed, and their effects on the speed of learning and on the retention of what was learned tested out. Such investigations of learning and arguments about the nature of reinforcement – e.g. what *constitutes* a reinforcer for a given species – were at the heart of theory and research in the period between Pavlov's pioneering work and Hilgard's review of the field in the mid-1960s.

The decline of learning theory

Part of the appeal of these approaches to the study of learning was the promise they offered of formulating theories that dealt only with directly *observable* and *manipulable* phenomena. By creating accounts concerned exclusively with 'objective' relationships between conditions of learning and observable responses it was hoped that a science of behaviour could be constructed that needed to make no appeal to 'subjective' mental states such as 'interest' or 'curiosity'.

Many of the contributors to Hilgard's volume had come to the conclusion that this general approach to the study of learning and the many seemingly intractable problems that it was facing was ceasing to be productive or profitable. The reasons for the rise in scepticism and a search for new concepts and methods were many, varied and complicated. We will not explore them in detail here. However, I will give a few examples to help to explain why the psychological territory of the time proved fertile to Piaget's ideas.

In one of the chapters in Hilgard's book, Pribram, an American psychologist, makes favourable reference to Piaget's theory and attempts to integrate some of its insights with his own ideas. Pribram had undertaken a number of research studies into animal learning. He cites observations which helped to convince him that external reinforcement was *not* a necessary condition for learning, thus questioning the very foundations of the then dominant theories of learning and instruction. In one study, for instance, a monkey was being conditioned to operate a bit of machinery that, when a lever was pulled, delivered a reinforcing peanut on an intermittent basis. The animal was left free to operate the lever for as long as it so 'desired'. When a reinforcer appeared, the monkey would often 'store' it in its foodpouch (located inside the mouth). It did not, then, always consume the peanut after a 'reinforced' response. Occasionally, when no peanut appeared after a pull on the lever, the animal would take a peanut from its pouch and eat it. In so doing, it reinforced itself after a supposedly non-reinforcing trial (thus somewhat defeating the psychologist's attempt to put it on a specific, pre-determined schedule!). As the experiment continued, there came a point at which the animal's food pouch was fully stuffed and its cheeks bulged to capacity. Despite being satiated and, hence, unlikely to profit from further 'reinforcement', it continued to operate the lever. Hands and feet stuffed with peanuts, the monkey began to chuck nuts out of the cage but still operated the lever to gain more.

Such observations led Pribram and many other psychologists of his time to question the assumption that external reinforcement of the sort implicated in some theories of learning was a necessary condition for learning to take place. One could speculate about Pribram's monkey in several ways. Perhaps the animal continued to operate the equipment not for nutritional gains but more for the 'pleasure' of playing with it. Was it trying to 'outwit' the schedule, like a gambler, by attempting to work out the 'rules' governing payoff? Whatever the reason, it seemed to Pribram that the *activity* itself held some *intrinsic* interest for the animal.

Piaget's theory, as we shall see, places *action* and self-directed problem-solving at the heart of learning and development. By acting on the world, the learner comes to discover how to control it. In human beings, learning how to act on the world and discovering the consequences of action form the bedrock of thinking itself. As psychologists studying learning began to entertain (or, more accurately, to re-entertain) ideas about intrinsic motivation and the importance of activity and mastery for its 'own sake', Piaget's theory provided a compatible and already well-developed approach to the study of learning and development. The time was right for the theory to be taken seriously.

Piaget's theory also seemed to provide answers to several other difficult problems. For instance, many references are found in Hilgard to the phenomenon of 'critical periods' for learning. Whilst animals and humans are able to learn some things with little effort at certain points in their life cycle, they seem incapable of learning the same things at other times. So, for example, learning to walk and, as we shall see, learning to talk, seem to follow a natural time-scale. Attempts to teach very young children to talk, for instance, will fail. Once 'ready', however, they seem to learn how to talk 'naturally' and without any deliberate or conscious teaching by adults. If exposure to a language is left late, say into puberty, the nature of any learning that takes place is of a different kind. Learning a second language involves psychologically different processes to those which make mother-tongue acquisition possible. Piaget's theory, as we shall see, offers a detailed and specific account of universal *stages* in human development which provided a possible explanation as to when and how a child is ready to learn or develop specific forms of knowledge and understanding. Attempts to teach the products of a 'later' stage before previous stages have been passed through cannot facilitate development nor can it foster understanding. So, Piaget's theory offered a 'ready made' explanation for critical periods in the development of human intelligence: its time had arrived.

Although Hilgard anticipated the surge of interest in Piaget's theory, he was not in a position to envisage the directions that debates and arguments about it would take. Indeed, many of the specific issues that have grown up around the theory find no mention in Hilgard's bibliography or index. One central theme that you will find running through the chapters of my book concerns the nature of the relationship between talking and thinking. Although 'verbal behavior' is listed in Hilgard's index the term 'language', and related words like 'talking' and 'listening', are not mentioned. This was a sign of the times. Psychologists interested in learning had, it seems, yet to read or to digest the early works of Noam Chomsky, an American linguist. These started to appear in print in the late 1950s. They were to inflict a serious, some would say lethal, blow to learning-theory accounts of how children learn their 'verbal behaviour'. Indeed, Chomsky's theory led some students of language development to reject the idea that children are *taught* how to talk at all, as we will see in chapter 4.

Piaget and Chomsky were united in their opposition to the view that human learning can be understood in terms of the reinforcement of connections between stimuli and responses, but offer very different perspectives on the nature of language and its development. Briefly, for we will look at the issue at greater length in later chapters, Piaget's theory leads to the claim that a child's ability to understand what is said to him and, in turn, his ability to use language informatively, depends upon his stage of intellectual development. This view leads to a number of *explicit* predictions about when children *can* learn how to talk and, when they do so, what they will understand by what they say and hear. Young children's understanding of terms like 'if . . . then', 'as much as', 'the same as', 'more than' and 'because', for example, differ from the meaning put upon them by older children and adults. At a deeper level, the theory also predicts that young children at certain stages of development are theoretically incapable of *expressing* ideas that involve the ability to understand the world from another person's point of view. What they are able to say is constrained by their stage of development. Chomskian theorists, on the other hand, argue that the course of specifically *linguistic* development, like the child's use and understanding of *grammar*, cannot be understood simply in terms of stages of intellectual development nor in terms of communication skills. The child, in this view, possesses a natural capacity to discover how language is structured. Language development is a 'special' affair and cannot be explained in terms of the child's general knowledge of the world. This seemingly remote and academic argument, as I hope to demonstrate later in the book, has important implications for the way in which we view children's abilities to think, learn and understand.

Another important series of questions and issues that received no mention in Hilgard's book but which have since achieved great significance, also revolve around arguments about the nature of language and its role in learning and education. In the 1960s the USA was, as it remains today, a multi-cultural and multi-lingual society. However, students of learning had yet to address the many important questions this state of affairs raises for education and teaching. In the UK, Basil Bernstein (1960), a sociologist, was about to announce what was to become an influential and controversial thesis about the relations between socio-economic class and language. He put forward the view that differences in the average levels of academic achievement attained by children from different home backgrounds could be understood and explained in terms of the ways in which language is used and structured in different social groups. Children from diverse social groups learn how to use and understand language in different ways. Such linguistic differences affect adjustment to, communication in, and learning at, school. Seizing upon these ideas, educational theorists and researchers in the USA extended them to provide 'explanations' as to why American black children fared less well in school, on average, than their white peers. This, as we will see in chapter 4, was to have a dramatic effect on political action in both the USA and the UK as both societies attempted to ensure greater equality of opportunity for less well-off children by state action designed, amongst other things, to overcome 'linguistic deprivation'. Here too, academic debate about the relation between language and thought, largely ignored until the late 1960s, spilled over into heated educational and political debate. Bernstein's ideas were also destined to come into conflict with those expressed by Chomsky and other linguists. Is it really the case that some children fail to 'learn' language as some American theorists seemed to suppose? If children acquire language naturally, as Chomskians argue, is it theoretically sound to assume that some families 'deprive' their children of language? Such assertions, from a Chomskian perspective, are literally nonsensical. We consider the arguments, and their educational implications, in chapters 4 and 8.

Learning and instruction

Piaget wrote very little about the educational implications of his theory. However, the idea that children pass through stages of development and the assertion that they cannot learn or be taught how to function at 'higher' levels before they have passed through the lower ones, was taken up widely and formed the basis for a new theory of learning *readiness*. Many psychologists and educators (e.g. Schwebel and Raph, 1974) explored the educational ramifications of Piaget's theory and transformed it into curricula, approaches to teaching and a whole philosophy of education. Developmental theory was en route to educational practice. J. S. Bruner, one of the American psychologists who contributed to Hilgard's book, was also beginning to formulate a theory of instruction which, though similar in some respects to Piaget's views, differed radically from them in a number of other ways, particularly in relation to the notion of developmental stages. Perhaps the different perspectives are best introduced with a very brief account of the intellectual background and motivation of these two theorists.

Piaget and Bruner

Piaget's academic roots lay in biology. As a teenager, for instance, he had undertaken and published the results of experiments on mollusc growth which gained international acclaim (Boden, 1979) and an invitation to become curator of a museum in Switzerland! His main quest, which motivated his studies of children, was to create an integrated theory of biology and philosophy of mind. For reasons we explore later, he went on to explain the evolution of mind and intelligence in terms of the development and realization of *logic*. He also sought common principles that would establish a theoretical continuity between biological and mental evolution and would help us to understand the origins and development of logical, mathematical and scientific thought. Though he studied the thinking and understanding of children and adolescents in breadth and depth, he did not, as far as I know, conduct any extensive or systematic studies of adult thinking. What he did do, however, was to provide explanations to mathematicians and natural scientists about the genetic and developmental foundations of their theories. For example, he lectured to physicists on the relation between time, velocity and distance and suggested that by looking at the formation of these concepts in children, they might understand how their own formal concepts of time and space evolved and discover their 'primitive' intellectual foundations. His views on concepts of time and space motivated Einstein to ask him if the origins of the theory of relativity could be understood in developmental terms. This question, according to Boden, led to theoretical work by Piaget's physicist colleagues who provided such an account.

Some of Bruner's early research was concerned with the study and analysis of adult reasoning. Working with others (Bruner, Goodnow and Austin, 1956) he undertook a series of experimental studies which convinced him that people do not utilize a single 'method' or 'logic' in reasoning and problem solving: instead they adopt one of a number of *strategies* that differ in scope, power and efficiency. Whereas Piaget was interested primarily in the *structure* of mature thinking, Bruner sought to describe the different *processes* that are implicated in creative problem-solving. Such processes, in Bruner's view, vary from individual to individual and from discipline to discipline (e.g. Bruner, 1966a, 1971).

The similarities between the two theories are, however, of equal interest. Both place emphasis on the importance of *action* and problem-solving in learning. They also adopted a similar position with regard to the different ways in which knowledge can be 'represented' or embodied, as we will see in chapter 7. Abstract thinking, in both accounts, should grow out of, be abstracted *from*, material actions. From both perspectives, teaching that teaches children only how to manipulate abstract procedures (e.g. learning how to solve equations) without first establishing the deep connections between such procedures and the activities involved in the solution of practical, concrete problems (which the procedures serve to represent at a more abstract level) is bound to fail. Children will only *understand* and generalize lessons about abstract mathematics, for example, if these are grounded in practical problem-solving. Where the two theories part company is in relation to the value of formal *logic* as a description of the ultimate 'destination' of intellectual development. Bruner argues that logic is not the basis for mature, adaptive thinking; rather, it is one of several 'special' ways of thinking. The rejection of logic as a framework for understanding the nature and development of thinking leads on to many other points of disagreement.

Another aspect of Bruner's psychology, in comparison to Piaget's, is a greater emphasis on the role of language, communication and instruction in the development of knowledge and understanding. For Bruner, the *processes* that underlie intelligent and adaptive thinking are not exclusive inventions of the child. Rather, they are *communicated*, albeit in subtle ways, from the more mature to the immature. Whilst Piaget does provide a role for social interaction and communication in his theory, it plays a far less important part in the development of intelligence than it does in Bruner's account. Another major theme, perhaps the main one, that permeates this book, is a discussion of these proposed relations between instruction, communication, learning and thinking. Different theories about the character of these relationships lead to radically different views on the nature and the importance of teaching in development, as we shall see.

Vygotsky and Bruner

Two years before Hilgard's book was published, Bruner had written an introduction to a book entitled *Language and Thought*, a translation of a work first written in 1936 by a Soviet psychologist, L. S. Vygotsky. Like Bruner and quite unlike Piaget, Vygotsky also placed *instruction* at the very heart of human development. Indeed, he defined intelligence itself as the capacity to *learn* through instruction. Vygotsky's views received no mention in Hilgard. Indeed, the assimilation of his thinking into Western psychology has been slow. With a few exceptions, like Bruner (and Piaget), students of human learning and thinking have made little reference to his ideas. The signs are, however, that interest in his views (and those of Soviet psychology more generally) is starting to feature more prominently in Western psychology. For instance, a book edited in 1984 by James Wertsch is dedicated to the exploration of Vygotsky's perspectives on human development and includes chapters by American, European and Soviet contributors. I will refer to some of its content later in the book.

Vygotsky's thinking on development is difficult to summarize in a few words. Let me make a few preliminary comments here to provide some sense of the directions that his approach points us towards. Like Bruner, who was influenced by him, Vygotsky puts language and communication (and, hence, instruction) at the core of intellectual and personal development. What is unique about Vygotsky's account is its scope and its philosophical foundations. Unlike Piaget, with a background in biology and natural sciences, Vygotsky's primary concern lay in understanding the nature, evolution and transmission of human culture. His early work included the study and analysis of 'representation' in art and literature. His perspective on psychology reflected his views on the *historical* and *cultural* origins of the way in which people in different societies come to act upon, construe and represent their world. So, where Piaget sought to unify biology, natural science and psychology, Vygotsky's quest was to integrate psychology with an analysis of history, art, literature, cultural activity and sociology. He sought nothing less than a coherent theory of the humanities and social sciences. As we shall see, these very different theoretical orientations lead to different images of childhood and schooling.

Uncertainty and information

The invention of Morse, radio, radar and other electronic means of communication has had, and continues to have, a profound effect on psychological theory. The development and perfection of electronic communication systems was made possible not only by the creation of new gadgets and hardware but also by the development of communications theory. As we will see in the next three chapters, some psychologists drew upon these theoretical developments in electronics to create new analogies for thinking about and constructing mathematical 'models' of human abilities. The conception of people as 'limited information processing systems' developed apace during the years of the Second World War when a generation of psychologists put their knowledge and skills to work in a number of areas such as the construction of tests for personnel selection and the development of training techniques. They also helped to design the machines of war and instruments of defence, detection and communication to take account of what has become known as 'human factors'.

Effective 'communication' between man and machine and the skilful control of complex systems demands designs that do not overtax or exceed people's abilities to attend to, monitor and react to the behaviour of the system under control. We are able to attend to just so much information at any one moment and the assimilation of information and adaptive responses to it demands time. Any system that provides too much critical information at any one moment or which leaves the human operator with too little time to interpret and react to it makes inhuman demands and cannot be controlled. So, for instance, the design of instrument panels in aircraft and the layout of aircraft runway lights incorporate results from psychological analyses of human information processing abilities (e.g. Gibson, 1950). These helped to maximize the probability of effective pilot reactions and to minimize the possibility of pilot error.

Information processing

During the 1950s and 1960s, the use of mathematical models to try to provide explicit, formal theories of human abilities became a major area of research in psychology. Although attempts to generate very precise models failed for a number of interesting (but currently irrelevant) reasons, the view of man as an information processor remains a powerful metaphor in the discipline. I think it is fair to say that the information processing approach in psychology provides a *language* for constructing 'models' of specific areas of human activity (for instance, to describe how we go about solving mathematics problems). It is not a 'theory' in the strong sense so much as a set of related terms and concepts that enable certain types of theory to be constructed. Don't worry if this seems rather abstract and vague at the moment: we will be exploring specific examples in later chapters.

The information processing approach in psychology provided a new language and an 'image' of man to rival S–R (Stimulus–Response) approaches. To illustrate the difference between the two perspectives, imagine the following. As I am writing this section, I have a cup of coffee by the side of my computer terminal. Every so often, I reach out to grasp the cup and take a swallow. Usually, I begin to reach out for the cup whilst reading what I have just written. Just before my hand reaches the cup, I glance towards it to make sure that I am poised in a suitable position to pick it up and lift it to my lips. One could describe my behaviour as a series of responses, each triggered by a specific stimulus. The language of information processing, however, provides a very different account.

Were my movements to be filmed, on several different occasions, each episode of picking up and drinking from the cup would be unique in some fine detail. My 'responses' may be similar in effect, but they are not identical in form. In what sense can they be called the 'same' response?

My *goal*, each time I reach for the cup, is the same and the achievement of that goal rests upon the same consequence (i.e. ingestion of coffee). However, the *means* to obtain the goal differ in detail on each occasion. The precise position of my body as I begin to reach, the exact location of the cup and the trajectory of my hand and arm towards it, vary each time. My cup-lifting behaviour, unlike that, say, of a two-year-old child, is usually extremely *skilful*, so much so that, again unlike a two-year-old, I do not need to pay much *attention* to the act of picking it up. Given that each action is unique, it is reasonable to assume that I must be exerting some continuous *control* over my movement. Should I, for example, over-reach and brush the cup with my sleeve, I am likely to switch my attention to take more 'care' over what I am doing. Although I do not appear to be attending to what I am doing, when things begin to go wrong my swift shift of attention betrays the fact that somehow I was monitoring my own activity whilst the main focus of my attention lay elsewhere.

Changing the description of human activity from one couched in terms of responses to stimuli to accounts which talk about more-or-less skilled *actions* aimed at goals, represents a major shift in theoretical orientation. The language of information processing, couched in terms like 'goals', 'attention' and 'control', invites one to think about behaviour in *purposive* terms. The 'same' goal may be achieved by different *means*. So, for instance, should my right hand be occupied when I want a drink, I may reach with my left, or ask someone to pick up the cup for me, and so on. I adapt *means* to *ends* in ways that reflect my interpretation of the current situation and this demands continuous control, even though I am not necessarily aware of being in control all the time.

Information processing theory led to the development of concepts like 'plans', 'skills' and 'strategies', and to a particular way of thinking about 'expertise', a term I will be using a good deal throughout the book. I use this word in preference to the term 'skill' for reasons that are perhaps best outlined here and now. In everyday talk the word 'skill' is usually applied to describe the quality of overt behaviour. We talk, for instance, about football skills, skilled back-hands in tennis or skilfully executed cover drives in cricket. However, the use of this term in psychology, at least since two influential books by Sir F. Bartlett (1932, 1958), also refers to *mental* activity. Bartlett argued that the identification of similarities between skilled physical and mental activities involves more than metaphor. Both involve common elements to do with timing, self-control, error detection and organization.

I use the term *expertise* to draw attention to the fact that *knowledge* and *action*, or concepts and procedures, are two aspects of a single process. Comparisons of expert performance with that of a novice, for example, reveal differences not only in the speed, smoothness and accuracy of their actions but also in the structure of their perception, memory and mental operations. Throughout the book, I will be exploring the notion that the difference between adults and children, in the ability to attend, concentrate, study, reason, talk and solve problems, can profitably be viewed as reflections of different levels of *expertise*. Looked at from this perspective, learning how to learn, think and communicate are described in terms of the acquisition of various kinds of expertise. How this might come about is a major question explored in later chapters.

In this brief opening chapter, I have tried to provide a short and selective overview of some of the perspectives and issues that have arisen during the past century in the field of child development. I have also used my opening pages to introduce most of the main characters and themes that pervade the rest of the book, on the assumption that even a little background knowledge about where different theorists 'came from', and some insight into the source of their interest in children and education, helps one to understand and to evaluate what they have to say. In the next chapter, we look in more depth at some of the 'images of childhood' implicit in the main theories introduced here and begin to explore their educational implications.

Chapter 1

Images of childhood and their reflection in teaching

In this chapter, I describe, in outline, three ways of thinking about the nature of learning and thinking. I try to present and discuss these views in terms of the way in which they invite us to think about the nature of the intellectual abilities of five- to eleven-year-old children. Theories that offer very different accounts of the way in which children think and learn also lead to alternative views on what is involved in teaching them. So, this chapter also revolves around a discussion of what roles the three images of childhood etch out for teachers.

The chapter is also designed to provide a guide to the rest of the book. Some of the ideas involved are difficult and they are often expressed in unfamiliar language. I have tried to keep jargon to a minimum. Where I have felt obliged to introduce uncommon terms, I have provided concrete examples and illustrations to try to convey their meaning. The main themes explored are discussed several times in later chapters, so it is not necessary to grasp or to remember all that is said here. I suggest a quick read to obtain a general sense of what is to come later in the book, rather than a close study of the contents of this chapter. Details come later.

Learning and schooling

About twenty years ago I read my first book on psychology and education. It was Bruner's (1966) influential *Toward a Theory of Instruction*. One of the observations he made in that book was that schools and the social roles they have created (such as 'teacher' and 'pupil') are relatively modern inventions. There are non-techno-logical cultures in which schools do not exist. Indeed, a number of languages have no verb meaning 'to teach' in their vocabulary. The notion that children must be taught in order to learn, let alone the expectation that they will do so in classrooms, is by no means a universal one. Rather, it seems to have been an invention of technological, schooled and literate societies. Another of Bruner's arguments is that the widespread availability of schooling involves far more than a change in the place where (some) learning and development take place. Rather, schools engender new and distinct *forms* of learning and lead to new *ways* of thinking. These contentions will be a major focus of the present book. We will be exploring the impact of formal education and, more specifically, teaching, on the development of children's powers of attention, concentration, memory, thinking, learning and language. I hope to show how a consideration of these topics bears directly on a range of practical issues having to do with children's adjustment to and, for some, problems in school. These concerns, in turn, will lead us to discussions about 'readiness' for learning, 'relevance' in the curriculum, 'discovery' methods in learning and factors that help to shape children's capacities for disciplined, self-directed learning and sustained, rational thinking.

Although I do not subscribe to the view that children are, in any simple sense, directly taught how to learn and think, I do believe that the development of certain ways of reasoning and learning about things is a direct product of both spontaneous and contrived social interactions between the developing child and more mature members of his community. By 'contrived encounters' I mean social interactions that come about as a result of *explicit* educational goals. Many interactions in school are, of course, of this nature. However, learning is obviously not synonymous with schooling. A great deal of what children learn occurs spontaneously outside the school walls as they play, observe, ask questions, experiment and make sense of the world around them. Similarly, many spontaneous encounters between children and their parents, relatives and peers involve an element of *informal* teaching. Suggestions, hints and warnings, conversation, practical tasks shared, family reminiscences and the like, all provide contexts within which the developing child's learning and understanding are orchestrated and extended through social interaction. Often, as we shall see, the formative influences of such interactions on the child's mentality are not *intentional* outcomes of what we seek to communicate to the child. Rather, they are products of implicit features of the social *practices* within which communication and attempts to teach take place. We are usually unaware of such things. They are, so to speak, like water to the fish, 'transparent' to the participants.

The child is not a passive nor always a compliant partner in such encounters. I share with Piaget and most contemporary theorists of child development the view that children actively 'construct' their knowledge of the world. I will discuss and illustrate this proposition in some detail. But I will depart from Piagetian theory in a number of important directions. I believe that adults, social interaction and communication play a far more formative role in the development of children's thinking and learning than his theory allows. Although Piaget accepts that social experiences and inter-personal behaviour are an important part of development, they play a rather limited and secondary role in his theory. The child's intercourse with the physical world provides the main constraints on and contributions to intelligence. Children construct their own knowledge by acting upon objects in space and time. Social interactions (particularly those which take place between children themselves) may facilitate the course of development by exposing a child to other points of view and to conflicting ideas which may encourage him to re-think or review his ideas. However, for Piaget, any social facilitation of development only works when the child's own understanding, based on his commerce with nature, is in an appropriate state of readiness for change. I will be arguing that social interaction plays a more important role than this view permits. Children's knowledge, I suggest, is often a product of the 'joint construction' of understanding by the child and more expert members of his culture.

I will also examine alternatives to Piaget's concept of knowledge, of what it is the child is learning about. These alternative views, we will find, question his account of young school children's ability to learn and think. Bruner and the Soviet psychologists such as Vygotsky and his colleague, Luria, place far more emphasis than Piaget does on the role played by culture and its systems of symbols (e.g. its languages, sciences, books, diagrams, pictures and other artefacts) in forming the child's intelligence. Such systems have a dynamic, structuring effect on learning and development. They are not to be viewed as the mere 'content' of thinking but seen as part of its structure and its activity. When the child learns a language, for example, he does not simply discover labels to describe and remember significant objects or features of his social and physical environment but ways of *construing* and *constructing* the world. When he watches television or examines pictures in books he is not merely experiencing another way of depicting things but is involved in medium-specific activities which, in time, generate mental 'operations' that become part of the fabric of his intellect. But I move on too fast.

From five to eleven

Theories of development and the evidence they have generated provide the framework for this book. The main *subject* explored is the study of learning and thinking in children aged between five and eleven years. It is not an easy topic. What we mean by 'thinking' and what is entailed by the term 'learning' are not easily expressed. Indeed, the meaning of such terms varies, often radically so, across theories of development. Similarly, our everyday usage of such terms also betrays a multitude of different attitudes towards, and implicit theories about, what thinking and learning involve and how they are fostered or nurtured. I do not think it would be useful to try here to outline and discuss definitions of thinking, learning and related aspects of our intellect. This, I suggest, is best achieved through a detailed consideration of concrete examples and illustrations. When we begin to weigh up the various interpretations offered to explain why, for instance, seven-year-olds are able to do many things that five-year-olds cannot do, we will, I hope, see how different theories offer us several ways of viewing and thinking about our own intelligence and its development.

Debates about the nature of development are inescapably and necessarily bound up with concepts of teaching. A book about the development of children's cognitive abilities, their powers of perception, attention, learning, memory, thinking and language, is also a book about teachers and teaching. Some theories afford only a supporting role for adults in the drama of development whilst others cast them into starring parts. What it means to be a 'teacher' rests, amongst other considerations, on how we construe children-as-learners. And how should we go about the task of creating the conditions under which teachers and learners are enabled to fulfil their roles? Do schools provide contexts within which anything approaching 'optimum' conditions for teaching and learning arise? What 'optimum' means depends upon how we choose to view the developmental process. At one level, then, it is impossible to divorce the academic study of children's thinking and learning from moral, political and economic issues concerning the resources we allocate to education and the way in which we train our teachers. Although it is not my intention to bring such issues to the forefront of attention, they will, inescapably, lurk in the background of many discussions.

Metaphors of mind: how do we talk about how we think?

When we think about what goes on in our minds and try to describe what takes place there, what terms do we use? How do we try to capture and describe the content and structure of thought? Well, we resort to metaphor; to phrases like 'in our minds'. If we are asked to describe what we are doing as we try to remember something, for instance, we often talk about 'searching', as though our memory is a 'place' or a 'store'. What we are 'looking' for is in a 'location', 'somewhere'. By talking about searching our memories, we invite comparisons with the processes involved in physical activities like searching a room, looking for a mislaid object. As we search our memories, we may know that something that we can't yet recall, but that we know we know, is 'at the back of our mind' and that we will recognize it when we 'find' it. Meanwhile, perhaps, another place or word that we have already thought about and rejected keeps coming to the 'forefront' of our thinking and, despite all our rejections, will not 'go away'.

When we talk about our reasoning, we often use expressions like 'imagining what would happen if . . .', 'picturing', or, particularly if one is a cognitive psychologist, of 'making a mental model of . . .' We may on other occasions be aware of a process that resembles 'talking to oneself' or like hearing an imaginary other talking to us. If during the course of our imaginings we think about a serious mistake, we might 'cringe' at its effect and feel the ghost of whatever feeling it would entail if we 'really did' what we 'thought to do'. As we reason, we reach decisions and make judgements, deciding, perhaps, that something 'will not work', 'doesn't fit', leads to a 'dead end' or that it takes us a 'step forward' and a 'stage further on'. We may chide ourselves for stupidity or praise our own ingenuity. If we are lucky, we may decide that we have 'made a discovery', 'got there', 'thought it out', 'found out' or 'done it'. Often, as many innovative thinkers have commented, following the feeling that an insight or solution has been 'grasped', 'seen' or 'felt' comes another period of often hard and protracted work as one sets out to *prove* or *explain* or *demonstrate* the fact that a solution has been 'worked out'. Reasoning, then, is often described in terms also used to talk about physical activity, discussion and inter-personal evaluations.

But we are not always 'in control' of our mental activity. When we are supposed to be thinking about one thing we may suddenly 'find ourselves' considering something else that we should not be thinking about and, probably, be unsure or mystified as to why and how we found ourselves doing so, or when we 'went off course'. Our concentration may lapse or we might 'lose hold' of what we were supposed to be 'working on'. On the other hand, a sudden idea, insight or solution may seem to 'come to us' in a 'flash of insight'.

The metaphors that we employ to talk about, describe and explain the invisible, often fleeting, processes that go on as we think are, not surprisingly perhaps, derived from the visible, talked-about aspects of our directed *physical* activities and our experiences in the real world. But are our descriptions and explanations anything *more* than metaphorical? Are they an adequate starting place for a psychological analysis of mind? Are there any fundamental and demonstrable connections between the spatial, temporal and cor-poreal aspects of practical activities and mental processes that we often describe in similar terms? One theory of human development which suggests that there are more than metaphorical relationships between the language used to describe mental processes and that used to talk about activities in the physical world is that of Vygotsky. Although, as we shall see, he did not claim that mental activities are direct 'enactments', 'copies' or 'recordings' of external activities, he did argue that their *nature and their structure* are derived from them. He explored the theory that activity in what he termed the external, social plane is gradually 'internalized' by the child as he develops until it *forms* his intellectual processes. When we speak, say, of creating a 'mental model' there is a real sense in which the 'imaged' actions that we perform and their 'imagined' consequences are derived from physical actions that have previously been done to real objects and whose consequences have been directly felt or observed.

Of course, we often make errors and misjudgements in reasoning. Our models of the world are seldom perfect replicas. We may find, when we try to 'really' act out what we previously thought of doing, it turns out that the world resists the enactment of our imagined actions, or that the result of our actions surprises us. Thought, thus viewed, is a *substitute* for overt action and permits 'trials' whose 'errors' are only imagined. Viewed in evolutionary terms, thought (up to now at least) has proved its survival value. Though not immune to error, it has, on balance, conferred evolutionary advantage. Thinking before acting must have proved sufficiently reliable and valid to enable energy to be saved (mental activity consumes less time and food than overt action) and dangers to be avoided. Perhaps, then, the use of words to refer to mental actions *as though* they are related to similar or analogous physical actions involves more than metaphor. However, as I have already warned and will argue later, establishing the *nature* of the relations between actions and thoughts is no simple matter.

Thought as internalized action

Piaget shares with Vygotsky a similar conception of the relations between action and thought. He also argued that the foundations of mental processes lie in action-in-the-world. His often cited, deceptively simple, statement that 'Thought is internalized action' declares his view that the analysis of human knowledge and intelligence must begin with a consideration of motor activity and practical problem-solving. It also alerts us to one of his important educational messages, which is that children have to be active and constructive in order to develop their understanding of the world.

Although this book is focussed on the development of children aged between five and eleven years, I think it is important when trying to grasp the significance of Piaget's analysis of the relation between acting and thinking to consider, albeit briefly, his observations of infants in the first year of their lives. The many examples he gave of babies' activities, play, imitation and problem-solving provide a concrete sense of the way in which he charted the beginnings of a transition from physical to mental activity.

Initially, the newborn's movements are reflex responses to internal and external stimulation. The infant may grasp a finger placed in his palm, respond to a light touch on the cheek by 'rooting' around, or blink in response to a puff of air. At first babies do not *anticipate* the impact of such stimulations, even when, so to speak, they can 'see them coming'. Things just happen to them. With experience, however, the infant starts to discover some of the *predictable* patterns in his experience. For instance, if a baby notices that a mobile placed over his cot moves when he happens to strike the cot side, he may well repeat the movement in order to maintain the interesting sight of the mobile in motion. At this stage, however, the infant is not aware of the fact that it is 'his' hand that has produced the effects on an object (i.e. the mobile). Both his actions and their consequences are part of a continuous flow; an undifferen-tiated experience or 'scheme'. However, this soon changes. When the infant starts to show evidence that he is *intending* to produce *anticipated* end results through his own actions, then true 'practical intelligence' has emerged. The infant's activity displays such intelligence when he begins to use different *means* towards a common *goal*. So, for example, an infant, having failed to reach up and touch the mobile, might push his mother's hand towards it, which is most likely to happen if both the mobile and her hand are in view at the same time. It is when the infant exhibits a *sequence* of different actions to achieve the same purpose that Piaget endows him with the beginnings of a practical intelligence. This intelligence takes the form of *anticipating* or desiring a state of affairs, being able to hold or represent what is sought 'in mind' and trying out various actions that, *in the past* have accomplished desired ends. Eventually, the child will come to 'reject' certain actions on the basis of mental activity alone as he imagines their consequences and mentally evaluates their desirability without actually performing them. Thus, interiorized or internalized *mental actions* start to substitute for (represent) physical actions; action is being internalized to form thought.

Several other theories of learning also offer explanations for such phenomena, and some of these (explicitly) proceed without making any reference to 'minds', infantile or otherwise. What is distinctive and original about Piaget's analysis is the fact that such 'elementary' learning is only one aspect of a much more elaborate theory of development. Sensory–motor schemes, the learned co-ordinations between actions and their sensory consequences, provide the bedrock of all knowledge, but the biology of human beings dictates that such sensory–motor learning is *structured* in the infant to form not only 'internalized actions' but, ultimately, *mental operations*.

I do not intend to go into detail here about Piaget's account of the operations of mind since this is best achieved after we have looked at some of the other observations that he used to illustrate the nature of children's thinking. These, I hope, will help to make his ideas more graspable. However, I do need to say a little about the distinction between mental actions and mental operations, both to explore Piaget's hypothesis that thought is internalized action and to help to show how his theory leads to a very different view of intellectual development to those provided by theories of learning that predated his.

Some actions in the world have rather special properties in that, for instance, their effects can be reversed (and observed). Imagine a child playing with a set of bricks. He has five of them, say. Each time he moves one, he changes the configuration and, hence, the *appearance* of the set of the blocks. He may pile them so that they get higher. He may then take the pile down and lay the bricks side by side so that they cover a larger surface area. Each of these actions leads to a perceptible change. To an adult eye, of course, whilst the appearance of the set of blocks changes, their *number* remains invariant. The adult appreciates the fact that any action can be 'reversed' to recreate an earlier configuration, for instance. Configurations are interchangeable and appearances are ephemeral but number is an *invariant property* of the set of blocks. Only if blocks are added or taken away, we realize, is their number changed. As we shall see in the next chapter, Piaget argues that young children (aged below seven years or so), do not appreciate the fact that actions which change the appearance of things do not also affect their number, because they can't grasp the concept of invariance involved itself. Recognizing the fact that certain actions are also *operations* which form logical groups and can be *reversed* or which may be 'offset' by other actions is a prerequisite for the ability to *understand* invariant properties like number. Whilst such mental operations are 'abstracted' from physical and mental actions, they have a special status. Although they are derived from practical experience they are not a direct product of 'learning' (or teaching) in any simple sense. One may observe an action but not an operation. Operations are 'mental constructions' which the child creates to make sense of his experience of the world. The transition in human development from an intelligence restricted to a capacity to perform single mental actions to one structured as systems of mental operations marks an intellectual *revolution* that occurs at about seven years of age (although Piaget himself was not over-concerned with 'dating' his stages). How and why the development of operations takes place is considered in the next chapter.

Piaget's analysis of the stages of human intellectual development emerged from a more over-arching endeavour, which was to understand the nature, structure and evolution of knowledge. Piaget was a 'genetic epistemologist', one who studies the origins and evolution of knowledge. He based his analysis of knowledge and his observations and interpretations of children's knowing and understanding on a theoretical framework derived from logic and mathematics (hence, he employed a 'logical-mathematical' approach). This framework led him to analyse and interpret children's development in terms of systems of logical operations that are taken to be the basis for rational understanding of the physical world and of mathematical systems for representing reality. Although it makes life difficult, we have to bear Piaget's main quest and his theoretical approach in mind. It is not possible to separate either an evaluation of his theory of development or its educational implications from a consideration of the value of using logic as a framework for thinking about thinking and learning. One consequence of Piaget's theory is the prediction that logical reasoning, described in terms of operations of mind, represents the culmination of intellectual development. As we shall see, the implication that mature thinking is adequately or even properly described in terms of logic has aroused a great deal of debate. If we decide that Piaget's view of logic does *not* offer an appropriate description of mature thinking, then we must question his interpretations of young children's abilities and, with them, the educational implications of his theory. Such questions are part of the agenda for this book.

Piaget's approach to language and cognition

Perception and thought

If Piaget places action at the foundation of thought, where do perceptual 'images' and verbal thinking come on the scene? Although there has been and continues to be much debate about the role of 'imagery' in thinking, many people report that they 'use' images when they think in order to represent or 'picture' a situation, object or event. How does Piaget's theory tackle the notion of mental images and what implications does his view have for teaching and learning?

Part of the answer is that Piaget 'relegates' perception to action. For instance, when the infant sees an object, what he perceives, recognizes and knows about it depends upon his past actions. An object is, so to speak, defined by the past actions that have been done to it. The 'sensory' aspects of experiences, such as what an object looked, smelled, felt, tasted and sounded like are consequences of what was *done* to that object. Thus, the sensory aspects of experience are 'classified' in terms of actions. Some objects can be sucked and others cannot. Some can be grasped and picked up whilst others resist such actions. Some materials can be stretched, others are not so malleable, and so on. A child's intuitive knowledge of the world is based on the actions that he performs on it, and objects are 'known' in terms of the repertoire of actions to which it can and cannot be 'assimilated'. This is one sense in which (past) actions dictate how children perceive the world.

Perception, for Piaget, also involves *activity*. One example of such activity is the movement of the eyes as a situation is inspected and observed. What we see is determined, in part, by where we look. What we remember is largely dictated by what we attend to. As we shall see in chapter 3, Piaget argues that a child's ability to *control* where and how he looks at things is itself determined by his stage of development. Pre-operational children, he argues (those who have yet to develop mental operations), cannot inspect situations *logically*. Thus, what they perceive is more unreliable and idiosyncratic than what is perceived by an 'operational' thinker, whose inspection of the world is guided by a logical understanding of it. The educational implications of this view of perception, as a process under the control of action and, eventually, mental operations, are profound and far-reaching. If Piaget's theory is sound, then it follows that young children are logically incapable of seeing the world as adults do. Any attempt to 'teach' them by demonstrating how things work is bound to fail if children do not possess the necessary mental operations to *make sense*, in logical terms, of what they are shown.

Language and thought

Piagetian views on the role of *language* in thinking are similar to those on visual perception. Language, for Piaget, is a system of symbols for *representing* the world, as distinct from actions and operations which form the *processes* of reasoning. So, for example, if we had asked the five-year-old child playing with the blocks 'How many?' he had, he would not have *understood* what we asked (at least, in our terms) because he lacks the operations that endow questions like 'How many?' with logical meaning. Suppose we *told* him that he had five blocks, taught him how to count them and managed to obtain from him the answer 'five' when we asked him how many blocks he had. Does the child understand what we said and did? Not according to Piaget – at least, not in the sense that the child shares our understanding of things. It is not the case that he now understands and has been 'taught' the *concept* of number. What the child has learned is simply a *procedure* (making certain sounds) in response to a question ('How many?'). He has not developed a *conceptual* understanding of number. Such an understanding demands that the child comes to the realization that many actions which change appearances have no effect on the abstract, invariant property that we call number. He will not understand such abstract concepts until he has reached operational thinking.

Thus, Piaget's theoretical arguments about the nature of thinking and of the relationships between what is seen, heard and understood have direct implications for teaching and its effectiveness (or lack of it). Attempts to question, show or explain things to children before they are mentally 'ready' cannot foster *development*, though the child may *learn* some 'empty' procedures. Indeed, premature teaching and questioning may demoralize or frustrate a child who can't begin to understand what he is being 'taught'.

A teacher can provide appropriate *materials* and contexts for development, and organize time and space so that children are free to act upon the world with objects and tasks that serve to foster the emergence of operations and an understanding of invariance. But the basis for such an understanding is constructed by the child through his own, self-selected problem solving; not through any direct efforts of his teachers.

Vygotsky: instruction and intelligence

Children who are unable to perform tasks, solve problems, memorize things or recall experiences when they are left to their own devices often succeed when they are helped by an adult. Piaget, as we have just seen, takes a somewhat negative view of such apparent successes, claiming that they involve the teaching and learning of procedures and not the development of understanding. He views 'genuine' intellectual competence as a manifestation of a child's largely unassisted activities. Vygotsky, on the other hand, argues that the capacity to *learn through instruction* is itself a fundamental feature of human intelligence. When adults help children to accomplish things that they are unable to achieve alone, they are fostering the development of knowledge and ability. Without a natural ability for teaching, as well as learning, human *cultures* would never have developed since they can only be perpetuated if the immature learn and the mature teach (though not in the narrow sense of these terms, of course). From this perspective, which places instruction at the heart of development, a child's *potential* for learning is revealed and indeed is often *realized* in interactions with more knowledgeable others.

One of Vygotsky's main contributions to educational theory is a concept termed the 'zone of proximal development'. This he used to refer to the 'gap' that exists for an individual (child or adult) between what he is able to do alone and what he can achieve with help from one more knowledgeable or skilled than himself. This concept leads to a very different view of 'readiness' for learning to that offered by Piagetian theory. Readiness, in Vygotskian terms, involves not only the state of the child's existing knowledge but also his capacity to learn with help. Two children at nominally the 'same' level of (unassisted) performance in a given task or discipline may differ in how much they are able to learn given similar amounts of instruction. A child's current level of performance must be distinguished from his *aptitude* to learn with further instruction. Some children have larger zones of proximal development than others even when their existing levels of performance are similar. Such children are able to learn more from instruction (though not necessarily in every domain of learning). Vygotsky's theory, then, offers a way of conceptualizing individual differences in 'educability' where Piaget's theory has little or nothing to say about the issue. Note, however, that this is not intended as a criticism of Piaget's theory. Piaget never set out to explore individual differences in rates of development so it is hardly surprising that he said little about the issue. Perhaps this explains why he wrote little about the educational implications of his theory, and even then apparently with some reluctance and late in life (Elkind, 1974). In chapter 3, we will see how Vygotsky's concept of differing zones of proximal development has led to important new techniques for diagnosing children's learning needs and to techniques for tailoring instructional methods to meet these.

For Vygotsky, then, *co-operatively achieved success* lies at the foundations of learning and development. Instruction – both formal and informal, in many social contexts, performed by more knowledgeable peers or siblings, parents, grandparents, friends, acquaintances and teachers – is the main vehicle for the cultural transmission of knowledge. Knowledge is embodied in the actions, work, play, technology, literature, art and talk of members of a society. Only through interaction with the living representatives of culture, what Bruner terms the 'vicars of culture', can a child come to acquire, embody and further develop that knowledge. Children's development thus reflects their *cultural* experiences and their opportunities for access to the more mature who already *practise* specific areas of knowledge.

In order to provide a flavour of Vygotsky's analysis of development and a sense of how it resembles Piaget's theory in some respects but differs from it in others, let me compare and contrast their views on the relation between language and thought.

Piaget and Vygotsky on talking and thinking

The most widely reported difference of opinion between Vygotsky and Piaget, about which they argued in print, concerns the nature of language and its effect on intellectual development. Piaget, as we have seen, argues that language exerts no formative effects on the structure of thinking. It is a 'medium', a method of representation, within which thought takes place. Mental actions and operations, the processes of thought, are derived from action, not talk.

Piaget's position is more subtle than this statement suggests, however. Although language does not create the structure of thinking it does facilitate its *emergence*. He suggests, for example, that it is through talking to others, particularly other children, that the child's thinking becomes socialized. What another child says about some event or happening may provoke thought, discussion or argument. It may lead both children to re-view and rethink their points of view. But it is the structure of the child's intelligence, based on activity, that determines when such collaborative exchanges come about. When Piaget analysed conversations between young children, for example, he found no evidence that they were able to discuss things rationally. Piaget writes, 'if, before the age of 7 or 8 children have no conversation bearing upon logical or causal relations, the reason is that at that age they hardly understand one another when they approach these questions' (Piaget, 1967).

What can be talked *about* is determined by children's stages of development. The pre-school child's thinking (and talk) is largely 'egocentric', reflecting the child's own thinking, activity and point of view. At this stage, the child may respond to what another person says, but he cannot stand in their shoes nor understand what they are saying from *their* perspective. Piaget writes 'Clearly . . . one must start from the child's activity in order to understand his thought; and his activity is unquestionably egocentric and egotistic. The social instinct in well-defined form develops late. The first critical period in this respect occurs towards the age of 7 or 8.'

One line of evidence that Piaget used to illustrate his views on language arose from observations of pre-school children at play. Although children talk as they play together, they do not, according to Piaget, really *converse*. The pre-operational child cannot think about what the world is like from another person's viewpoint. To do this, he must be capable of ignoring his own physical and mental position and be able to 'construct' situations as they appear from other perspectives. For various reasons discussed later, children can only perform such constructions when they have developed mental operations. Before this stage is reached, they assimilate what is said by another person, adult or child, to their own point of view, often 'distorting' the meaning of much that is said to them. The impact of language on the child, then, is limited to what he can assimilate, and this is determined by the structure of the child's thinking. True 'reciprocity' and attempts at mutual understanding only emerge with the development of concrete operations, at around age seven. This is why young children playing and talking in each other's company are usually involved in 'collective monologues' rather than true dialogue.

Vygotsky's theory shares a number of similarities with Piaget's but differs radically in its treatment of language and its influence on thinking. He agreed with Piaget's view that children do not think like adults and applauded the fact that, unlike most child psychologists before him, Piaget did not simply set out to discover what children could *not* do in comparison with adults, but sought to find out what they could do and what they actually did. However, childhood speech, in Vygotsky's view, is not a personal, egocentric affair but the reverse: it is *social* and communicative in both origin and intent. Vygotsky also observed what Piaget termed 'collective monologues' by young children but he gave them a different interpretation. For Vygotsky, they represent an important stage of transition between two quite different *functions* of language. In the beginning, speech serves a regulative, communicative function. Later, it also serves other functions and transforms the way in which children learn, think and understand. It becomes an instrument or *tool* of thought, not only providing a 'code' or system for representing the world but also the means by which *self-regulation* comes about. The initial motivation for gesture and speech is to control the world through the agency of other people. The infant is weak and cannot sustain himself. Consequently, many of the things he wants or needs have to be met with the help of others. Gestures and speech serve this role, giving the infant a way of influencing the course of his immediate future which he could not achieve otherwise. Speech, like any system of movement, is a physical *activity*, a way of controlling one's own body in order to achieve goals and avoid discomfort. The overt activity of speaking provides the basis for 'inner speech', that rather mysterious covert activity that often forms the process of thinking. For Vygotsky, then, not only do physical actions that serve to manipulate and organize the world get internalized to become (non-verbal) thinking: the physical activity of speaking, which serves to regulate the actions of others, also becomes internalized to create verbal thinking. All forms of thought, then, are *activities*.

The 'monologues' produced by pre-school children, such as those observed by Piaget, lie midway between the social and intellectual functions of speech. For Vygotsky, the child who is talking to himself is *regulating* and planning his own activities in ways that foreshadow verbal thinking. As the child discovers how to control the actions of others through speech, his developing knowledge of language 'acts back' on him in that others can also regulate his actions through speech. As he discovers how to gain people's attention by speaking and learns how to direct their attention to features of the shared physical world – to solicit specific actions and services, inhibit, refuse and so forth – he becomes subject to the same regulative forces through the speech of others. They can begin to control and direct his attention, solicit his services and inhibit his activities. Alongside 'other-control' by verbal means comes verbal 'self-control-by-others'.

As such developments are taking place on the linguistic front, the child is also developing his non-verbal knowledge of the world through his own activities. In relation to this aspect of early development, the Soviet emphasis on activity is similar to Piaget's concept of sensory–motor development. At around three years of age, a merging and integration of the two streams of development, non-verbal and verbal, begins. The pre-school child's verbal commentaries on his own activities are evidence of the emergence of *linguistic control* over his own non-verbal activities. In 'talking to himself' the child is playing two roles; that of the regulated and the regulator. In the past, other people played one of these roles. Sometimes the child regulated their actions, at other times they regulated his. The pre-school child is beginning to play both parts before 'internalizing' the process to become a verbal thinker.

Children's monologues, for Piaget, reflect the egocentric nature of their thinking. When at around age seven or eight, genuine discourse is made possible by the development of logical operations, language starts to become rational and social (though egocentric thinking does not disappear entirely). Egocentric speech disappears from the scene because the child is now aware of the need to make what he says accessible to his listener and has the intellectual competence to start to learn how to make himself intelligible.

Vygotsky argues, however, that egocentric speech serves an intellectual purpose for children and does not 'disappear' at age seven but is internalized to form 'inner speech' and verbal thinking. When Vygotsky and his colleagues observed pre-school children they also found evidence of egocentric speech, but noted that this was most likely to occur when some *frustration* or difficulty arose. For example, when a child discovered that he did not have a blue pencil to colour a drawing he said 'Where's the pencil? I need a blue pencil. Never mind, I'll draw with the red one and wet it with water; it will become dark and look blue' (Vygotsky, 1962, p. 17). So, egocentric speech often serves a *planning* and *self-regulating* function and is stimulated by problems and frustrations.

In this way, speech comes to form what Vygotsky referred to as the higher mental processes. These include the ability to plan, evaluate, memorize and reason. Note that these processes are *culturally* formed in social interaction. Looked at in this way, language does not simply *reflect* or represent concepts already formed on a non-verbal level. Rather, it structures and directs the processes of thinking and concept formation themselves. Where Piaget views young children's play and talk as a manifestation of a natural desire to manipulate and assimilate the physical world, laying down the sensory–motor and intuitive foundations for mathematical and logical operations, Vygotsky sees it as a product of social experience and evidence for the emergence of intellectual self-control.

Processing information: on becoming an expert

One of the influences that helped to shape the development of Piaget's theory was a discipline called 'cybernetics'. This arose in the 1940s, fathered by a mathematician, Norbert Wiener, and a physician, Arturo Rosenbluth. It is defined, in modern terms, as 'the science of effective organisation' (Beer, 1977). The initial aim of cyberneticians (the term is derived from the Greek word for 'steersman') was to identify the fundamental and universal principles governing the development and functioning of all complex systems, be they organic, physical or mechanical. Are there universal laws which govern how such systems must be organized and structured in order to work effectively in any environment?

The concepts of *information* and information *control* are employed by cyberneticians to analyse the workings of natural systems such as the human brain, and to design efficient and workable man-made systems such as computers, large industrial organizations and so on. How should information be distributed, processed and controlled in order for such systems to work? In company with another set of concepts, derived initially from electronic engineering and called information theory, the ideas and terminology of cybernetics have been absorbed into psychology to provide a theoretical *language* for the study and analysis of human intelligence.

Piaget's interest in cybernetics stemmed from his desire to create a field of study, genetic epistemology, that would cross the traditional boundaries separating several disciplines (biology, psychology, philosophy, the natural sciences, mathematics and logic). Like the cyberneticians, he wanted to discover general principles of *organiz-ation* that applied to all living systems and which would establish theoretical connections between biology and knowledge: how has the evolution and structure of biological systems led to the emergence of rational intelligence? The study of 'self-organising systems' that develop towards stable and efficient functioning, governed by universal principles of structure and function, was of central relevance to his endeavour, so it is no surprise that he should have been attracted to the ideas of cybernetics.

Other psychologists also adopted the concepts and the language of cybernetics and information theory. Although, as we shall see, they put them to uses that are different from Piaget's, their main motivation was also to explore the nature of human cognition viewed as a system organized to process information in order to adapt, learn and understand.

In engineering, information theory has been used to study, design and evaluate ways of transmitting information between two points without distortion, loss or degradation. No information processing system, be it telephone, radio, television or whatever, is perfect. Information may be lost during the encoding phase (consider, for example, how a voice over a telephone compares with the 'real thing'), or it may 'leak' or be distorted by noise (like the 'crackle' on a telephone line). The role of the information theorist is to provide the means to measure and improve the performance of systems that transmit, process and store information and the engineer's task is to design and make systems that minimize distortion, loss and noise and which work fast.

The term 'information' used in this sense has a more precise, technical meaning than that implied by its use in everyday talk. Imagine, for instance, that I have drawn a single card from a normal deck of playing cards. I ask you to discover what card I am holding. You ask if it is a red card. I inform you that it is not. You have been given an item of information that rules out one-half of the set that the card was drawn from. More formally, I have given you one 'bit' of information (short for 'binary digit'). You next ask if the card is a club. I say that it is not. You can now rule out from the set of candidates for the card I am holding a further 50 per cent of the possibilities (i.e. you now know it must be one of the thirteen spades). I have now given you two bits of information overall. In short, any item of information that reduces uncertainty about an event by a half conveys one bit of information. Of course, when an electronics engineer calculates the amount of information being conveyed in a complex system, the maths become somewhat difficult!

What has all this got to do with the psychology of learning and thinking? Well, do we discover anything by thinking about human beings as 'information processors'? Is it useful, for example, to look at human speech as a system for transmitting information? Can the workings of the brain be analysed usefully as an information processing device like a computer? Do children become better at 'processing information' as they develop? Can learning usefully be viewed as information processing, memory as information storage and knowledge as information structures?

These are, in fact, controversial questions in psychology and I will not attempt to answer them in detail here. I list them to provide some sense of how and why information processing theory has been embraced by many psychologists. An important paper, written by George Miller in 1956, paved the way for many insights into the nature of human intelligence based on the image of 'man the information processor'. Let me say a little about the background to and content of this paper before discussing what it might have to tell us about the nature of learning and thinking.

If adults are asked to remember random strings of digits (i.e. to transmit information about them from one moment in time to another) they usually manage to handle sets of six or seven items without making many errors. Increase the number of digits and they begin to make mistakes (they lose information and introduce 'noise'). Imagine tasting two drinks which vary in saltiness. You are presented with each in turn and asked to describe them to some- one or, perhaps, to press one of two keys to signal which you have just sampled. Adults find this task easy. Increase the number of drinks to three (high, middle and low in saltiness). Then move on to four, five, six, seven, and so on. Here too we find that adults can usually 'transmit information' without error in situations where they are exposed to six or seven different degrees of saltiness, but once the set exceeds seven then errors, information loss and noise creep in. Miller, who drew attention to these and many similar phenom- ena, suggested that whatever the nature of the stimuli used in such situations (they may be sounds, tastes, degrees of brightness, colour saturation and so on), provided that they are 'random' and that the sequences used have no meaning (e.g. tones that do not form a recognized tune), we find that mature people can 'transmit', without loss or distortion, information about sets of stimuli that number somewhere between five and nine. The title of his paper was 'The magical number seven, plus or minus two'.

Why is this interesting? Well, described in the language of information theory, it demonstrates that adults have a limited and relatively fixed *channel capacity*. We are only able to transmit information, without loss or distortion, about a specific number of (unstructured) items. It follows that if people are put into unfamiliar situations and expected to take note of and react to (i.e. to process) more than a relatively small number of elements, they will be overwhelmed by information and uncertainty ('What do I attend to next?', 'What should I do about it?'). They will make mistakes. In such situations, *training* and/or *experience* will be needed before anything approaching error-free performance can be achieved.

The analysis becomes more interesting when we consider the answers to two questions. The first asks if children have the *same* channel capacity and information processing limits as adults. The second concerns the nature of *expertise*. What happens with training or experience that enables people to *overcome* their information processing limitations? Why is it, for example, that a concert pianist may be able to sight-read a piece of music that involves, say, sequences of eight-note chords in a novel combination? The pianist is transmitting far more information than subjects in the experiments just outlined, but how? How is practice and experience translated into expert performance? What is being *learned* and how is it remembered?

First consider the question about children. If three-year-olds are asked to remember strings of digits, they begin to falter when the set exceeds three items. By five, children can handle about five items. By age eight or so, mature levels of performance are reached. There is debate about exactly what happens during development to explain this phenomenon, and I will discuss both the arguments and their educational implications in the next chapter when I explore the view that children have to learn *how* to memorize such things. For the moment, the important point is that children have a smaller 'channel capacity' than adults do. Consequently, in unfamiliar, uncertain situations, they are less able than the mature person is to attend to, memorize and respond to events. Perhaps we should explore the view that five-year-olds (but not seven-year-olds) fail to solve many problems because they lack the *information processing capacities* needed to do such tasks. This I also do in the next chapter.

In thinking about the nature of expertise and how it is learned or acquired, consider an example. We find a chess Grand Master willing to take part in an experiment. We show him or her a chess board on which pieces are arranged in a 'state of play'. We show them the board for a few moments and then ask them to turn away and then to recall the positions of the pieces they were shown. They are likely to perform this feat without error even when the board has on it most or all of the pieces. Ask a novice at chess to do the same task and he or she is unlikely to remember more than a handful of pieces (Van De Groot, 1965). Does the chess Grand Master have a phenomenal memory? Is this why he or she was able to achieve Grand Mastership? No: outside their area of special expertise, the Grand Master suffers from the same information processing limitations as the rest of us. Their feats of perception and memory are *specific* to chess boards and pieces.

More detailed studies of how they manage this feat illustrate the important and far-reaching connections between what may appear to be 'fixed' or 'natural' capacities – like the ability to see and memorize – and 'higher mental processes' – such as learning and thinking. What the expert, but not the novice, 'sees' when he or she inspects the chess board are *configurations* of pieces, or in Miller's term, 'chunks'. These configurations, in turn, represent familiar, recurrent patterns that occur as an outcome of particular strategies of play, or some pattern that shows an 'interesting' departure from such prototypical configurations. Experiments designed to analyse the way in which experts perceive the structure of chess games (Chase and Simon, 1973) show that they have memorized a huge repertoire of such configurations. In other words, the chess Grand Master can recognize a very large number of different patterns that are typical or interpretable states of play. Whereas the novice 'perceives' isolated pieces which, perhaps, he or she can barely recognize or identify, the Master recognizes individual pieces as parts of larger configurations. Put in information processing terms, the expert and novice share the same channel capacity, but the six or seven chunks that the expert encodes are meaningful configurations, not isolated chessmen. Through playing chess, and the observation of others at play, the expert has not only discovered clever strategies and good tactics of play but also developed an *organized memory* which enables them to assimilate much more of what they see than the novice. This also means that they are better able to *plan* and think ahead because their representation or model of the chess board is robust, accurate and enduring. So they are also able to think more clearly and in greater depth.

The differences exposed in such studies between experts and novices are found in many other contexts. Indeed, there is a fair case to be made for the assertion that they are typical of differences found between experts and novices in *any* field. The expert reader, for example, perceives and processes larger units of text than the beginning reader. An adult can look at an array of objects and 'subitize' them – perceive them in groups of certain size (e.g. as sets of three) – whilst a young child cannot. Thus, the speed with which we are able to 'encode' what we see, the *organization* of what we see and the amount of information that we can memorize are related to and symptomatic of the *structure* of our knowledge.

Children are novices at life in general and find many of the tasks and demands they face in school novel and full of uncertainty. They are more limited than adults in how much they can attend to and memorize in unfamiliar situations. Perhaps, then, it should not be surprising to find differences between the mature and immature in the ability to profit by a specific experience or to solve an unfamiliar problem. It may be that what is at stake in such situations is not young children's inability to perform *logical operations* but their general lack of *expertise* which leads them to perceive situations in different ways to the adult.

An informal, but telling, finding that emerged from studies of chess players was their inability to identify, describe or articulate how they were 'seeing' chess boards. Surely, much of our expertise is like this. Our knowledge is 'tacit', locked into the way we act and perform and not easily articulated or described to others. Experts may find the problems of the novice puzzling or even infuriating if they do not recognize that novices do not perceive situations in the same way as they themselves do. It should come as no surprise, for example, to find that even when the expert *points out* things to be attended to, the novice may not be able to 'take in' what they are shown because they lack the prerequisite *knowledge* which would enable them to perceive and memorize configurations. If so, it is also not surprising that the expert's ability to *act* and *think* is surer, smoother and more accurate than that of the novice.

Viewing children as limited information processors who have yet to learn or acquire expertise offers a third image of the child as learner and thinker. This makes no recourse to 'large-scale' concepts like logical operations, but suggests that knowing how and what we are about is far more *domain-* or task-specific. Children's ability in one area, be it chess, arithmetic, reading or whatever may not reflect their abilities in others if their *expertise* in different subjects and activities varies. This view makes no use of concepts of *stages* of development: however, it does agree with Piaget's view that perception, memory, knowledge and understanding are all deeply related and change with learning and development.

Piaget, Vygotsky and Bruner: a brief comparison and summary

Before moving on to the next chapter, I will summarize some of the main ideas we have just considered. Rather than simply repeat myself, I will try to re-examine these ideas whilst exploring a little more of the biography of the three main characters I have introduced.

I have outlined three main perspectives on the development of learning and thinking. These will be explored in more detail in the following pages. One view, which stems from Piaget's theory, holds that all children pass through a series of stages before they construct the ability to perceive, reason and understand in mature, rational terms. In this view, teaching, whether through demonstration, explanation or asking questions, can only influence the course of intellectual development if the child is able to assimilate what is said and done. Assimilation, in turn, is constrained by the child's stage of development. This leads to a specific concept of learning 'readiness' and, as we shall see, holds out many implications for the design of curricula and the timing of formal instruction.

A second perspective, introduced by Vygotsky, shares some important areas of agreement with Piagetian theory, particularly an emphasis on *activity* as the basis for learning and for the development of thinking. However, it involves different assumptions about the relationship between talking and thinking. It entails a far greater emphasis on the role of communication, social interaction and instruction in determining the path of development. Vygotsky died in his late thirties in 1934. His death came after ten years of illness from tuberculosis. In that ten-year period, Vygotsky wrote about a hundred books and papers, many of which have only recently been published and translated into English. Many psychologists, including some of his own former students and colleagues, recognize that much of what he wrote was speculative and, in places, self-contradicting. Unlike Piaget, who worked on into his eighties and lived to see a dramatic expansion in the field of developmental psychology, Vygotsky did not have access to what has become a vast literature on child development. Consequently, whilst many of the ideas we will explore later in this book are consistent with his general position, and were sometimes stimulated directly by it, we are left to guess at what Vygotsky himself might have had to say about them.

Bruner, influenced as I have already said by Vygotsky, was constructing the foundations of his theory of instruction in the 1960s when the assimilation of information theory into psychology was under way. Unlike both Vygotsky and Piaget, Bruner came to the study of child development after extensive research into adult thinking and problem-solving. Although sharing with Vygotsky a stress on the importance of culture and cultural history in the formation of mind, his background provided him with a more detailed sense of the *processes* involved in mature, socialized cognition. His theory, unlike either Piaget's or Vygotsky's, was grounded in the language of information theory. For instance, he entitled one of his early papers 'Going beyond the information given' (Bruner, 1957). In this, he explored the nature of creative thinking and originality in terms of our ability not only to acquire information but also to 'go beyond' it by inventing codes and rules. Learning involves the search for pattern, regularity and predictability. Instruction serves to assist children in the formation and discovery of such patterns and rules. We return to a fuller discussion of these ideas in chapter 7.

Like Vygotsky, Bruner is convinced that social experience plays a major part in mental development, though his theory of the way in which social experience is involved in development differs from Vygotsky's account in a number of ways (not least by being informed by research findings that Vygotsky did not live to study). For example, throughout his writings on human development Bruner lays considerable stress on the importance of acknowledging not only the role of culture and social interaction but also the influences of biology and evolution. He often draws parallels between the abilities of humans and other species when he theorizes about the formation of mind: 'I take it as a working premise that growth cannot be understood without reference to human culture and primate evolution' (1968, p. 2). Vygotsky also acknowledged the importance of biological study in the creation of psychological theory. He distinguished between what he called the 'natural line' and the 'cultural line' in development. But he did not live to provide a synthesis of the two streams of growth. Indeed, unlike Bruner, he largely 'ignored' the natural, biological line in his desire to establish the importance of historical, social and cultural influences on human development (Wertsch, 1985, p. 8). You will find that discussions of the interplay between biology and social experience pervade this book.

Looked at in one way, then, Bruner's theory seems to stand between those of Piaget and Vygotsky. Like Piaget, Bruner emphasizes the importance of biological and evolutionary constraints on human intelligence. At the same time, and more in sympathy with Vygotsky, he lays stress on the way in which culture forms and transforms the child's development, and he gives a more central role than Piaget does to social interaction, language and instruction in the formation of mind. Bruner employs the language of information processing in formulating his ideas and, in so doing, offers us an opportunity to integrate the findings from work on adult cognition with those arising from the study of children. All too often, cognitive psychologists who study adult intelligence ignore the process of development and education. They often leave one with the impression that mental activity springs, fully formed, out of a developmental vacuum. Bruner, however, seeks to ground his account of the 'processes of mind' in a theory of culture and growth, often drawing and building upon insights delivered by both Piaget and Vygotsky.

The main focus of disagreement between Piaget and Bruner revolves around the issue of stages of development. These, as we have seen, are central to Piaget's analysis of human growth but are rejected by Bruner. In the next chapter, we look with more care and in more detail at this issue.

Chapter 2

Are there stages of development?

This relatively brief chapter includes a more detailed consideration of some of the issues raised in the Introduction (I promised to be repetitive!). More specifically, we examine Piaget's proposition that a major change occurs in children's thinking and in their readiness for certain types of learning at about seven years of age. The aim of the chapter is not simply to provide a more detailed and extensive account of Piaget's theory of stages. It also considers and illustrates some of the major criticisms that have been levelled against his views, and examines alternative descriptions of the nature of development and learning during the first years of schooling. By looking in detail at the demands placed on children in experiments that are designed to study their thinking and analyse their understanding, we can gain some insights into the complexities of adult–child communication in formal, contrived encounters. These suggest a number of ways in which children may misunderstand what adults ask them to do which may have nothing to do with their possession, or lack of possession, of logical competence. If one accepts these alternative explanations then one may reject the notion of stages of development and accept a more central role for language, communication and instruction in the development of children's thinking and learning than that portrayed in Piagetian theory.

Appearance and reality in the development of understanding

A central aspect of Piaget's theory is the proposition that children's thinking is different *in kind* from that of more mature individuals. All children develop through the same sequence of stages before achieving mature, rational thought. The structure of children's thinking at each stage is distinctive, the same for all children at that stage, and different from that of children and adults at other stages. Development, for Piaget, is not simply the continuous accumulation of things learned step by step. Rather, it involves a number of intellectual 'revolutions' at specific junctures in the life cycle, each one of which involves important changes in the structure of intelligence. Each stage yields a different way of thinking about and understanding the world to that it grows out of and replaces.

Several important arguments about children's ability to learn flow from the theory. The effects of a particular learning experience on a child's knowledge and understanding varies according to his or her stage. Whilst a young child might learn or be taught how to solve a given problem, to provide what sounds like an appropriate answer to a difficult question, or to execute a particular routine (counting or adding numbers, say), the impact of such experiences on the child will be different in kind from that experienced by one at a later stage of development. The status and significance of what children learn is a direct function of their stage of development.

It follows from this view that the impact of lessons taught by parents or teachers also varies as a function of a child's developmental stage. Indeed, a major implication of the theory is that the effects and effectiveness of teaching are fundamentally constrained by the structure of the child's intelligence. Recall the example given in the last chapter. It may be possible to teach a five-year-old child to recite the words one to five, but it does not follow that he or she understands numbers. Learning routines by rote (repetition and drill), and discovering how some properties of sets of objects remain invariant despite changes in their appearance – one of the preconditions for achieving numeracy – are worlds apart. When we teach the young child to recite numbers and, later, attribute her eventual numeracy to our own instruction, we are, in Piaget's view, falling into the trap of 'magical thinking'. We have done things to and with the child. In time, the child changes and learns. Therefore our actions 'caused' the child's development. No, says Piaget: the child's understanding arises out of his self-directed *actions* upon the physical world.

The question we must turn to now is how self-directed activity leads the child to *construct* his or her own understanding of natural phenomena. We also consider how they come to question and reject the assumption that changes in the appearance of things entail a change in their nature or substance. To address these questions, I need to introduce and explain some of Piaget's theoretical terminology.

Two key Piagetian terms: assimilation and accommodation

In the last chapter, I outlined the way in which an infant might perceive objects in terms of the past actions that she has exerted on them. Objects become 'known' and 'recognized' in terms of the actions that serve to *assimilate* them to the fulfilment of intentions. So, for example, a bottle may be known and perceived in terms of activities like grasping, bringing it to the mouth, sucking and swallowing. To the extent that any new 'container' can be assimilated successfully to these schemes in order to fulfil the desire to drink, then it too will be 'known' in terms of 'bottle-related' actions.

At one level, of course, every action we perform is unique. When the infant grasps, lifts and drinks from a particular bottle, containing a certain amount in it, from a specific surface, in a given context, her actual performance will vary in minor detail from other, similar performances. Put in Piagetian terms, every act of assimilation involves an element of *accommodation*. Piaget uses this term to refer to the changes, often minor ones, that have to be made to pre-existing schemes of activity in order to make possible the assimilation of a new experience. Imagine, for example, the infant trying, for the first time, to pick up and drink from a full, pint-sized container. She tries to assimilate this new object to her existing schemes of grasping and drinking but finds that the object *resists* her efforts and begins to tilt and spill. She will eventually come to know that some things are too heavy for her to lift. Indeed, this experience is laying the developmental foundations for the concept of weight itself. She is learning that some things cannot be picked up unaided. The child cries out or in some way requests assistance. Her father helps her to lift the container until it is in a position that enables her to fulfil her intention to drink (to assimilate the object). She has now *accommodated* her activities to this new experience. The realm of objects that can be assimilated to the activity of drinking is now split into those that can be assimilated by the original schemes of grasping and drinking, and others that require other means (e.g. a call for help) to enable assimilation. The child would probably centre on size as the perceptual cue which discriminates one sub-class of things that afford drinks from others that only do so with help.

Some accommodations require dramatic changes in the structure of the child's understanding of the world, particularly those which herald a change in stage. To understand how and when these revolutionary changes come about, we need to delve deeper into the theory.

More technicalities: centration, disequilibrium and de-centring

When a child is trying to do something, whether her intention arises as a consequence of her own activities or is stimulated by a request

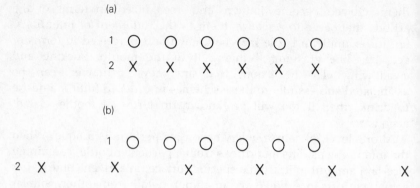

Figure 2.1 Conservation of number: (a) prior to transformation; (b) after transformation

or question from another person, what she *attends* to in the situation will be dictated by the *actions* that, in the past, have served to achieve similar intentions. So, the child's past activities dictate what is perceptually *salient* to her.

Suppose we show a five-year-old child two lines of coins laid out as shown in figure 2.1a. We ask her if one set contains more coins than the other. The child is likely to say that they have the same number. Since the sets of coins are essentially similar in all respects, whatever the child looks at in comparing one set with the other will probably lead her to a judgement of equality. We now rearrange the coins so that one set is longer than the other (figure 2.1b). Are they still the same? The child will, in all probability, decide that the longer set contains more coins. Presumably, length is taken as an index of 'amount' or 'number' because, in the past, this dimension proved a reliable guide to relative amount. What the child does not *notice* is the fact that whilst the length of one line has been changed, this change was, so to speak, 'offset' or 'compensated for' by an equal and opposite change in the relative *density* of objects in the two sets. What seems salient to the child is the change that occurs in length or extent. Relative length can be estimated by comparing or centring on the end points of the two sets. Estimating relative density, on the other hand, demands more intense and systematic scrutiny of the objects in the two sets.

What the child is unable to do, then, is to take account of and 'co-ordinate' two or more changes that occur *simultaneously* as the coins are moved about. Similarly, she cannot co-ordinate her initial judgement (the sets have the same number) with the final one (one has more). She does not sense any discrepancy or 'illogicality' in her two judgements because the act that changed appearance also changed the 'number' of objects. Her judgements, from her own perspective, are not inconsistent since appearances *have* changed.

Similarly, if we put the pennies back into line again the child will say that both sets are the same again, but not appreciate any inconsistency. Each judgement that the child makes involves only *one* centration; a single act of observation and comparison. Thus, any change in appearance of necessity involves a change in amount. Asking questions, shuffling pennies, drawing the child's attention to the relative 'density' of the two sets, will not teach her otherwise because she cannot *co-ordinate* her judgements nor her observations in order to detect any discrepancy or conflict.

Nature, however, will not 'tolerate' the assumption that any obvious change in appearance always entails a change in the 'nature' of things. As the child plays with sets of objects, be these blocks, beads, coins, animals, marbles, people or whatever, and rearranges or sees them rearranged, she will eventually and inevitably encounter a situation in which her tacit assumption about the nature of change will be violated by events. This could happen in an indeterminate number of ways. Perhaps she *discovers* the fact that two sets of objects which looked different actually fulfil some common purpose (e.g. filling a small container). Or her joy at increasing her wealth by enlarging the area of floor covered by her savings might be dashed when she finds they can only buy the same amount, however she lays her money out. Who knows? The argument is that, nature being what it is, the child must discover some situation that will challenge her assumptions. She then enters a state of *disequilibrium*. She is confused as her assumption is brought into question by the reality of events. This mental state is intolerable and motivates thought and action. Eventually, the child will discover a more embracing or 'over-arching' idea or mental scheme which will restore equilibrium. She might realize, for example, that if she takes account of *both* linear extent and density, her confusion begins to lift. She is *de-centring* herself and moving away from an *intuitive* understanding of number, involving centration on only one thing, to judgements based on the *co-ordination* of several acts of centration.

Now mental *operations* appear on the scene. Mental actions involve single action–consequence relations (e.g. when pennies are moved a line gets longer or shorter). Mental operations are *classes* of actions that are integrated with other (logically related) operations. In other words they appear as *systems* not, like actions, as isolated entities. Perhaps I can help to explain this difficult notion. The ability to 'see' that changes in length are offset by changes in density (co-ordination and compensation) is part and parcel of understanding that fact that the effects of an action (e.g. extending the line of coins) can be *reversed* by an equal and opposite act (aligning them again). Actions *become* operations when they are embedded in systems of thought that are co-ordinated and reversible. Thus, the ability to *conserve* abstract properties, like number, emerges as a part of a new system of understanding that involves operations. Once the child's thinking becomes co-ordinated and reversible, for instance, she 'knows' that changes in appearance may be deceptive and realizes that in any situation number *must* remain invariant (i.e. two sets remain equivalent) if nothing is added or taken away. Indeed, by a similar line of argument, the *concept* of adding and taking away is now *understood* in relation to invariance. All these aspects of understanding co-emerge as part of a system of thinking: concrete operational intelligence has been constructed. Learning arithmetical concepts can begin.

Piaget's theory (and evidence) suggest that the ability to coordinate, compensate, reverse and appreciate the nature of invariance (to conserve) emerge in relation to several areas of knowledge at about the same time in development (usually around age seven). Piaget suggests that the ability to conserve (grasp invariance and equivalence) involves similar intellectual abilities (e.g. co-ordination) whether we are dealing with concepts of number, area, volume, weight, quantity or whatever. This explains why a child who lacks such abilities cannot grasp any of these abstract notions. A child who displays understanding in one area, however, possesses the necessary competence to develop an understanding of other 'invariances'. She has entered the stage of 'concrete operations' and begun her career as a 'conserver'.

Not all conservations appear at the same time. Some, like conservation of weight (realizing, for example, that changing the shape of a lump of clay does not also change its weight) come later than others (e.g. conservation of quantity). Piaget's argument is that the same logical abilities are involved: some things are more difficult to learn (for reasons that are not always clear), and are assimilated to concrete operational thinking later than other things, but, they are nonetheless assimilated to the same system of understanding. The notion that intelligence can be analysed in terms of such 'general purpose' mental abilities is, as we shall see, one of the most controversial features of Piaget's theory.

Before moving on to consider the educational implications of Piaget's theory and alternative explanations for children's learning and understanding, let me discuss another example of the transition from pre-operational to operational thinking. This should help to show how Piaget identifies the same intellectual abilities at work in superficially quite different domains of knowledge to give credibility to the notion of stages of development.

Suppose we show our five-year-old two identical beakers filled with liquid and she judges that they contain the same amount to drink. Then, in full view of the child, we pour the contents of one into another vessel with a different shape. Imagine that it is thinner and taller. We ask the child to judge whether the new container contains the same amount of liquid as that contained in the beaker left untouched (are the two quantities equivalent?). The child is likely to say that the thinner one, in which the liquid rises to a greater relative height, contains more. Why does the child make this judgement? Why can't she 'see' that the two vessels must contain equivalent amounts?

As we have seen, the child's thinking, intuitive at this stage, is perceptually dominated and limited to judgements based on a single point of comparison across the two objects. She sees and appreciates the fact that the action of pouring leads to a change in appearance, in relative height, but what she does not (and, of course, cannot) appreciate is that several changes in appearance occur simultaneously. Consequently, her judgement of quantity is based on only one of the simultaneous changes that occur. When the two vessels are identical, a judgement based on any coupled centrations (i.e. on an inspection of two similar aspects of the two vessels) will result in the 'correct' answer. When the vessels are different, however, attention to only one dimension gives the 'wrong' answer. The child does not understand the notion of quantity nor can she appreciate the fact that this remains invariant when pouring occurs.

The child's thinking and understanding are the same here as in the number conservation study. Whilst pouring is taking place she can only attend to one dimension of change. When pouring is finished and the child is asked to compare the two quantities she also fails to appreciate the equivalence of the two quantities because her visual inspection is limited to a single act of comparison. Reminding her of her previous judgement is also ineffective because, lacking the capacity to co-ordinate her answers and believing that changes in appearance entail changes of substance, the child does not experience any sense of conflict or discrepancy in her answers. When the child achieves *operativity*, she can 'perceive' the fact that pouring leads to simultaneous changes in several aspects of a phenomenon and discover the fact that one change offsets, or is compensated by, another. When she has constructed systems of operations her perception of the world is, quite literally, transformed.

Conflict, instruction and accommodation

Imagine a child who has entered the stage of concrete operations presented with the quantity conservation task. Although she has not seen this phenomenon before and has never been confronted with the problem of conserving continuous quantity, she *is* able to perceive and co-ordinate simultaneous changes in appearance. She also knows that changes in the way things look do not necessarily mean that they cannot be equivalent. She is able to co-ordinate her answers to questions posed before and after pouring and, being logical, will not tolerate any inconsistencies between them. She also knows that if liquid is poured back any changes in appearance can be reversed to retrieve the initial state of affairs. In consequence, while the problem is just as novel for her as for the five-year-old, the intelligence she brings to bear on it and what she 'sees' are different in kind.

If she has only recently achieved operational competence, the solution to the problem may not be immediately apparent to her, but she is intellectually ready to *discover* its solution. At this stage a teacher (or another child) may say and do things which *conflict* with our child's interpretation of events. For instance, if one child suggests that quantity has changed because liquid in one glass is higher, then the other person, drawing her attention to opposing differences in another dimension (e.g. the other glass is wider) or reminding her of her previous judgement (that both held the same amount), may activate a sense of conflict. Since she is beginning to perceive things that, hitherto, she was unaware of and realizes that more is going on than used to meet her eyes, it is possible that this conflict will set her thinking and trying to solve the puzzle facing her. She sets out to resolve any contradiction and achieve some degree of coherence in her theory of what is going on. The way out, the way to accommodate the conflict, is for her to restructure the way she thinks.

Restructuring

Social experience, then, may help a child to restructure her thinking by inducing disagreement and cognitive *conflict* that mobilize thought and help to bring about the next stage of development. But children have to be in an appropriate state of intellectual readiness for such social facilitation to take place. They can only experience conflict when their intuitive view of the world is beginning to break down. Even here the restoration of equilibrium, and the restructuring of knowledge that makes it possible, are a product of the child's own thinking. Illustration, explanation and interrogation might help to mobilize the child's problem-solving, but only she can discover the solution.

A critique of Piaget's theory

The great power of Piaget's theory stems from his identification of structurally different, pre-operational and operational, structures of mind. The *universal* nature of a stage, the fact that it structures everything the child perceives and thinks, provides a general explanation for the fact that, in many different situations, seven-year-olds are likely to think quite differently from their younger peers and are 'ready' for a different stage of learning. The promise of *generality* is what makes Piaget's theory so attractive and important.

However, there are many people who do not accept Piaget's theory. As early as 1936, for instance, Susan Isaacs reported many observations of children in her nursery school at Maltinghouse in Cambridge. Her pre-schoolers, she argued, displayed clear evidence of rational thinking. Her observations and her interpretations of what these implied for Piaget's theory anticipated many contemporary arguments in child development. There is now a significant body of opinion which holds that Piaget's methods and demonstrations led him to underestimate or misconstrue the nature of children's thinking. Let us consider some alternative explanations for children's 'failures' in tasks demanding 'operational' thinking.

Did Piaget underestimate the importance of language?

Think again about the demands being placed on the young child in Piaget's task situations. The experimenter obviously has to *communicate* the nature of the problem being set to the child, and we can analyse the process of communication into a number of levels. A *breakdown* in mutual understanding between adult and child at any of these levels might account for children's apparent illogicality.

First, we obviously need to consider the actual words and grammar involved in what the adult says to the child. In the quantity conservation task, for instance, we find expressions like 'as much as', 'same amount to drink', and so forth. Do children actually *understand* these words and expressions in the way that the adult intends? Young children may appear to understand and use them in familiar situations, but are the meanings that they carry in everyday talk between adults and young children the same as those involved in contrived, experimental tasks? If we examine and analyse children's linguistic development will we discover that they do not, in fact, really understand the language involved in experimental tests?

Let me provide an illustrative example. Another of the intellectual structures that Piaget analysed to reveal marked differences in the thinking of five- and seven-year-old children involves concepts of 'classes' and 'class inclusion'. To the mature mind, a given object (e.g. a chair) or a class of objects (e.g. animals) can, at one and the same time, be members of any number of more inclusive categories. So, a chair is also a member of the class 'furniture' or of 'man-made

Figure 2.2 'Are there more flowers or more tulips?'

artefacts' and so on. Categories like 'animal' can be subsumed under more inclusive labels (e.g. living beings) and decomposed into more exclusive ones (e.g. canine, feline). For an adult, such classifications exist as enduring, organized structures of knowledge. Saying that a dog is an animal or a member of the canine family does not change the *thing* being referred to. The same concept can belong to any number of classes at the same time.

But pre-operational children cannot co-ordinate different judgements or acts of centration. So, for example, a tulip cannot be conceived of as *both* a tulip and a flower at one and the same time. This demands co-ordination which, as we have seen, pre-operational children cannot do. So, if we show the pre-operational child the set up illustrated in figure 2.2 and ask her 'Are there more flowers or more tulips?' the child will probably say 'More tulips'. 'More' is interpreted as a reference to the largest available sub-class (of flowers). Since there are more tulips than daisies, there are more tulips. Piaget's interpretation of this phenomenon is that the child cannot 'see' or, rather, cannot *organize* what she sees, so that the same entities (the tulips) are *simultaneously* both tulips and flowers.

Questions like 'Are there more flowers or more tulips?' sound distinctly odd! However, before we look into rather murky linguistic depths to analyse the nature and consequences of their strangeness, let me consider the issue of class inclusion with what looks like a much simpler example. A child (one of Piaget's own), aged two-and-a-half, is often taken for a walk by her father along a particular road. This road is often infested with slugs. The child sometimes points to a slug saying (in French) 'There's the slug again.' Her father asks (since she had pointed out another slug earlier) 'But isn't it another?'. The child went back to the first slug encountered, and was asked 'Is it the same?' – 'Yes.' 'Another slug?' – 'Yes.' 'Another or the same?' . . . The questions, Piaget concluded, 'obviously had no meaning' for the child.

What does 'the' mean? When the child says 'There's the slug again' is she, perhaps, using the word 'the' as part of the act of pointing to and talking about an object in the situation? But when Piaget asks if it is 'the' same slug (i.e. as a previous slug) he is using the word to refer *back* to a previous experience. These two uses of words like 'the' are quite different and children develop an understanding of the first 'the', as something being pointed at, a long time before they learn how to use and understand the second 'the', which is used to refer back to an earlier utterance or experience. Even if the child is aware of the fact that a slug is both itself and a member of the class 'all slugs', she would not understand the question because she does not and cannot understand the *language* involved. Are we, then, dealing with absence of *logic* or a failure of communication based on the child's stage of language development, or both? Piaget's observation does not allow us to answer this question.

Suppose we find, in general, that specific problems in understanding language can explain why children fail to answer Piaget's questions. Would this mean that we have sufficient evidence to reject Piaget's explanation for their 'errors' of reasoning? Well, not really. It might still be argued, for example, that understanding a word like 'the' in all its meanings demands concrete operational competence. Part of the elegance and power of Piaget's theory is the way in which it integrates many aspects of development, including the relationship between intellectual and linguistic understanding. One might argue, for example, that understanding the second form of the word 'the', to refer back to previous experiences, demands an ability to co-ordinate judgements, which explains why young children cannot understand it when it is used in this way (although this explanation is hard to sustain, as we will see in chapter 5).

Piaget's theory also leads directly to the prediction that pre-operational children will *not* understand phrases like 'as much as' used in conservation tests in the same way that adults do. Mature understanding of what such expressions mean demands the capacity to co-ordinate different judgements, so of course the child doesn't understand the words involved. If we are to reject Piaget's account we must provide an alternative and equally robust theory of how the child comes to understand language, and provide evidence that it is *language* or communication abilities as such that create problems for the child, not his or her inability to reason logically. We have to find some way of distinguishing linguistic problems from intellectual problems. Perhaps we could try to provide evidence that when linguistic problems are avoided, the young child can reason rationally. Or we might try to demonstrate that the acquisition of linguistic knowledge involves 'special' features that are not simply reflections of the difficulties a child faces in understanding the concepts or ideas embodied in language. Put another way, does the development of thinking dictate the development of language, or are some features of language development independent of intellectual growth? Or is the capacity to use language itself the basis for understanding and grasping concepts like equivalence and classification?

To investigate the theory of stages and all its educational implications we must, then, examine alternative accounts of linguistic development, and of the relationships between language and thought, to those espoused by Piaget. This we do in chapter 6.

Can children make sense of Piaget's questions?

I have already drawn attention to the fact that communication between adult and child in Piagetian tests of class inclusion sound, to say the least, rather strange. Even if the child, in one sense, understands the *words* and the grammar involved in such questions, there is still a question mark over what they think the questioner intends to *mean*. What does the child think is going on in the experimental situation? How does she interpret the performance of the experimenter? How do the 'social practices' that govern interactions between adults and children in the world at large influence how the child *interprets* what the experimenter expects of her?

First, note that the child is often asked a similar question at least twice in such experiments. In the test of conservation of continuous quantity, for instance, the child is usually asked something like 'Are they the same or different?' at least twice: once before the liquid is poured into the new container and once after pouring has taken place. What *function* does the repetition of a question usually serve in everyday encounters between adults and children? Blank, Rose and Berlin (1978) suggest that a repeated question is usually a signal that the *first* answer given was wrong, inaccurate or inappropriate. If so, perhaps the child in conservation experiments is thrown, not by the 'logical' demands of the task, but by her interpretation of what she assumes the adult is *implicitly* communicating. There are now several experiments which have shown that changes in the way such problems are presented to children which ensure that only one question is asked (e.g. the second of the two questions mentioned above, asked after pouring has taken place) lead to a greater chance of 'correct' or conserving answers from young children. So perhaps breakdown of mutual understanding, rather than logical incompetence, explains the child's apparent 'errors' of reasoning.

The issue of questioning draws our attention to 'pragmatic'

features of communication about which I will have a good deal to say in this book. 'Pragmatic', in this sense, refers to the way in which the meaning of an utterance is influenced by its social context and by the relationship between the speaker and hearer. For example, if a teacher asks a child 'Can you close the door?' he or she is unlikely to be enquiring about the child's physical prowess in the practice of door-shutting (unless, of course, there is some reason to doubt that the child can do such things and the teacher really wants to know if he or she can do so). Many utterances involve 'indirect' acts of communication. The example above, for instance, is probably a request or order 'disguised' as a question. If a child fails to comply with or fails to understand a request or question from an adult, we must ask whether any 'indirect' or 'hidden' meanings are implicated. The meanings associated with utterances in everyday interactions may differ from those implied in experimental tasks, leading to confusion for the child and a breakdown of communication. Such features of communication are complex and of immense importance in evaluating what a child knows and understands, as we shall see.

Thus, when we begin to explore the interaction between experimenter and child as a *social encounter*, and one that displays some 'special' and, from the child's perspective, unfamiliar properties, a number of questions arise. Until we consider and resolve these, we would be unwise to draw inferences about children's intellectual ability and logical competence.

Another concrete example illustrates how pragmatic aspects of everyday social practices influence children's interpretation of experimental or 'contrived' situations. In a quantity conservation study, Light, Buckingham and Roberts (1979), performed the usual transfer of the contents of one container to another, but they incorporated an important modification to Piaget's method. One of the two identical beakers had a broken, razor-sharp rim. The children's attention was drawn to this flaw, and the potential danger it presented was given as a reason for transferring its contents to another (differently shaped) container. Asked to compare quantities after pouring in this context, children were more likely to be successful than they were when no such reason for the experimenter's actions was given. One interpretation of this finding is that the explanation for changing glasses made the experimenter's actions *sensible* to the child. Put another way, the child's everyday social experiences render what the experimenter does intelligible. She sees no reason to assume that he is showing her something unusual that demands an explanation. When no such reason is given, perhaps the child (erroneously) believes that there must be some hidden reason that she does not understand. Adults usually appear to know more than children do. When children cannot infer a sensible reason for the adult's behaviour, they may think that there is more to the problem than 'meets the eye', perhaps assuming that there is something they do not understand and need to learn.

Finally, a rather different illustration of the way in which children's interpretations of what an experimenter is getting at can influence their apparent competence. If ten-year-old children are asked to compare two sets of ten objects (these are arranged in two haphazard sets) in order to find out if they comprise the same number, they usually perform the task accurately. However, if the experimenter asks 'Why are there more in this set than that set?' many ten-year-olds, like younger children, will give an explanation based on appearances, even when the sets are equal. That is, they will choose the set that *looks* more numerous. But when the experimenter says 'I *think* there are more in this set than that one', most children count the set and disagree (Hundeide, 1985). Consequently, it is not the case that children are not prepared to challenge an adult's judgement or opinion. Rather, when they are asked to *explain* something by a question like 'Why are there . . . ?', they take *on trust* the fact that there is a difference to be explained. The experimenter's question does not reveal a lack of logic in children's judgements. Rather, it illustrates how people's *interpretation* of what others mean by what they say involves more than the words or questions involved: mutual understanding rests on a range of conventions and expectations which are often violated in experiments. As we will find in chapter 7, they are also frequently violated in classrooms.

Do children understand Piaget's tasks?

Another criticism that has often been levelled against Piaget's studies is that many involve tasks that are 'artificial' and unfamiliar to children, and that this explains why they make errors. For example, one of the predictions that arises from Piaget's theory is that pre-operational children are psychologically 'egocentric'. He argues that they are incapable of conceptualizing a situation from any perspective other than the one they themselves are occupying. Their thinking is dominated by their perceptions and, since they are unable to co-ordinate judgements based on different observations, when they move from one position to another they can't integrate judgements made at different times to achieve an 'objective' view of situations. They are always dominated by their own perceptions and hence cannot construct a view of things as seen from another point of view.

One experiment designed to test and display this feature of pre-operational children's thinking involves the situation illustrated in figure 2.3. Children are shown a model of three mountains together with a number of pictures that depict how the mountain scene

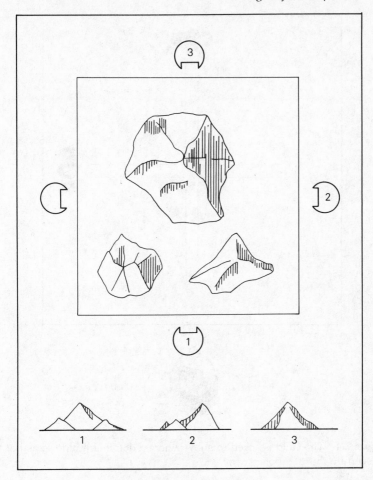

Figure 2.3   The three mountains problem. A child is positioned at location 1. She is asked to select from a group of drawings the view of the mountains that would be seen by persons at locations 1, 2 and 3

appears from different positions of observation. Imagine that a child is looking at the model from position 1. She is asked to pick out the picture that represents what another person would see if they were to look at the same model from position 2 or 3. Children below the age of seven years or so, who have yet to develop operational thinking (pre-operational children), are unlikely to succeed in this situation and will probably choose the drawing that represents what they themselves see of the three mountains. They are unable to conceptualize or form a mental representation of what the model looks like from other than their own point of view. This task, for Piaget, illustrates pre-operational children's egocentrism and demonstrates that their concept of space is subjective and centred on

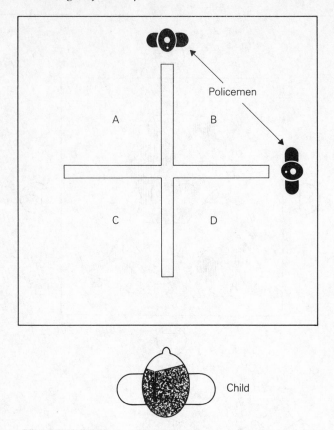

Figure 2.4   The child is asked to show where a doll might hide so as not to be seen by the two policemen

their own body. Unlike adults, they cannot conceive of space in 'objective' terms: they cannot construct an interpretation of what 'their' space might look like from another perspective, for example.

Although, as with most of Piaget's demonstrations, many other experimenters have reaffirmed his findings with children from several different cultures, other researchers have shown that so-called pre-operational children can conceptualize viewpoints other than their own when the problem makes more 'sense' to them. Figure 2.4 illustrates a task used by a group of psychologists working with Donaldson (1978) in Edinburgh. The child's task here is to decide where to place a doll in the set-up so that it can 'hide' from the two policemen. To solve this problem, the child has to relate the points of view of the two police dolls to discover the region of space that neither can see and in which the other doll can hide. Many pre-operational children succeed in solving this task. Donaldson's interpretation is that where the actions of the characters in the problem are interpretable to the child, where they refer to experiences that are relatively familiar and involve actions that the child can make sense of, then the child is not egocentric nor limited to a subjective concept of space.

Is the evidence against Piaget conclusive?

Conclusive though such evidence may seem on first sight, it is not, in fact, so easy to 'disprove' Piaget's theory. In his explorations of children's thinking, Piaget was not simply concerned to find out whether they got a particular problem right or not. He usually went on to investigate children's reasons for giving the answer provided in an attempt to explore their *understanding* of the situation. There are many ways in which a particular problem might be solved: by chance, 'intuition', learning or through instruction. Success alone is not a sufficient criterion for attributing logical understanding to a child. Only when a child is able to provide a rational *justification* for her judgements is any success interpreted as 'operational' in nature. Many studies that have attempted to 'disconfirm' predictions from Piaget's theory have not explored children's justifications, concentrating simply on whether the answers they give are correct or incorrect. From a Piagetian perspective, such studies do not demonstrate logical competence in young children.

On the other hand, Piaget's demand for verbal explanation and justification introduces additional problems of language and communication into the situation. These may serve to obscure rather than to uncover children's understanding. The subject of discussion, explanation, justification and understanding is also a later focus of this book.

Summary

The examples and illustrations I have just discussed identify a number of factors that we need to consider and evaluate in trying to make a decision about Piaget's proposal that the structure of children's thinking moves from an intuitive, pre-logical grasp of reality to a logically constrained, more realistic view of the world at around the age of seven. If children do not understand the words and expressions involved in attempts to test their understanding; if they are so unfamiliar with the task they are asked to perform that they do not know what is relevant to the questions asked and, hence, cannot analyse and grasp what they need to take into account; if they are unsure of the experimenter's motives or misled by the way in which the interaction is conducted; if they assume that there is more to the problem than meets the eye; then they may appear logically incompetent.

Piagetian theory can and does provide explanations for some of these phenomena. Children cannot understand many things that adults say because they lack the necessary intellectual structures to make sense of what they mean. They may well misunderstand an experimenter's intentions because they are 'egocentric' and cannot diagnose what the experimenter intends. They are unable to analyse tasks into their important elements because they cannot 'de-centre' from their own viewpoint. If we accept these explanations, then we also accept the stringent notion of readiness for learning and the relative unimportance of language, communication and instruction.

If we reject these explanations, then we must find others. Vygotsky's theory invites us to consider the possibility that children understand those things that are common features of their social experience. Learning *how* to think about and learn about things that are relatively *unfamiliar* are not 'natural' achievements that occur with time, but special forms of 'self-regulation' which rest on *relevant* experiences. In the next chapter, we consider the proposal that these experiences are provided by schooling. If we accept this line of argument, then it follows that any changes that occur in children's ability to learn, think and understand may, in part at least, be a *product* of schooling.

Another question, examined in detail in chapter 6, when we will have discussed the evidence and examples needed to explore it fully, asks whether looking at intellectual development as a process of the construction of *logic* and logical operations is useful. If we do not begin with the assumption that *adults* reason by means of logical operations, then the issue as to whether the seven-year-old's thinking is logical and that of the five-year-old is intuitive may not arise. But if intelligent, adaptive thinking is not based in logical operations what *does* it involve? How does it develop? To what extent is it a product of communication and teaching?

Chapter 3

Learning how to think and learn

Piaget's analysis of pre-operational thinking suggests that young children tend to form their judgements about the nature of things on the basis of single acts of centration. He argues that their perception is thus 'dominated' by what they happen to attend to. They cannot 'de-centre' their thinking or co-ordinate their mental actions to achieve stable, logical judgements. Only later, when they have constructed logical operations, do they develop the capacity for sustained and systematic perceptual analysis and rational thought.

Whilst the changes in children's ability to perceive, analyse and remember events that Piaget identified are consistent with the results of many other experimental studies, interpretations of how such changes come about vary. Research in the 'information processing' tradition, introduced in chapter 1, provides a different account of the mental activities involved in development. Research in the Vygotskian tradition offers yet another view of the origins and nature of children's abilities. Vygotsky argued that mature mental activity involves adaptive 'self-regulation' which develops through social interaction. In this view, instruction and schooling play a central role in helping children to discover how to pay attention, concentrate and learn effectively. These ideas, and some of the research they have motivated, are the focus of this chapter. We also begin to explore the relationships between the child's perception of the world and his understanding of it.

Attending, concentrating and remembering

When teachers are asked to evaluate a child's likely potential in a particular subject or discipline, their answer is likely to relate to a specific feature of the child's classroom behaviour: the child's willingness or capacity to *concentrate* on tasks relevant to that subject. Those children who spend most time 'on task' in the classroom are most likely to be judged capable of doing well in the subject or discipline being taught. More importantly, if we monitor the children's progress we will find that teacher predictions are, more often than not, borne out. Concentration is a good indicator of interest and potential (Keough, 1982). There are several reasons why teacher judgements, children's powers of concentration, and school achievement might be related in this way. One possibility, considered in more detail later in the book, is that teachers are in the business of fulfilling their own prophecies. Perhaps they treat children they perceive as more likely to succeed differently from those they think are less likely to do so and, in so doing, foster the expected patterns of achievement. While we may not rule this factor out entirely, I will be arguing later that such an explanation is far too general and even simple-minded to be convincing. As I will try to show in this chapter, many factors influence children's powers of concentration and thereby exert a marked influence on how much and how readily they learn.

It will come as no surprise to find that, on average, children's concentration span increases with age. But why does it? Well, anyone who has worked with children might observe that younger children are usually more 'distractable' than older ones. Again we ask, why? What is it about young children that leaves them relatively open to distraction? To answer this question, we need to look at the general nature of young children's powers of perception, attention and memory and at their knowledge and 'planning' abilities. The ability to keep on task and to ignore distractions is, in fact, a symptom of the structure of the child's intellect, and changes in concentration span are related to intellectual development. Consider some experimental evidence which illustrates and supports this proposition (see Kail, 1979, for a more detailed and very readable account).

Learning to remember: rehearsal and organization

If five-year-old children are shown a set of 20 pictures and asked to predict how many of them they will be able to remember, they are likely to grossly overestimate their own capacities and may claim that they will remember them all. If we ask eleven-year-olds the same question, their assessments will probably prove accurate. Again, perhaps unsurprisingly, older children will remember more than the younger ones. Thus, changes in the ability to memorize go hand-in-hand with more accurate and realistic assessments of one's own mental abilities. Deliberate attempts to commit information to memory are not the product of a 'natural ability' but involve learned *activity*. In fact, they involve a series of activities. The skill in undertaking each of these increases with age throughout the early years of school and beyond.

I think we often mislead ourselves by describing our own psychology using nouns like memory, perception and attention when we should be thinking in terms of verbs such as memorizing, perceiving and attending. Intellectual processes take time to execute and, like manual skills, can be organized and executed more or less effectively. Deliberate memorization involves such skills. It does not emerge full blown at some point in life but involves a series of interlocking activities which eventually become automatic and often seemingly effortless, but which in reality take years of learning and practice to develop and acquire.

The five-year-olds' unrealistic estimates of their own powers of memory are reflected in their concentration or habits of study. Whereas older children distribute their attention carefully between the different things they are trying to memorize, and spend time in so doing, the younger ones are likely to make a cursory and non-exhaustive inspection before deciding that they are able to remember. As they gain in proficiency, children not only learn how to commit things to memory, they also become more aware of and accurate in their assessments of their own memorial powers. They also become aware of what they do and do not know and this leads to the development of more effective concentration and study skills. For example, if we ask a five- or six-year-old to commit a series of familiar objects to memory we will find that they will recall, on average, about four. Suppose we then ask the child to have another go. Will he pay more attention to the ones he failed to recall the first time round? No: he will probably be *non-selective*, and just as likely to attend to those he remembered the first time around as to those that he did not memorize. The eleven-year-old will be reasonably selective and proficient in such circumstances, and hence will further outstrip the performance of his younger peers.

Two of the most well established principles of human memory are that 'rehearsal' is a powerful aid to deliberate memorization and that the imposition of some structure or meaning on what we seek to memorize also determines the likelihood of successful recall. Rehearsal refers to the continuous repetition, out loud or under the breath, of what one is trying to hold in mind (obvious examples are the repetition of a shopping list or an unfamiliar telephone number whilst dialling). Five- or six-year-olds asked to remember a set of things that can be named and, hence, rehearsed will probably not rehearse them. It is possible to help them to use a rehearsal strategy and this increases their chances of success, particularly if they are asked to say words out loud so that they can be corrected if they miss one or more things out. However, even after being taught how to rehearse and having experienced evidence of its success, children will *not* usually rehearse spontaneously when they are asked to memorize other material. The use of rehearsal as an aid to memorization might appear to be a simple, self-evident and obvious way to aid learning. However, children learn how to do it gradually, throughout the early years of school.

Even adults, to whom such tactics may seem obvious, often fail to use rehearsal when it would aid their attempts to learn. Investigations into the study techniques of undergraduates, for example, suggest that they often do not rehearse what they have been taught. Listening to a lecture or reading a text, understanding what is heard or read and believing that understanding implies learning, students fail to rehearse and then pay the penalty later. In one study, groups of students were asked to recall a lesson. Some were asked after a day, others after several days and some several weeks following the event. The amount recalled 'decayed' sharply over the first few days, but more interesting was the finding that students who, early on, were asked to recall and recount the lesson showed very little subsequent forgetting over a period of several weeks. Going over notes, thinking and rehearsing what has been heard or read, greatly facilitates how much is memorized. This may seem like common sense, but experience and evidence suggest that even people who are able to use rehearsal strategies fail to do so.

Imposing some *structure* or organization on what we are trying to learn is another seemingly obvious strategy for improving performance, and one that seems to come naturally. But it does not. Imagine giving a number of objects to be remembered to an eleven-year-old. These can be grouped into a set of categories. Suppose, for example, the child is presented with a number of toy animals, toys which represent various forms of transportation, and some toy pieces of fruit. The child is likely to recall them in organized sets: he may, say, give first a set of animal names, then a set of transport names followed by fruit. Similarly, if we allow the child to move the objects around he or she is likely to group them physically into categories as an aid to improved memorization. So the eleven-year-old exploits the fact that organizing material to be learned into well-established groups or categories increases the chances of successful recall. Five-year-olds, on the other hand, are unlikely to exploit this kind of categorical organization even when they can, when requested, arrange the objects into categories. Although they know how to group objects, and can be helped to improve their learning by instructions to arrange the objects into groups before trying to learn them, as with rehearsal they will not exploit the strategy spontaneously when they are presented with another set of objects.

Memorizing: one activity or many?

But, you might ask, are we really dealing here with changes in memory skills? Might it not be the case that children simply don't understand the instructions given? Perhaps the five-year-old child does not understand the meaning of words like 'remember'? Well, the evidence suggests that we are dealing with changes in the child's cognitive skills and not simply with linguistic development. There are situations, for instance, in which pre-school children show that they understand what an instruction to remember entails (at least in one sense). Imagine placing a sweet beneath one of a set of upturned cups that are identical in appearance. We ask a two-year-old to remember which cup the sweet is placed under. Then we tell the child that we have to go and fetch something from another room and that they must remember where the sweet is until we get back. Surreptitiously, we arrange for someone to observe the child while we are away. What we are likely to find is that our preschooler will keep touching the appropriate cup from time to time. The child uses his digits to 'keep hold' of the information he has to remember, literally 're-mind-ing' himself of it by physical means (i.e. putting his finger on it, hitting it on the head; the source of many a metaphor). Young children do, in some senses at least, understand what it means to remember. What they learn with age are more powerful and efficient strategies for memorizing and learning; they learn *how* to control or regulate their own performance more effectively.

Let us consider another example of the preschooler's powers of memory which helps to illustrate other aspects of the 'natural history' of memory development. Imagine a playground with a series of fence posts around its perimeter. An adult is going to walk with a group of preschoolers from one post to another attaching coloured pieces of paper to each post. When they reach, say, the third post, the children are told that when they have attached paper to all the posts they will have their photograph taken. They are shown the camera to be used which is removed from a bag held by the adult. The adult then hides the camera when the children are not looking. When they reach the last post, the adult laments that the camera has been lost. Now, what do the children suggest and do? Do they simply begin to search at random for the camera or, perhaps, go back to the first post? Or do they remember the fact that the camera was last seen at post number three? They are more likely to return to the scene of the event, post three. They remembered where they last saw the camera and also *infer* that this is the best place for a search to commence. They are making intelligent use of past experience to formulate a plan of action – evidence of both memory and reasoning.

Why, when preschool children seem so competent in such situations, do five-year-olds seem to perform so poorly in the experiments I outlined earlier? Well, such differences in children's apparent competence are symptomatic of important features of human memory and cognition. They also help to illustrate the *multiplicity* of intellectual activities that we commonly (and mistakenly) lump together under headings like 'memory'. The abilities deployed by preschoolers in the situations just outlined are different in kind from those demanded in the first experiments presented, which demanded 'deliberate' memorization. Basically, what young children learn and remember are things that arise as a 'natural' and often *incidental* consequence of their activities. No one needed to alert the preschoolers in the playgroup to the fact that they would be expected to remember the location of an object. Setting out deliberately to commit a body of information to memory is a quite different affair to such examples of natural or spontaneous remembering, where what is subsequently recalled is something one literally handled, attended to or in some way had to take cognizance of in the course of doing a practical activity. Perhaps another example will illustrate the distinction I am attempting to draw.

Recall that earlier in the chapter I outlined the five-year-old's relative incompetence when asked to make judgements about his or her own memory ability, and the resulting poor performance. Suppose instead of *asking* the child to remember objects we ask him to *do* something with them. We might, for example, ask him to point to and label every animal in the set of toys. Subsequently, we ask him to recall what he has seen (and touched). We will find that the number of items recalled by the child is superior to that achieved when we simply *ask* him to memorize. The task of pointing and labelling encouraged the child to attend systematically to the objects, and led to activities or *interactions* with the material destined to be remembered. The child's active involvement with the material and his concentration on the task at hand helped him to 'encode' or become consciously aware of the objects handled. In such circumstances, memorization usually takes place quite spontaneously. Similarly, in the playground experiment, children were actively involved in tasks (e.g. putting paper on posts, searching for a misplaced object) that made sense to them and were comprehensible. Furthermore, as in the cup experiment with the preschooler, the object to be remembered was *external and spatial*. Such tasks both provide concrete external cues that prompt recall (which help to remind the child) and involve practical demands in their performance which lead the child to act upon the material to be remembered. Young children's spatial memory is, in such circumstances, good. Contrast such situations with the task of deliberately committing to memory discrete sets of objects through rehearsal when there are no simple, physical locational cues to aid memorization or recall, and there is no purpose, other than memorization itself, being served.

So, in tasks where *memorization* is an end in and of itself, rather than an incidental product of activities that are instrumental in achieving some practical end or objective, young children do not know how to proceed. Special skills in rehearsal and some form of (self-induced) interaction with the material in order to 'make sense' of it (e.g. grouping it perhaps, or forming the elements into a story or some other pattern) take time to learn and perfect.

It follows that if we help the young child to make sense of a task by asking him to group objects together into appropriate sets, or by embodying the objects to be remembered into a story or pattern for him, then we may facilitate his performance of the task. However, as with rehearsal, simply exposing children to such strategies does not lead to their immediate adoption and generalization. If we want children to learn and remember things, we must often 'scaffold' the process for them by setting tasks, arranging materials, reminding and prompting them. Eventually, they will come to do such things for themselves (at least, on occasion) and will discover how to rehearse and so on. Put another way, the teacher's role in facilitating learning and memory will change as a function of the child's age and capacities.

A pause for review

Before moving on, let *us* rehearse some of the arguments I have been putting forward. Attending, concentrating and memorizing are *activities*. Simply asking a child aged five or six to pay attention, concentrate, study, learn or remember is unlikely to bear fruit. Unless we embody the material to be learned and remembered in a task that makes sense to the child, one that involves objectives he can realize and that draws his attention 'naturally' to the elements we wish him to take in, our imperatives to concentrate, memorize or learn are almost bound to fail. Young children can and will concentrate and remember but will often need the support of a more knowledgeable and intellectually skilled assistant. Such assistants in a real sense act as external aids to memorization, as 're-mind-ers'. At the same time, they provide living illustrations of the processes involved in memorization which eventually the child comes to 'internalize' and exploit himself. Looked at in this way, the processes involved in deliberate memorization and contrived or formal learning situations take place first in external, observable and social terms before being internalized by the child to become personal, mental activities. More mature individuals or adults who are involved with children in shared projects and activities provide children with the means to become autonomous and self-regulating. The importance of such shared social activities as a basis for mental development is, as you will find when you read on, a recurrent theme of this book.

Memory and schooling

If the assertion that certain powers of concentration and memory are fostered in social interaction has any value, then it should follow that the development of such powers will vary from one culture to another to the extent that the social practices which help create them are different in those cultures. There is evidence to support this case. It comes from comparing the memorizing activities of adults in our own society with those of adults from non-schooled/non-literate cultures. I will refer several times to such comparisons at various places in the book where they both help to illustrate the *social* origins of mental life and assist us in our search for the specific features of social practices that influence the development of mental abilities.

In a number of studies of non-schooled, non-literate societies (Cole and Scribner, 1974) some marked differences (and important similarities, that we consider later) have been revealed between the characteristic ways of memorizing found there and in Western technological cultures. There is a growing body of evidence, for example, to show that rehearsal is *not* a feature of deliberate attempts at memorization by people in non-technological societies and, further, that strategies like grouping familiar objects into categories to aid memory are also the product of schooled, literate cultures. In the past, such differences between the mature people of different societies, and what appear to be similarities in performance between young children in our kind of society and adults in 'traditional' cultures, were regarded as evidence that characteristic modes of thinking in these other cultures are 'childlike'; 'non-rational' or in some other way less developed than in our own. Such views, at least in informed circles, have been revised of late as more sophisticated ways of studying and theorizing about culture and cognition have been developed. What I think we may conclude from such observations is that deliberate attempts to memorize 'arbitrarily' sets of information, i.e. memorization for its own sake, is a product of technological societies and more specifically of schooling and/or literacy. Perhaps if we ask ourselves a different set of questions these rather puzzling differences and their implications will become clearer.

First, we must ask ourselves what possible *need* an individual in a traditional society would have for deliberate memorization of the sort we have been discussing. Certainly, they need to remember places, routes, seasons and those practical skills and knowledge that enable them to survive in their own environment. Studies of the navigational powers of people in fishing and trading cultures, for example, reveal extremely complex and intricate systems of mapping and navigation which demand considerable powers of memory and planning. As children go about daily life in these cultures they 'naturally' or 'incidentally' acquire such knowledge as they observe, imitate or are helped to perform necessary tasks by the more knowledgeable and mature. But they do not sit down in a specially constructed building with teachers to be shown about and told about things outside their common cultural experience. Sitting, attending, listening carefully, or diligently watching a performance by an adult, in relation to a task that the adult has set, leads to demands on concentration, memory and thinking that are not a feature of incidental learning. As I pointed out in the Introduction, the notion that children learn by being deliberately 'taught' by adults is by no means universally shared.

Indeed, as Newson and Newson (1974) have pointed out, contemporary Western concerns with issues like the psychological well-being and educational potential of children are of historically recent origin. Compulsory schooling for all is a relatively modern cultural invention and with it has come a new range of questions and concerns. In the eighteenth century, for instance, parents were understandably more concerned with the physical well-being and survival chances of their offspring, since life then, by modern standards, was far more hazardous, particularly for young children. Only with good medical and nutritional care and all the other achievements of modern societies have we come to worry more about the mental welfare of children. The invention of schooling and the creation of roles such as 'teacher' and 'pupil' has led to new demands on adults, as they try consciously and deliberately to 'transmit' their knowledge and culture. It has also created special demands on children as they attempt deliberately to learn, memorize and think in specially constructed buildings, away from and out of contact with adult activity. In non-schooled societies children are gradually acculturated, socialized and 'educated' by becoming progressively more involved in adult economic activity until they eventually learn and inherit their social roles. Our own children, meanwhile, are effectively excluded from centres of adult activity and learn, not by doing the things that their parents are involved in, but by listening, reading, experimenting and solving problems set for them by a 'specialist' teacher. Since members of non-schooled cultures have no need to develop skills such as those involved in deliberate memorization, it is perhaps unsurprising that, when confronted by a strange Western person with his odd questions and peculiar demands, they are unable to perform what are culture-specific and culturally transmitted skills that take children in our own society years to master.

We are used to thinking about bits of machinery, architecture and technology as special, cultural inventions. We accept that each upcoming generation of our society will need to learn about new things, and develop new skills in order to operate and work new instruments of production. It is strange, perhaps, to think of what seem to be 'natural' aspects of our mental life as cultural inventions in the same vein. Strange though it may seem, I suggest that it is nonetheless the case.

Paying attention

One reason why older children are likely to be able to sustain longer periods of study and concentration than younger children is that they have discovered how to exploit strategies such as rehearsal and organization of material for learning. Lacking such skills, the child below age eight or so is often likely to appear more impulsive and capricious than the older child whose attempts to regulate his or her own learning or memorizing take time to execute.

If we look in more detail at how children distribute their attention – to examine, for instance, what they look at when they are trying to solve a problem or answer a question – we find other important differences between the performances of children who have just entered school and those aged around seven to eight. Where the older child's patterns of attention are becoming systematic and exhaustive, and reflect a sensitivity to the demands of the task facing them, the five- to six-year-old's attention seems impulsive and brief. Why? Before discussing possible answers, let us consider a few examples which illustrate how children's powers of attention emerge and develop through the years of schooling.

Inspect the three pairs of drawings shown in figure 3.1 and spot any differences between each pair. When children aged between three to six years are asked to do this, we find that they are unlikely to be very accurate. If we observe their eye movements as they compare pairs of figures, we discover that they tend to compare only one or two features of the drawings before reaching a decision. If they happen to compare two points which reveal a difference, then they make a correct decision (showing that they understand what the experimenter means by 'different'). However, since their inspection is brief and not exhaustive, they are unlikely to 'see' differences and instead judge that pairs which are different look identical. Figure 3.2 illustrates the inspection pattern of a four-year-old: compare it with that shown for an eight-year-old child. Older children are more careful, analytic and exhaustive in their inspection of the figures. Not surprisingly, their judgements are more accurate. When they say that two drawings are identical it is on the basis of a

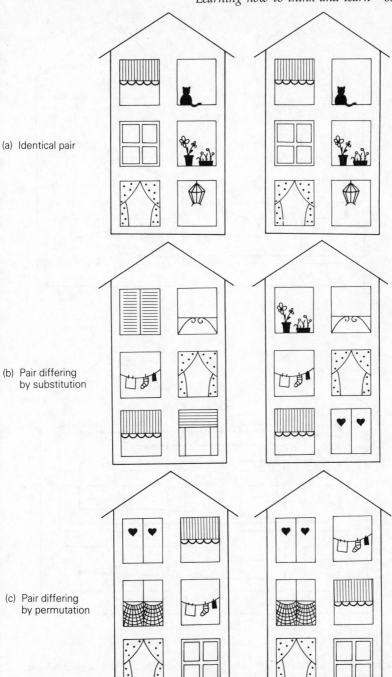

Figure 3.1 Children are asked to compare each pair of drawings to say whether they look the same or different: (a) identical pair; (b) pair differing by substitution; (c) pair differing by permutation

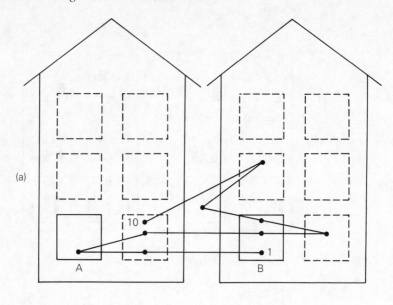

(a)

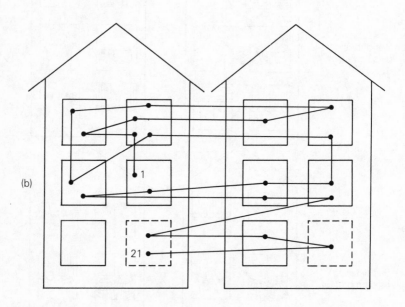

(b)

Figure 3.2   Children's inspection patterns faced with the drawings illustrated in figure 3.1. Dotted lines illustrate windows that *differ* from one house to the other; the children's eye movements start at 1: (a) a child of 4 y 4 m judges in 10 eye movements that the two houses are 'the same' on the basis that windows A and B look similar; (b) a child of 8 makes 21 eye movements before deciding that the pair differ

more thorough search. Performance on this task keeps on improving up to age eight or nine years, as children become increasingly cautious and careful in their perceptual activity (Vurpillot, 1976).

As we observed for tests that required deliberate memorization, children below the age of seven or so often appear impulsive when asked to undertake unfamiliar tasks. As children grow through the early years, we find increasing evidence that they are learning or discovering how to control their own attention, learning and problem-solving in situations where other people set them tasks to perform. Paying attention, like deliberate memorization, is an *activity* that can be executed more or less skilfully. There is an implicit *plan* in the eight-year-old's inspection of the figures that is lacking in the five-year-old's attempts to do the task. What might appear at first sight to be a simple issue of perception, of 'seeing' a solution, turns out on closer inspection to involve intelligence, knowledge and skill in self-regulation.

When we ask young children to look at a situation and, say, ask them a question about what they are 'seeing', we cannot assume, simply because they turn heads and eyes to look at what we are showing them, that they will perceive the situation in the same way as ourselves. The relationships between requests, questions and other utterances, and the systematic search for information that these utterances are designed to stimulate on the other, change with age towards increasing degrees of accuracy, or what Bruner terms greater 'analytical competence'. Understanding the demands of a question, such as 'Are these the same?', and undertaking a systematic search for information to answer it, are two interlocking aspects of knowledge.

But, you might ask, aren't children younger than eight years of age capable of using pictorial aids to instruction in some situations? What about jigsaws, model-making or following Lego instructions? Surely children are able to guide their own activities in such tasks before age eight? Yes they are. Indeed, in a series of studies, we have found that children as young as four years of age are reasonably adept at using pictorial aids to help them put together quite complex construction toys (Murphy and Wood, 1982). We gave them a series of nine photographs (figure 3.3) and asked them to make the model depicted. Although four-year-olds almost never completed the task successfully, when we looked at their eye movements to see how they 'interrogated' the pictures, we found that they did usually look at a picture that was relevant to what they were trying to do with the blocks.

The differences between model-building tasks and the 'inspection' tasks discussed earlier are similar in some respects to those between 'natural' and 'deliberate' processes of memorization. Tasks like assembling models and making use of pictures to put together

Figure 3.3   Photographs showing stages in the construction of the pyramid

jigsaws are relatively common activities for many children in our society. So when they were asked to make up the model in our experiment, they had some intuitive sense of what we meant and relevant past experiences to draw upon. They came equipped with enough experience to make sense of what we asked them to do. The photographs were used as an aid to their own practical activity. In the comparison and questioning tasks there were no external guides to provide children with feedback about the success or otherwise of their efforts (unless, of course, an adult were to help them by pointing out relevant features that they had overlooked). Unlike the model-building tasks, where the results of their activities were visible and could be compared with the photographs, the inspection problem demands that the child make a judgement about how and when he has satisfied the requirements of the questioner. The ability to make such decisions, coupled with the more 'abstract' nature of the inspection tasks, is what marks off the performance of eight-year-olds from that of younger children.

I will explore ways in which others help children to overcome their limited knowledge and inexperience in analysing, planning and regulating their own activities later. For the moment, I want to return to consider cross-cultural studies which reinforce the argument that understanding and using media like photographs involve knowledge of conventions and learned skills of analysis and planning. To the trained user of such artefacts, perception and recognition of what is illustrated in a photograph or picture might seem automatic and hence 'natural'. But this is not the case. When people from non-pictorial cultures, who have never seen or used paper to represent or depict objects, are asked to identify drawings or photographs of familiar objects or animals they cannot do so. Pictures are two-dimensional representations of things that, in the real world, occupy three dimensions. Real objects are solid and have depth. When we look at a picture we have to *infer* solidity and depth from cues like the relative size of different things in the picture or from differences in texture, perspective cues, overlap of parts of one object by another and so forth. Perception of such things is neither 'natural' nor automatic. Rather, the implicit conventions governing the interpretation of drawings and photographs have to be learned. When children in our society use pictures to help make things, look at family snaps, watch television or are involved in the many experiences in which pictorial materials intrude into their lives, they are learning how to interpret what is being depicted. Lacking such experiences, people from non-pictorial cultures cannot 'make sense' of such representations and only after a period of training can they learn to 'see' what we see (Serpell, 1976). Next time you visit a good art gallery compare the way in which, say, geometric perspective has been represented by painters across the centuries. Conventions for trying to capture the three-dimensional world on two-dimensional canvas have undergone several revolutions over time and, following each revolution, people have had to 'learn to see' paintings in the new ways intended by the artist.

Perceptual/attentional activities take time, demand guided selection, memory and interpretation. Perhaps it becomes less surprising, then, to find that young children in the first years of schooling still have much to learn about how to attend to and interpret their world in the same way that more mature members of their culture do. When we ask a young child to 'pay attention' we should recognize that any failure to comply might not result from boredom, wilfulness or 'distractability' but from the fact that he lacks the necessary knowledge and skill to bring to bear on the task or topic at hand. This is not to say that young children (like all of us) might not concentrate or attend because they are uninterested in what is going on, or because they prefer to do other things. However, we have to recognize that when we ask children to pay attention and concentrate on tasks that we have set and which provide little by way of concrete, perceptual support, they may find it impossible to comply with our demands.

Wholes and parts: theories of perception and understanding

In this section, I want to discuss another dimension of what is involved in learning how to attend and understand, which brings us back to the study of children's thinking and reasoning and to arguments about the relationship between perception and knowledge. So, far, my discussion of children's development has been largely descriptive and has avoided theorizing. Now we must start to consider explanations for the nature of young children's abilities and discuss some of the factors that different theorists believe influence and promote development and learning. Different theories, as we shall see, have quite different implications for teaching.

Suppose we show a young child the picture illustrated in figure 3.4 and ask him to describe what he sees. If the child is aged below five years, he will probably identify the various objects (such as the light bulbs) in the display but will not 'see' the larger figure that these suggest. He seems unable to 'synthesize' the objects into a larger configuration. When the individual elements are meaningful, have an identity of their own, the child is likely to focus on each in turn and cannot 'stand back' in order to see the more all-embracing figure. A minority of five-year-olds, however, may report seeing the larger configuration. They will not be able to 'see' or identify the smaller objects. Briefly, children aged below seven tend to 'centre'

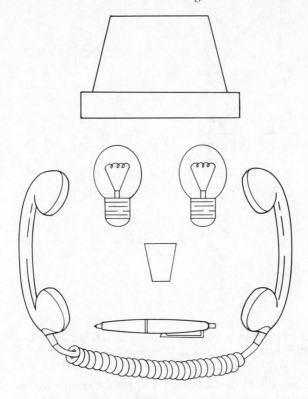

Figure 3.4 Children under the age of 7 years are unlikely to see the figure as a face

upon either the overall configuration or its parts. What they cannot do is attend to or perceive both at the same time. It's a case of one thing or the other.

In other situations, children of this age seem unable to break down a larger figure into its constituents or to perceive a part of a figure as 'belonging' to two or more larger units. Examine the diagrams illustrated in figure 3.5, for example. Such illustrations, called 'embedded figures', are used in some tests of intellectual maturity. A child aged below seven is unlikely to be able to trace the contour of the figures shown in set A when they are 'embedded' in the complex line drawings of set B, even though four-year-olds are able to trace the outlines of the simple shape shown in sets C and D. Such simple forms, or *Gestalten* (well-formed, regular shapes), seem to have a 'natural' identity. Young children can perceive such shapes when they are hidden by other lines, but unlike older children are incapable of analysing more complex figures.

In some situations, then, the young child cannot *synthesize* meaningful elements into larger units. In the 'embedded figures'

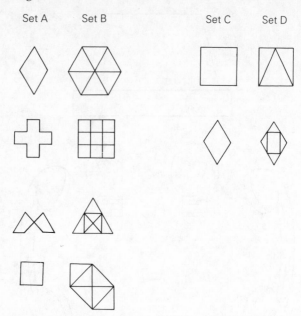

Set A   Set B   Set C   Set D

Figure 3.5 The child is asked to outline, in sets B and D, the figure that matches the shape in sets A and C respectively

problem he fails to break down or *analyse* complex forms into their elements. In both situations, the child seems incapable of perceiving a given element as a constituent of two or more configurations at one and the same time. Once the child perceives something in a particular way, he seems unable to 're-view' it from a different perspective. After the age of seven or so, children not only become more systematic and accurate in their perceptual judgements but also display greater flexibility. They are, in Piaget's terms, able to de-centre themselves to view a task from more than one point of view. Such experimental findings are consistent with Piaget's prediction that pre-operational children *cannot* entertain the idea that an element of any task or situation, whatever its nature, can belong at the same time to two or more categories or classes. What the child 'sees' is determined by how he thinks.

Are young children illogical, or 'limited processors of information'?

If children are more limited than their elders in their ability to attend, memorize and generally to regulate their own learning, problem-solving and thinking, then it may be that they often fail where older people succeed, not because they lack 'logic', but because they do not possess the relevant experience and expertise. If so, it may be possible to help them to learn and to understand situations which, left alone, they cannot master, by helping to augment their limited expertise and trying to teach them how to control their own intellectual activities. If this is possible, we might wish to claim far more importance for teaching in development and a greater potential for learning through instruction in young children than Piagetian theory suggests. Let us consider some examples to see if this is the case.

One of the many tasks that Piaget invented to study the transition from pre-operational to operational thinking involves the ability to place objects of different sizes into order from small to large – so-called 'seriation' tasks. Imagine, for example, five sticks each of a different colour and length. We show a child aged five an arrangement of these sticks in serial order and ask him to reproduce the configuration with another, similar set of sticks. The child cannot do it. He may produce the odd pair of sticks, one small and one large but he cannot, for example, insert a third stick *between* these to produce a longer series. Piaget's explanation for this phenomenon is consistent with those given for children's failures in conservation experiments. To insert a stick between two others in the appropriate sequence, for example, demands the ability to view it *at one and the same time* as a stick that is longer than one of the pair and smaller than the other. It has to be viewed simultaneously in two ways. This demands intellectual *co-ordination* of perceptual judgements which, as we have seen, pre-operational children cannot achieve. Similarly, if we tell the child that one stick is longer than another which in turn is longer than a third one, he cannot draw the *logical inference* that the first must be longer than the third, because such inferences also demand co-ordination of the statements given.

Bryant (1974), however, suggests that young children's inability to draw such inferences and solve seriation problems is not due to the fact that they are pre-logical. Rather, their failure is due to the fact that these sorts of problems overload their mental capacities. To solve such problems the child has to examine carefully, compare and *memorize* the relations between the five sticks in order to draw any inferences. We have just seen that each of these demands creates difficulties for children and that they are unlikely to rehearse spontaneously, so they will probably spend little time on the task, be unsystematic in their inspection of the sticks, and lack the powers of rehearsal needed to solve the problem set. If we help them to do these things, will we discover that they are more likely to draw inferences? Yes. To demonstrate this, Bryant showed children five sticks of different colours and sizes, but only as ordered pairs. So, for instance, the child might be shown a red and a blue stick where the red was longer. He is then shown the blue stick compared to a smaller green one, followed by the green paired with yellow and then the yellow with the shortest stick, say orange. Bryant repeatedly showed the pairs of sticks to children until they could tell him (before seeing each pair) which was longer. Having thus ensured that the child had *memorized* the information needed to solve the problem he asked them which was longer, the blue stick or the yellow stick. Many children were able to give the right answer.

Thus where the experimenter helps the child to pay attention to, rehearse and memorize the 'propositions' from which he will be asked to draw inferences, the child succeeds. Piagetians could argue, I suppose, that this is an example of rote learning and that the child's answer was based on an ability to form a picture of the abolute length of each of the coloured sticks, in which case children are not drawing inferences at all. But the issue is not nearly so clear-cut. In chapter 6 we will explore the way in which adults solve problems that involve logical inferences. These challenge the view that *adults* usually solve these problems by thinking, for instance, 'if blue is longer than green and green is longer than yellow, then blue is longer than yellow'. If we are to evaluate the performance of Bryant's children, we need to look in more detail at the way in which adults go about drawing inferences and ask if they reason 'logically' in the sense that Piaget's theory seems to suggest.

Many other attempts have been made to 'train' young children in ways of performing Piagetian tasks. The argument motivating many of these studies is that children do not pass through a pre-operational stage of development in which they are unable to learn or be taught how to reason 'logically'. Rather, the argument proceeds, the tasks used are so unfamiliar to children and make such (for them) unusual demands that failure is attributable to a lack of relevant *experience*, not to intellectual incompetence.

Some attempts to teach children how to solve Piagetian-style problems have produced positive effects, others have not. Deciding whether such results confirm or disconfirm the notion of a pre-operational stage of development is not a straightforward affair. In the first place, what we mean by 'teaching' is problematic. Do some attempts to teach children fail, for instance, because the teaching techniques they use are weak? How can we evaluate the quality of the teaching styles used by experimenters? What criterion do we set up to evaluate success? Is it simply enough to show, like Bryant did, that children can be helped to do things that they cannot do on their own, or do we demand that children so taught must show that they can *transfer* or *generalize* what they have been taught to another situation before we say that they 'really' have learned a lesson?

Trying to answer one difficult question (can children reason logically?) thus confronts us with three other issues. How do we define effective instruction? How and when do children *generalize* what they are taught to new problems? Do adults reason logically in the manner implied by Piagetian theory? Let us start with the first question.

What is effective instruction?

Any theory that presents a view of how children learn or develop implies a theory of instruction. Although Piaget did not attempt to explicate in detail the implications of his analysis of development for a theory of instruction, several of his followers have attempted so to do (e.g. Schwebel and Raph). Other learning/developmental theorists (e.g. Skinner, Gagne, Sheffield, Vygotsky/Luria, Bruner, to name but a few) have worked out in some detail the educational ramifications of their ideas. It is not my intention here to review and evaluate all these points of view, although in later chapters I will discuss some of the research they have inspired. Rather than attempt to deal with them all here, I have decided to concentrate on three approaches, trying to synthesize the insights they have generated. The three in question are Bruner's steps towards a theory of instruction, Soviet developmental theory (inspired by Vygotsky's writings), and research that has grown out of the information processing paradigm outlined in chapter 1. First, let me reiterate and underline some of the things I have already said about the nature of *expertise*.

Expertise

Experts in a discipline, game, sport, craft or whatever are able to perceive and memorize more accurately and fully than a non-expert any phenomenon that is relevant to their area of expertise. I have already discussed chess as a paradigm case. An expert's knowledge endows them with the ability to perceive *organization* and *structure* where the novice's perception is piecemeal and fragmented. What we perceive in a situation is *motivated* by our immediate purposes or interests. What we consider salient and worthy of attention is dictated by what we are trying to do. To the extent that we are expert at fulfilling our intentions in a situation which 'lends itself' to the fulfilment of our goals, we usually perform well. We are able to think and act relatively quickly, smoothly and accurately. Because of this, we are also more likely to notice any *departures* from our expectations than the novice. Imagine, for instance, watching a game of American football with an American fan. Then think about watching a game of cricket. Who responds to the novel and unusual? The person who already knows the rules and existing *practices* of play. Unlike the novice, whose concentration is likely to be fully engaged in monitoring and making sense of immediate events, the expert can appreciate what is currently happening in a wider context; he is likely to appreciate strategies of play and clever tactics. He will probably remember more about what takes place. He is also more likely to spot any mistakes made or to notice any unusual happenings that occur.

In saying that the expert perceives and memorizes more, whether it is the expert at chess or an expert musician listening to an orchestra and detecting the odd wrong note or poorly tuned instrument, I am talking *literally*. A good mathematician can perceive and recall more of the structure of a maths problem than a novice. A computer programmer shown a program written in a language familiar to him or her will perceive and memorize more of the *structure* of the program than a novice programmer, who might remember the first few lines of code but none of the program's structure. Expertise structures the process of perception and memorization. This makes thinking and acting fast, smooth, accurate and sensitive to error, novelty and unusual events.

When we help a child to solve a problem, we are providing conditions in which he can begin to perceive regularities and structure in his experience. Left alone, the child is overcome by uncertainty and does not know what to attend to or what to do. Instruction can help in a number of ways. When we point things out to the child, we help to highlight what he should attend to. By *reminding* children we are helping them to bring to mind and exploit those aspects of their past experience that we (as experts) but not they (as novices) know to be *relevant* to what they are currently trying to do. If the task involves a number of steps, the child, whilst concentrating on how to execute one, may forget about things he has already done. He may also lose his sense of 'direction' and, whilst working on a part of the task, lose sight of the whole problem. By drawing his attention back to what he did earlier and reminding him of what the ultimate goal is, we help to maintain his 'place' in the task and prevent him from total submersion in his immediate activity. When the child performs some activity that takes him closer to success, he may not recognize the significance of what he has done, particularly if he has lost sight of the overall goal. Here, praise and reassurance confirm the relevance of what he has done and act as a signal that he should move on.

Looked at in this way, many of the seemingly simple and even trivial things that the more mature do as they help children in everyday activities take on an important significance. Pointing out, reminding, suggesting and praising, all serve to orchestrate and structure the child's activities under the guidance of one more expert. By helping the child to structure his activities, we are helping him to perform things he could not do alone until such time as he becomes familiar enough with the demands of the task at hand to develop local expertise and to try things alone. By breaking complex tasks down into manageable, smaller problems, we help the child to detect regularities and patterns in his activity that he is unlikely to discover alone. We are also providing living examples of the way in which more expert people go about the task of regulating and managing activity in conditions of high uncertainty. When we suggest, remind, prompt or whatever, we are providing insights into processes that usually take place 'in our head'.

Vygotsky, as we have already seen, argues that such *external* and *social* activities are gradually internalized by the child as he comes to regulate his own intellectual activity. Such encounters are the source of experiences which eventually create the 'inner dialogues' that form the processes of mental self-regulation. Viewed in this way, learning is taking place on at least two levels: the child is learning about the task, developing 'local expertise'; and he is also learning how to structure his own learning and reasoning. Piagetians are likely to see direct instruction and attempts to help children who are not ready to do things alone as premature, misguided efforts that result in rote learning or the acquisition of empty, 'procedural' knowledge; but Vygotsky (and Bruner) see them as the 'raw material' of learning and development. In such encounters, the child is developing expertise and is inheriting culturally developed ways of thinking and learning.

Experts and novices as teachers and learners

Providing such a general, theoretical account of the ways in which an expert can assist a novice is one thing; translating it into recommendations for the education of a particular child or group of children is another. Common experience suggests that not all experts can teach, and that many attempts to help children to learn do not succeed. Lack of success may be attributable to many factors. The child may not be able to assimilate what we seek to teach because he lacks the relevant and necessary prior knowledge. The teaching itself may be inadequate or inappropriate: a teacher might, for instance, rely too much on demonstration, which demands from the would-be learner close and sustained attention, and a capacity to 'parse' or break down what is shown into component operations or actions. It demands sufficient prior knowledge to memorize and recall what is shown and may prove too difficult to assimilate. Alternatively a teacher might talk too much and make excessive demands on children's linguistic understanding.

In chapter 7, we will look in some detail at these issues and consider various lines of evidence which suggest that the effectiveness of demonstrations, explanations and illustrations as aids to teaching vary as a function of the learner's aptitudes and prior knowledge. For the moment I want to discuss a more specific question. How can we conceptualize and analyse the process of instruction in order to determine whether or not what is being taught is also being learned?

Children are often able to perform, given help, tasks that they are unable to do alone. Vygotsky, as we have seen, coined the term 'zone of proximal development' to refer to these 'gaps' between unassisted and assisted competence. How can we determine whether or not instruction is *sensitive* to a child's zone of development? When does it make demands beyond his potential level of comprehension? How can we be sure that instruction does not underestimate his ability? I and some colleagues have explored these questions in a number of studies of teaching and learning interactions (e.g. Wood, Wood and Middleton, 1978). In one, we asked mothers of four- to five-year-old children to teach their child how to put together the construction task that was illustrated in figure 3.4. The task makes many demands on children: they have to select objects according to their size and shape, assemble them in a specific sequence, orient the assemblies in a particular way and, finally, they have to pile the blocks in a series graded by size. When children are shown the pictures illustrated in figure 3.4 and asked to construct the assembly shown, the chances of total success (i.e. completed assembly) are low until around age seven to eight years. However, taught well, four-year-olds can learn how to complete all or most of the assembly on their own. But what does it mean to be taught 'well' in this context?

Consider how we might go about teaching a child how to do this task – what should be said or done first? Imagine a four-year-old looking at his mother and not yet trying to do anything with the blocks. There are no pictures available in this study: mothers provide all the information. A mother might say 'Why don't you try to put some blocks together?', or 'Can you find the four biggest blocks?' Alternatively, she might add to what she says by pointing to blocks or picking them out saying, perhaps, 'Let's try to put these big ones together.' She may go further, by both selecting the blocks and lining them up so that they are ready for assembly, rather like the state of affairs shown in figure 3.4. Or she may decide to demonstrate how a set of four blocks fit together, doing several operations herself while the child looks on.

The five instructional options, summarized below, enabled us to classify all that the mothers did and said in teaching their children.

Levels used to classify teaching in the pyramid task
Level 1   General verbal encouragement
Level 2   Specific verbal instruction
Level 3   Assists in choice of material
Level 4   Prepares material for assembly
Level 5   Demonstrates an operation

Note as we come down the list how the *amount* or specificity of instruction increases while, by the same token, the degree of *responsibility* for what happens next conferred on the child decreases. Some mothers attempted to teach children by relying almost exclusively on demonstration. Their children learned little. Others tried to talk children through the task, doing little by way of pointing or showing, and their children also managed to achieve little when asked to do the task alone. The children who learned most about the task were exposed to a style of instruction that combined showing and telling in a specific pattern. The mothers of the children who learned most might, for instance, try to suggest or tell the child what to do next, but if he did not understand what was said, perhaps choosing blocks different in size or shape to those she described, his mother would immediately offer more help. She might point to one of his blocks and say 'This doesn't look quite right. Why not try [pointing at a block] that one?' When the child succeeded in following a suggestion, however, the mother would step back and let him take more responsibility for what happened next. If she did make a suggestion, it was usually a less controlling one than she used in her previous instruction. By teaching children 'contingently' – that is, by making any help given conditional upon the child's understanding of previous levels of instruction – these mothers ensured that the child was not left alone when he was overwhelmed by the task, and also guaranteed him greater scope for initiative when he showed signs of success.

When we trained someone to teach children using different instructional 'styles' we found similar effects. Attempts to teach children verbally did not work and usually demoralized the child and led him to withdraw. Children would try to follow verbal instructions like 'Find four big ones' or 'You need one with a peg on it', but were soon swamped. Either they were unable to understand what was said, could not memorize it or (more likely) couldn't pay attention, simultaneously, to all the relevant aspects of the task. For example, implicit in an instruction like 'Find one with a peg' is the implication that the child should also keep in mind the size of the blocks he is currently working on. Children might pick up a block with a peg on it following such an instruction, but it was the wrong size. Having 'failed' to understand what the instruction given meant, they had to be given another one, perhaps 'No, you need a larger one with a peg', and so on. Typically, verbal instructions proved too much for children of this age. They encountered failure upon failure and eventually most gave up.

Children taught by demonstration watched what the teacher did and were keen to have a turn when their chance came, but they had clearly been unable to take in much of what they had been shown. They usually got the idea that pegs fitted into holes and that they had to pile the blocks up. All the finer points to do with size, orientation, sequences of moves and the like were lost on them. They often finished up with a haphazard pile of blocks not assembled into levels. Children taught contingently, however, gradually learned how to do the task with help and, as the sessions proceeded, they began to understand what the teacher *meant* when she said things like 'Get the four next ones' because previous instruction involved an element of *showing* which made such verbal instructions contextually 'meaningful'.

One way of conceptualizing contingent instruction is offered by the studies of children's information processing abilities outlined above. Contingent teaching helps children to construct local expertise – expertise connected with that particular task or group of tasks – by focusing their attention on relevant and timely aspects of the task, and by highlighting things they need to take account of. It also breaks the task down into a sequence of smaller tasks which children can manage to perform, and orchestrates this sequence so that they eventually manage to construct the completed assembly. We have used the metaphor of 'scaffolding' to describe this aspect of the teaching process. Built well, such scaffolds help children to learn how to achieve heights that they cannot scale alone (Wood, Bruner and Ross, 1976).

I have outlined this example to provide a concrete instance of the difficulties involved in evaluating the question of whether instruction is important for learning. After the age of seven, most children can do this task on their own, following the 'instructions' implicit in a series of photographs or in a filmed demonstration. Since the task involves demands, like seriation, which children don't usually master on their own until about the age of seven, we might argue that this finding offers support for Piaget's theory, showing that seven-year-olds are 'ready' to do and understand this task since they have achieved operational competence. If the criterion for learning *competence* is the ability to do the task *alone*, then it could be held that these results support Piaget's theory.

If we consider only children taught by demonstration and verbal instruction (which, incidentally are teaching techniques that have been used, unsuccessfully, to see if 'training' helps preschool children to learn how to do seriation tasks), then we might also argue that pre-operational children do not have the competence to learn how to do such tasks. However, taught contingently, children can learn. Contingent teaching, as defined here, involves pacing the amount of help children are given on the basis of their moment-to-moment understanding. If they do not understand an instruction given at one level, then more help is forthcoming. When they do understand, the teacher steps back and gives the child more room for initiative. In this way, the child is never left alone when he is in difficulty nor is he 'held back' by teaching that is too directive and intrusive. This formula sounds simple, even trite, but putting it into practice is anything but easy. Even with our relatively simple task, the person trained to teach contingently in the study I have just outlined often 'violated' the rules. Sometimes, for example, she repeated an instruction at the same level when she should have given more help. On other occasions she gave help where none was called for. Understanding the 'rules' of contingency and *teaching* according to those rules are two quite different things.

In the 'real world' of the classroom, of course, the problem of achieving contingent instruction is far more difficult. In the first place, many lessons taught in school often involve tasks that do not have a clear, obvious structure and may not yield single 'right answers'. Even mathematics, which seems well structured, does not have a single clear-cut structure as we will discover when we consider mathematics teaching and learning in chapter 7. There is, for instance, no one sequence in which a mathematical concept or procedure can be taught that is suitable or 'optimal' for all children. Another obvious fact about most classroom teaching is that it takes place with *groups* of children. How do studies of one-to-one teaching relate to the instruction of classes of children? Does it make sense to talk about contingent teaching in a situation where many children are being taught simultaneously? We address this issue in the two final chapters.

Whilst far removed from the demands of the classroom, our studies of teaching styles and their effects do, I hope, serve to illustrate a number of arguments. Four-year-olds *can* be taught to do tasks that, alone, they will not master until around age seven or eight. For them to learn, however, instruction must be geared to their (changing) level of competence. When this condition can be and is achieved, young children can be taught and do learn.

Learning and generalization: first thoughts on a thorny issue

We do not usually set out to teach children how to do strange things like conserve continuous quantity or weight nor, in any direct way, do we teach them how to seriate objects. Yet, by the time they are seven or eight years of age, children in many different countries confronted, for the first time in their lives, with these Piagetian tasks, manage to understand them and may be able to explain why and how they do so. If they have not been 'taught' how to do such things in any simple sense, it follows that we do not have to concern ourselves with 'teaching' them either at home or in school. Most children come to understand them 'naturally'.

What is at issue is not whether Piaget's tasks should be on the school curriculum or be taught. The question is how and why children develop the intelligence to *achieve* understanding. What knowledge and experience are they *drawing* on and *generalizing* from in order to understand? For Piaget, the schemes of knowing that make possible the understanding and generalization of experience are rooted in actions on the world. For Vygotsky and Bruner, the intellectual 'tools' and activities which form the basis of understanding arise out of social interaction and largely informal teaching. The language of information processing, concepts of uncertainty, limited channel capacity, chunking and expertise, offer a way of describing what children can and cannot do. The social and historical perspective offered by Vygotsky and Bruner, expressed in the language of information processing, provides an account of learning that differs from Piaget's (in some important respects) in terms of the mental activities that are believed to underlie learning and thinking, and in the experiences that lead to their acquisition and perfection.

If we accept the Piagetian view that children aged below seven or so cannot profitably be taught tasks and concepts (like number and arithmetic, for instance) because they lack the competence to learn such things, then we accept a very different set of constraints on the nature of schooling than if we believe Bruner and Vygotsky. I have given a few examples of research which suggests that young children can profitably be taught how to do things that they cannot do alone. If you accept Vygotsky's analysis of development, such demonstrations do not merely show that children can learn through instruction. They also illustrate the kinds of interaction between adults and children, experts and novices, that are *necessary* for the transmission of knowledge. If we believe that learning how to learn and how to think about things arise through social interaction, then the *relationship* between the young child and his teacher is different in kind to that implicated in Piaget's theory. For both Vygotsky and Bruner, interactions between the young child and his teacher in which both *co-operate* in the development of mutual understanding are the 'stuff' of development and learning.

The way in which children come to profit by experience and attain the ability to tackle and master new situations and problems is thus a subject for debate which revolves around the part played by social and cultural influences. Vygotsky argues that the child not only learns and internalizes lessons about specific tasks when he co-operates with more knowledgeable others, he is also exposed to and internalizes the instructional *process* itself. He discovers how to plan, regulate and organize his own practical and cognitive activity. If this is the case, why do some children seem to retain and generalize what they are taught whilst others find it difficult to remember and exploit what they learn? This question becomes central to the consideration of the nature of educability, discussed in chapter 8, but let me begin the discussion here.

Piagetians might argue that many 'failures' to remember and generalize lessons are attributable to the fact that premature teaching serves only to inculcate empty procedures or learned tricks. Only when the child constructs his own understanding would we expect him to remember and generalize what he has been taught. Evidence that intellectual *development* rather than procedural *learning* has occurred is revealed by children's ability to understand and grasp several related phenomena. So, for example, once a child achieves concrete operational competence he should be able to develop an understanding of a whole range of phenomena like how number, quantity, area, weight and volume are conserved; he discovers how to create ordered series, construct complex systems of classification and draw logical inferences. Lessons taught about such things to pre-operational children will not foster development – something that will be revealed when children, apparently taught how to solve problems in one domain (e.g. seriation), fail to extend or generalize what they have learned to others (e.g. concepts of number).

The issue is more complex than this argument suggests. In the first place, we would only predict and expect such large-scale generalizations to occur if we already accept the claim that the *same* intellectual abilities (i.e. being able to co-ordinate, reverse, compensate etc.) are implicated in understanding each of these (and many other) concepts. If we do not subscribe to this view, but believe instead that *local expertise* is what is needed to understand these different concepts and that they do not involve general-purpose operations, then we would not necessarily *expect* children to transfer what they learn from one area to another. If it were the case that children *did* show 'immediate' or ready generalization across all Piaget's tasks, then this argument would be difficult to sustain. However, generalization from one domain to another is *not* immediate: for example, the conservation of weight usually occurs after the ability to conserve continuous quantity has been achieved.

Piaget's theory accepts this state of affairs. He employs the term 'horizontal decalage' to describe the gradual extension of competence from task to task. The child assimilates some phenomena before others, so the transition from stage to stage is not a sudden all-or-none affair but somewhat gradual. This makes clear-cut predictions about when and how children will display logical understanding of different tasks difficult. Added to this uncertainty are findings which show that the path of decalage predicted by Piaget's theory does not fit the developmental facts. So, for example, he predicts that class inclusion (the ability to conceptualize the same object in relation to two or more categories) should occur before, and provide an intellectual basis for, the development of number concepts. Until a child understands the fact that the number six, say, is at one and the same time both smaller than eight but larger than four, then no grasp of number concepts can take place. Yet the study of children's development of number concepts suggests the opposite state of affairs, with the understanding of number predating the ability to solve Piagetian tests of class inclusion. One suggestion (Lunzer, 1973) is that the child's knowledge of number helps him to understand class inclusion problems.

On the basis of Bruner's theory, what we would expect a child to learn and generalize are not grand, underlying logical structures but processes of self-regulation. He argues that effective teaching in school, for example, exposes children to *ways of thinking* that characterize different disciplines. The 'syntax' of a subject – its formal structure, facts and 'solutions' – is only one aspect of what a child needs to learn. Teaching of procedures, facts, dates, formulae and so forth will not engender understanding or facilitate generaliz-ation unless the child understands the intentions and purposes that motivate both the discipline and the people who practise and teach it. Ways of thinking, in mathematics, history, geography or whatever, have developed to achieve certain ways of making sense of and understanding the world. Unless the child *practises* the role of being a mathematician, historian or geographer, learns the issues that excite such people, the problems that interest them and the tools that help them to resolve and solve these, then the child may only learn empty tricks or procedures and will not inherit the *discipline* itself. If we accept such views on the nature of what it is children learn when they are involved in both informal and formal instructional encounters, then we would expect to find important, far-reaching differences in the way the children from different cultures, sub-cultures and social groups develop and learn.

Whilst all three theorists, Vygotsky, Piaget and Bruner, emphasize the centrality of purposive activity in learning and development, the roles they portray for social interaction and instruction are quite different. So too are their predictions about the impact of culture and social experience on cognition. Piaget leads us in search of cultural universals revealed by common stages of development. Vygotsky and Bruner prepare us to find different ways of thinking and construing the world that arise out of cultural knowledge and different ways of socializing and educating children.

Before we try to make up our minds about such complex and difficult issues, which we return to in chapter 6, we need to consider more evidence. This takes us first on an exploration of language and its impact on the development of thinking, understanding and knowing.

Chapter 4

Language and learning

This chapter addresses a range of difficult and controversial topics that revolve around competing views of the relationship between language, learning and educational achievement. You might find it hard going in places. I have already identified some of the theoretical issues surrounding theories of language and thought. I have asked, for example, if the problems that children face when we attempt to test their ability to reason logically stem, wholly or in part, from misunderstandings created by problems of communication and language. Do children, as some students of development believe, have to develop special ways of communicating and thinking in order to learn in school? If they do not learn, are their problems of an intellectual kind or do they arise from poor communication skills? If so, where are the roots of such problems to be found: in the home, or in school, or both?

Children enter school speaking a range of different accents and dialects. These are often associated with variations in social background and parental occupation. As we shall see, some educational theorists believe that important and far-reaching effects on educational performance result from variations in the way that children from different backgrounds use language. Opposed to such views is the argument that such linguistic variations need exert no direct effects, positive or negative, on children's ability to learn and think. Rather, the argument proceeds, any connection between variations in language and school performance are caused by differences in the effectiveness of schools and teachers in their ability to reach and teach children from some social and ethnic backgrounds. Advocates of this second point of view have often appealed to linguistic theory to support their case. Consequently we must consider, albeit briefly and selectively, ideas from linguistics that are central to arguments about the basis of educational success and failure. The inclusion of this aspect of development contributes to the difficulty of some parts of this chapter.

Bernstein's analysis: restricted codes and elaborated codes

Churchill once suggested that Britain and America are two countries divided by a common language. Basil Bernstein, a less well-known student of the English-speaking peoples, went further. He argued that the people of Britain themselves are divided by language, at least in relation to educational achievement and vocational opportunity. Others have argued that the same holds true of people in other societies.

Bernstein, a sociologist, attempted to explain the well-known and widely documented relationship between children's school performance and their socio-economic background in terms of variations in the uses and forms of language found in different social classes (e.g. Bernstein 1960, 1961, 1970). He argued that children from middle-class homes are likely to be socialized, controlled and talked to in different ways to working-class children. These variations in language lead children to different 'world views', aspirations, attitudes and aptitudes for learning and, eventually, to different levels of school performance. The vocational opportunities open to the two groups of children are constrained by their academic qualifications, so they tend to gravitate towards different forms of employment. Middle-class youngsters are likely to find themselves in white-collar managerial roles while the working-class child is probably destined to follow her parents into manual occupations. Thus, generations move in cycles through time. Social classes tend to perpetuate themselves by means of differences in language and child-rearing practices.

Bernstein's views, first expressed in the 1960s, were met with both enthusiasm and hostility. On the one hand, his theory offered a degree of hope for those striving to create fairer schools and a more egalitarian society. His explanation for differences in school performance suggested that they are a product of social experience, not attributable to biological differences in native intelligence – the explanation favoured by some students of human nature. If social class differences in school performance did rest on problems associated with language and communication, then it might be possible to overcome them to ensure greater equality of opportunity and achievement. Perhaps the 'cycle of disadvantage' could be broken, and hitherto self-perpetuating patterns of social class differences eradicated. His theory gave some educators grounds for hope and inspired enthusiasm.

On the other hand, intentionally or not, Bernstein's thesis implied that the seeds and causes of educational success or failure were to be found in the home. Whilst education might provide a means to help children overcome disadvantage, the implication was that schooling for children from some social backgrounds was to contain an element of remediation and repair. Whilst denying variation in educability due to biological differences, his theory still implied explanation by 'deficit'. The roots of disadvantage were to be found, not in the genes, but in the family and local community. Herein were the sources of hostile reactions from some people.

For reasons I will come to later, many linguists, sociologists and educationalists rejected Bernstein's apparent attempt to explain patterns of achievement in terms of factors located 'in' the child. There are, of course, audible differences in the accents and dialects that children bring into school. These reflect language variation across different regions and communities and are likely to *identify* a child's socio-economic background. Some ways of talking, revealed in pronunciation, vocabulary and in the use of certain grammatical devices (such as 'Ain't got none', for instance), announce regional and perhaps socio-economic origins.

Bernstein's theory went beyond such surface differences in speech, however, to suggest more fundamental and far-reaching variations in the way language is *used* and *structured* in different social groups. He suggested, for example, that children from better-off homes, whose parents are likely to have had a relatively extensive education and hold white-collar jobs, are exposed to what he termed an 'elaborated code' of the English language. Working-class children, on the other hand, are more likely to experience and learn to use a 'restricted code'. These codes were supposedly revealed by a number of characteristic differences in ways of talking.

A restricted code user is likely to frame what she says in such a way that her listener must be aware of or share her physical situation in order to understand what she means. The use of 'non-determinate' ways of referring to things (for example, 'this', 'that', 'those' and 'them') are typical of restricted code language. To understand what is being referred to, a listener must know what the speaker is thinking about, looking at, touching or in some way indicating non-verbally. The elaborated code also uses such terms but in such a way that the thing they refer to is first established *verbally*. For instance, if one heard something like – 'John brought his new bike to school. "Look at this", he said proudly' – one might reasonably assume that 'this' refers back to (is a 'pro-form' for) the object 'bike'. The elaborated code user, the argument proceeds, speaks in such a way that her listener need not share her physical *context* in order to understand what she says. In this and other respects, elaborated code language is more similar to written text than is restricted code language.

Because the elaborated code is more verbally specific, precise and less physically 'context dependent', it forms a much more effective mode of communication in situations where speakers cannot resort to non-verbal communication or to common shared experience in order to make what they say mutually understandable. Since school teaching confronts children with speech that is often, even usually, independent of the immediate physical context, children who are fluent in elaborated code language will find communication and learning relatively easy in comparison to those whose major experiences of language are confined to a restricted code. Consequently, children from different social backgrounds come to school more or less prepared for the communicative and linguistic demands they will encounter. This is one reason why a child from a middle-class background is likely to learn more readily in school than her working-class peers.

There are many more facets to Bernstein's description of language codes than their different relationships to context and non-verbal communication, and I will consider some of these later. The important thing for the moment is to understand in general terms how the theory predicts that differences associated with accent and dialect coincide with more important differences in language *use*. These differences, in turn, arise from the linguistic and personal demands associated with different roles and occupations within society.

Bernstein's theory and educational politics

Although Bernstein's theory was developed to explain differences in the educational achievement of British children, it was also embraced by educators and politicians in the USA, where it was extended to explain differences in the educational achievements of black and white children. There has been considerable controversy about the extent to which Bernstein's ideas were misunderstood and exaggerated by educationalists who made use of them to explain educational inequalities. Beyond noting the fact that some people did seem to adopt a far more radical stance about the linguistic abilities of black children than his theory implies, however, we will not be concerned with the details of this argument.

Bernstein's theory appeared at a time of Government affluence and public optimism in both the USA and the UK. In the United States, the poverty amongst many black Americans was a subject for heated political debate. Action through education seemed to some politicians the most direct way to tackle the problems of inequality and poverty. Similarly, in the United Kingdom, 'Educational Priority Areas' were identified and targeted for additional financial help and action designed to help children from economically poor homes.

The political will to act coincided with, and was no doubt partly shaped by, theories and findings emerging from several disciplines, sociology and psychology in particular. These suggested that differences in intelligence and educability were not innate but direct products of early social experiences. Poverty, it was claimed, depresses children's health, motivation, intelligence and language. Bernstein's views on language, coupled with psychological studies of intelligence (including Piaget's), provided a theoretical rationale and, perhaps, a stimulus for political action to wage a 'war on poverty'.

In 1965, President Johnson announced the launch of 'Project Head Start' in the USA. This was a federally funded venture designed to provide educational opportunities for pre-school children from poor homes. It also financed improvements in medical, social and family support systems. Johnson was reported by Mohr (1965) in the *New York Times* as follows:

> 5- and 6-year old children are inheritors of poverty's curse and not its creators . . . Unless we act, these children will pass it on to the next generation, like a family birthmark . . . We have taken up the challenge of poverty and we don't intend to lose generations of our children to this enemy of the human race . . . Before this summer, they were on the road to despair . . . But today . . . children who have never spoken learned to talk. Parents who were suspicious of school authorities came to see the centres and they stayed on to help the teachers. Teachers tried new approaches and learned new techniques.

This speech was made less than three months after the Headstart programme had been initiated! The quote is important in the present context because it betrays some of the attitudes and theories that shaped educational policy. Note the assertion that 'children who have never spoken learned to talk' (in three months?). The belief that many poor children, particularly black ones, were not only exposed to a different dialect but were in fact *mute* clearly went far beyond Bernstein's views on class and codes. Where did such an opinion come from? Well, there were a number of empirical studies which seemed to suggest that pre-school black children could not talk or were able to understand and say very little. In 1966, Bereiter and Englemann, for example, concluded, on the basis of experimental investigations, that

> the speech of severely deprived children seems to consist not of distinct words, as does the speech of middle-class children of the same age, but rather of whole phrases or sentences that

function like giant words . . . these 'giant word' units cannot be taken apart by the child and recombined; they cannot be transformed from statements to questions, from imperatives to declaratives, and so on. Instead of saying 'He's a big dog', the deprived child says 'He bih daw'. . . . Instead of saying 'That is a red truck', he says 'Da-re-truh' . . . the listener . . . may believe that the child is using words like *it*, *is*, *if* and *in*, when in fact he is using the same sound for all of them – something on the order of 'ih'. (Reported in Brown et al., 1984, p. 29)

A note on 'dialects' and 'creoles'

Such sweeping generalizations about the linguistic abilities of many black American children and children from economically impoverished homes provoked many strong reactions. They represent an extreme environmentalist point of view, i.e. that children are *taught* to speak. Perhaps they coincided with stereotypical views of what life was like for children whose parents were in poverty. They were also totally at variance with what was, in the 1960s, fast becoming the dominant theory of language and its acquisition. This theory, developed by the American linguist Noam Chomsky (e.g. 1957, 1965), was destined to change radically and, I suspect, irrevocably our views on language and learning.

From Chomsky's theory there came the argument that children are not *taught* to speak at all, nor, in any simple sense, do they *learn* language, by imitation, say. Rather, children *acquire* their mother tongue(s). Furthermore, although children obviously develop different accents and dialects depending upon the social group within which they live, there is no theoretical justification for the view that such differences are in any sense for 'better' or 'worse'.

A similar line of argument has been extended to the language of children from ethnic groups who use 'creoles'. Briefly, a creole emerges when users of two different languages live side-by-side over long periods of time. The 'dominant' language, that used by the group with economic and political power, is learned by the non-dominant language group. The first generation to learn this new dominant language do not acquire it as a 'mother tongue' but as a foreign language. Historically, such languages were not formally taught in schools, but 'picked up' in the course of everyday social contact. The first generation learning in this way develop what is termed a 'pidgin' version of the new language. However, when they go on to use this new hybridized language with their own children, the subsequent generations acquire it as a mother tongue. This new language form is what is referred to as a 'creole'. Consequently, the form of English used by children from some ethnic groups (e.g.

those whose ancestors were of Afro-Caribbean origins) has emerged, over time, as a product of interactions between people from two or more different language groups. The same phenomenon, 'creolization', has occurred many times in the past, of course. The history of the British Isles, for example, has seen the influx of several different conquering groups (e.g. Norse, Saxon, Norman). Each brought a different language and new customs which have blended over time to form British culture and the English language. Regional dialects represent audible, historical traces of past invasions. Regions of settlement by different invading groups, speaking different languages, varied, and influenced the development of regional accents and dialects.

Although no language is ever static (consider, for example, the familiarity of Russian words like 'sputnik' and its 'creative use' to produce new terms like 'refuse-nik'), English and the languages of 'developed' countries have achieved a high degree of stability and uniformity. The use of what is termed 'received pronunciation' and the 'standard' form of a language (in England, this corresponds to so-called 'BBC English') is likely to say a lot about a person's social and educational background. However, according to most students of language, it does not follow that the person using this socially 'dominant' dialect has a *superior* grasp of 'English'. No one dialect of English, in any *linguistic* sense, is superior as a means of communication to any other. Although dialects and creoles vary in pronunciation and grammatical structure (due to their distinct historical origins) they are no less *grammatical* than Standard English. All languages, dialects and creoles are governed by rules of grammar and whilst the rules may vary from one dialect to another, they are all 'equally' grammatical. In this view, the fact that one way of speaking is viewed as superior, more intelligent or more 'proper' than another is not a *linguistic* phenomenon, but a *political, social and economic* affair. A particular way of speaking has become *dominant* because those who speak it have risen to power, and control functions like education, mass communication and the means of production. Such a view, which we will explore more fully in a moment, leads to a rejection of the notion that some children are 'linguistically deprived' or their language 'impoverished' if they happen to speak with a particular dialect or creole.

Why then did experimentalists conclude that some children are deprived of language; that they come to school mute or, at best, inarticulate? Perhaps because such children did not want to talk to them. For example, black American children, when addressed by a white middle-class academic in formal laboratory settings, said little and appeared monosyllabic, but were found to be loquacious, witty and capable of rational argument when observed on their own territory in the local community. Labov (1969), who pioneered such observations, concluded that whilst their speech might sound different from that of white middle-class people, these children's command of language was no less articulate, rule-governed, complex or rational. Labov's argument, which he extended against Bernstein's thesis, was that the way in which people talk, and what they do or do not say to each other, is fundamentally affected by the *social and institutional* context in which they are observed. The 'register' of language used – say, by a black child talking to white middle-class representatives of authority – is a socio-political phenomenon. In this last case the child, he would argue, is well advised to say little and hold her peace. She is in a 'no win' situation in which anything she says and does is likely to appear 'wrong' or incompetent. However, in situations where the child feels relaxed and in control, her 'register' of speech changes to reveal her linguistic and intellectual competence.

Extensions of this argument into the classroom lead to a very different interpretation of the relationships between language, learning and educational achievement to those entailed by theories of linguistic deprivation. Before considering these, let me outline, briefly, some of the main elements of Chomsky's theory of language and give some sense of the impact that his ideas have had on the study of child language. We can then return to reconsider and extend our discussion of the relationships between language, learning, intelligence and school achievement.

The Chomskian legacy

Our thinking about the nature of language and its acquisition, as I have already said, has been revolutionized since the formulation of Chomsky's theory, aspects of which were first published in the late 1950s. Although, as a theoretical linguist, he was involved in a rather different quest from those that concern psychologists and educators, it soon became clear that his views on the nature of language could not be ignored by those who were interested in the study or cultivation of human abilities.

Like Piaget, Chomsky rejected as inadequate those psychological theories of learning that had become prominent and dominant by the 1960s. Both theorists argued that exclusive attention to the 'stimuli' that children experience and the 'responses' these evoke provides an inadequate conceptual framework for the study or analysis of intellectual abilities. Piaget, as we have seen, argued that children not only learn responses or actions but construct operations. Chomsky, theorizing about language, argues language cannot profitably be viewed as vocal 'responses' to 'stimuli'. Rather, language involves a system of grammatical *rules*. These enable a user of language to *generate* novel utterances that they may never have heard or produced before. He argued that the study of language must concern itself with discovering the grammatical rules that we use when we speak and listen. What kinds of rules do children acquire when they discover how to understand and produce speech? How and when are these rules acquired? These were the kinds of questions that Chomsky's theory stimulated.

Where Piagetians and Chomskians seem to differ radically is in their views on the relations between language and thought, and the way in which the development of one influences that of the other. Piaget's theory predicts that the use and understanding of language is constrained by stages of intellectual development. Chomsky, on the other hand, argues that language has a 'special structure' that involves systems of specifically *linguistic* rules that cannot be 'reduced' to cognition. More about this later.

These extremely complex theoretical arguments about the nature of language and its development are of central importance to our discussions of the relationships between language and learning. Though very academic and abstract in nature, they are of relevance to urgent educational arguments about the reasons why children from some social groups generally do less well in school than those from other backgrounds. The two theories also invite us to explore different explanations for the finding that children of different ages may appear more or less logical and able to learn things. For if language acquisition *is* partially or wholly independent of cognitive development, then it follows, as I have already argued, that children may fail to solve a problem being set by an adult or misunderstand something being taught or explained to them not because they lack certain intellectual abilities but because they don't understand what is being said to them. Furthermore, if language acquisition is a natural and largely automatic process, as some students of Chomsky have suggested, then it follows that differences in language, dialect and the like are unlikely to be primary causes of communication and learning problems, as linguistic 'deficit' theories imply. No language is more or less 'efficient' than any other. A child's ability to learn and understand should be quite independent of the particular language or dialect that she happens to speak. Here, Piagetians and Chomskians are likely to be in agreement in their opposition to deficit theory, though for somewhat different reasons.

It is not my intention to explore Chomskian theory in detail, but we do need to consider some of the arguments favouring the view that language acquisition cannot be explained either in terms of teaching and learning or by stages of cognitive development.

Ambiguity and paraphrase: evidence of structure

The relationships between an idea to be communicated and vocal sounds that we make in order to achieve communication are complex and rule-governed. The same idea can be expressed in many different ways. Even what may seem to be a description of a simple scene can be said in many different ways (e.g. 'A cat sat on a mat by the bed', or 'By the bed was a mat that a cat was sitting on', and so on). So there is no single or direct relationship between a 'stimulus' (e.g. an object, event or happening) and the 'response' (a particular pattern of vocal movements) that is made to represent or refer to it. The fact that *paraphrase* is a central and general feature of language demonstrates that the relationship between an intended *meaning* and the sounds used to *express* it are too complex to be explained in terms of learned connections between words and things. Rules are involved in both producing and analysing language. By the same token, the same string of words (a famous example is 'They were flying kites') may express several *different* meanings depending upon the interpretation put upon it or, in other terms, upon how the listener 'parses' the utterance. 'They' might refer to people involved in the activity of kite-flying or to kites in flight. Thus, the same sound, 'flying', may be understood as a verb or adjective respectively, depending upon the overall meaning put upon the utterance.

Paraphrase and ambiguity are two pervasive and universal features of speech that must be acknowledged and explained by any theory that promises to provide an adequate analysis of language. Learning theory, Chomsky argued, is incapable of accommodating such creative, 'generative' aspects of language. Any theory that sets out with the assumption that the meaning of speech can be explained by patterns of associations between objects and sounds put together into a learned sequence (e.g. phrases, sentences) cannot, he argued, begin to provide a useful account of the nature of language. Such theories begin with an incorrect conceptualization of what language *is*.

Chomsky argued that a valid theory of language must include a distinction between what he termed the 'deep' and 'surface' structure of utterances. The surface structure is the physical manifestation of an utterance (i.e. a series of sound waves or a sequence of letters in print). Since a similar meaning can be conveyed by quite different sound and print patterns, there cannot be a simple relationship between surface structure and meaning. The same set of sounds can have more than one meaning (ambiguity) and the same meaning can be expressed by different surface structures (paraphrase). Consequently, there must be a 'deeper' structure underlying speech. This deep structure, the terrain explored by structural linguists like Chomsky, and out of bounds to us, must be related to surface structure by *rules* which specify how meaning is mapped onto speech and which explain, amongst other things, paraphrase and ambiguity. Chomsky created a theory about the nature of these systems of rules.

A competent user of a language may produce an utterance that has never been spoken before and a competent listener is able to understand what is said. Any language enables its users to 'generate' a theoretically infinite number of (structured and rule-governed) utterances. Any number of sentences in this book, for instance, may never have been generated before, but a competent (and literate) user of English is able to understand their meaning (at least, I hope so). Such abilities also imply that language competence involves sets of rules. These rules are sensitive to the *structure* of language and enable us, for example, to understand which word or words in an utterance serve as the subject and the predicate, which act as verb and which as object.

This is not to say, of course, that we are consciously aware of working out verbs, objects and the like when we communicate. We, like the child acquiring language, may not even understand what such terms mean. However, our natural language abilities enable us to analyse utterances into their grammatical constituents 'automatically' and unconsciously. Linguists, in this view, have invented terms like 'grammatical subject' to refer to and develop theories about the natural processes that make the production and analysis of language possible.

Chomsky's theory thus puts generativity and creativity at the very heart of language ability and, as we shall see, at the heart of language development too. What the structural linguist attempts to do is to construct a working theory or 'model grammar' of a language which can produce and 'parse' (analyse) a potentially infinite number of utterances. This model grammar should only produce utterances that a native speaker of that language will accept as being 'well formed' (grammatical), and should not itself accept as grammatical an utterance that would not be accepted as such by a native speaker. To the extent that these conditions are met, the model represents a theory of what goes on in the human mind in the production and analysis of the grammar.

Perhaps you can see why linguists and computers got together! Computational linguistics, the attempt to program computers that can generate and analyse human language(s), is a new approach to the study and analysis of language. If successful, it will enable machines and people to 'communicate' directly in natural language. The practical importance of this field of study is self-evident. Think how much easier it would make 'man–machine communication'. I have a specific reason for mentioning it here. Chomsky and many structural linguists (though not all) are not concerned with 'real' speech. By this, I mean that they are not studying things like the way in which people hesitate, pause, make false starts and correct themselves when they talk. Nor are they concerned with the way in which gestures, pointing and other non-verbal aspects of communication aid mutual understanding. There are many such features of language *performance* that are not of direct interest to theoretical linguists who are trying to construct 'ideal models' of grammar. The different objectives being pursued by these linguists and by people who are interested in 'real life' discourse have led to many arguments and misunderstandings. I will not be concerned with these in this book, but I think it is important to keep in mind the fact that Chomsky's quest is somewhat *different* from that of most educators. Put another way, whilst it is useful and informative to see how far theories of grammatical structure help us to understand everyday uses of language, we should not be too ready to criticize such theories for being inadequate to fulfil our needs. They are not *intended* to do so.

Let us ask, then, what impact structural linguists have had on our knowledge of children's language development, keeping in mind the rather different nature of their goal and our current concerns.

Language acquisition and the LAD

Chomsky's analysis offered not only a dynamic new view of language but also changed attitudes towards and research into language acquisition. His theory displaced the image of the child language 'learner' who develops language by being taught and reinforced, and substituted it with the theory of a language 'acquirer' who discovers and makes creative, generative use of *rules* from the very start of language development. These rules, even before language is 'fully' mastered, enable the child to produce and analyse a theoretically infinite number of utterances. Child language study was thus transformed into a search for the 'rules' that children acquire and involved attempts to write 'child grammars'. More about this later.

In rejecting the theory that the capacity to learn how to speak and understand speech is in any sense taught, Chomsky leads us to a view of the language acquisition capacity that is rather like a 'mental organ' (Chomsky, 1980, p. 188). The way in which the eye and the nervous system respond to light of different wavelengths to produce the sensations of colour vision, for example, is a property of the way in which the visual system is structured. This sensory system is genetically determined and a fruit of evolution. Perhaps the processing of speech in the nervous system proceeds along similar lines. Speech sounds stimulating the auditory nerves are 'processed' naturally to uncover (eventually) the rules by which that speech is structured. Although languages obviously differ in the word sounds they use and the grammatical rules they embody, Chomsky believes that they all share certain universal properties, which an innate system – what has been termed the 'Language Acquisition Device' or LAD (McNeill, 1970) – has evolved to produce and acquire. The automatic workings of the LAD are such that a child 'knows' that the speech signal is the product of another similar system which generates sentences, words, and so on. Thus the child does not have to 'learn' that speech is built out of words and sentences that possess components like subjects and predicates or verbs and objects. The LAD ensures that she perceives speech sounds in this way (though she still has to discover the specific rules underlying her 'host' language and learn the relations between words and the things to which they refer).

Meaning and 'structure dependency'

In the 'flying kites' example already introduced, recall how the same word (flying) changed its grammatical category and hence its meaning according to the chosen meaning of the *sentence* as a whole. This is symptomatic of another universal feature of languages. Meaning involves much more than simply stringing words together: it is *not* simply the sum of word parts. Rather, the meaning of words themselves is constrained by the overall structure of the utterance in which they are embedded. Put another way, meaning is 'structure dependent'. This is one reason why a Chomskian view of language leads to the assertion that children are innately equipped to 'parse' utterances naturally into linguistic units. Only a system that is sensitive to such higher-order structures, the argument proceeds, could ever discover what speech means. In this way, Chomsky turns the behaviourist analysis on its head. Language development does not proceed from learning isolated words to the discovery of progressively longer word–word combinations. Instead, the child 'expects' to hear units of meaning which are structured by rules. Similarly, when the child produces her first words and word combinations these should not be viewed as simple responses attached to isolated things but more like embryonic sentences. The child is communicating ideas or deep structures, albeit, in the early stages, through single words. Any theory which holds that utterances are learned by building up or stringing together single word units cannot capture such structural, rule-governed features of language.

Perhaps a final example will help to underline this point.

Compare 'Green ideas sleep furiously' with 'Furiously green sleep ideas'. Although both strings of words are meaningless, are you prepared to accept that the first sounds more 'grammatical' than the latter? If so, it follows that knowledge of grammatical structure is independent of meaningfulness. We recognize grammatical structure *itself* even though we are not able to describe the rules that create such structures. We can recognize and use the rules but cannot articulate them.

Chomsky's theory has kept linguists and psycholinguists in business for many years and it has been used to make a number of predictions about language use and its development. Since Chomsky inspired but does not necessarily agree with what people (particularly some psychologists) have done with and to his theory, I'll talk about 'Chomskian' theory from now on to signal the fact that such work may not be consistent with his 'pure' theory.

Some examples of the early stages of language development

Having read Chomsky, researchers were obviously going to look at children's speech to ask if it displayed any evidence of rule acquisition or use. Motivated by notions of an innate Language Acquisition Device of the sort Chomsky seemed to envisage, they searched for common patterns, structures and stages in the linguistic development of all children. If, as the theory implies, children do their own language *acquisition*, researchers were bound to ask if it follows that adult talk to children is largely irrelevant to their development.

Given these concerns with the notion of 'innateness' and the rejection of teaching and learning in language acquisition, it is perhaps not surprising that the bulk of research into child language development has concentrated on the very early stages over the first three years of life. Many detailed observations have been made of children's first 'words' and their early word combinations. Numerous attempts (none entirely successful to date) have been made to write 'child grammars' (Crystal, 1976). Basically, such attempts involve the formulation of rules that will 'predict' which categories of words children will put together and in what ways, and, at the same time, will never produce an utterance with a structure that they never utter. Although most of this work of early language development and child grammar is not directly relevant to our current educational concerns, some of the issues, findings and ideas that have emerged from it are.

There seems to be general agreement that young children do acquire 'rules' in learning to talk (although many would argue that these are not of the type predicted by Chomskian theory). One line of evidence for this assertion comes from the common finding that children often produce utterances that, though systematically related to their stage of language development, are extremely unlikely to be the result of imitating adult speech. For example, some children produce plural forms like 'mouses' and 'catses' even though earlier in life they may have used the correct forms, 'mice' and 'cats'. Studies of the way in which children come to master the rules involved in creating plural forms illustrate a *general* phenomenon that recurs time and time again in language development right through to adolescence. Children pass through a series of stages or phases as they encounter and master (learn?) how to use and understand many aspects of language structure. Let me outline the proposed stages involved.

Language: stages in the development of expertise?

I have already said that children often use words like 'mice' and 'cats' appropriately before they begin to make 'errors' like 'mices'. In this early stage children do not seem aware of the fact that plural forms like 'cats', 'bats', 'bikes' are composed of *two* elements. Rather, they seem to treat all word-like sounds as though they are *single* elements of meaning (Gleitman and Wanner, 1982). Many words contain two or more 'morphemes' (i.e. units of meaning), like 'cat-s', 'walk-ing', 'un-cover-ing' and so on. Some of these units (sometimes referred to as 'free morphemes') are free to stand alone, like cat, walk and cover, but others (like '-s', 'un-' and '-ing') are bound to occur in combination with free morphemes (hence so-called 'bound morphemes'). Children, though producing a few 'multimorpheme' words at this stage, do not seem aware of the fact that these can be 'decomposed' to reveal two or more units. When they *do* discover the fact that such words can be broken down, they come to realize that prefixes like 'un-' and suffixes like '-s' and '-ing' have very *specific* meanings. Having, so to speak, 'detached' such morphemes and discovered what they mean, the child proceeds to *generalize* the 'rules' for using them to produce words like 'undress' and 'rats' but she may also combine them with other words to produce 'errors' of overgeneralization. So she might add '-s' to 'mice' producing 'mices', 'un-' to 'wipe' producing 'unwipe', and '-ed' to 'went' giving 'wented'. Although the child is unlikely ever to have heard such words, the fact that so many (though not necessarily all) children produce them at the same *stage* of development suggests strongly that they are inferring and generalizing rules.

Stage 1, then, involves the limited use of a relatively small number of words in 'non-rule-governed' ways. Following the discovery of new features of speech (like a particular prefix or suffix) and their meaning, the child moves into a second stage which may be marked by errors of overgeneralization. As the child discovers irregularities like 'mice' (which is already a plural form) and 'went' (which is already a 'perfected' verb form), such errors disappear and the child moves on to a stage where a more mature understanding of the various linguistic rules involved is perfected.

This process is not nearly so 'automatic' an affair as some early students of Chomsky seemed to suggest. It certainly implies that the child has to *work* on the problems involved in achieving mature understanding of language and that *learning* is implicated (though not necessarily teaching – please read on). Though this form of learning (discovery of rules through problem-solving) is a very different affair to that implicated in 'response learning' theories, it is not, I suggest, very different from the learning processes described in the development of expertise. More about this later.

I have suggested that this pattern of stages (limited, non-productive mastery of a few forms followed by the discovery of new linguistic features and possible 'errors' of generalization prior to mastery and perfection of mature rule systems) is a general and recurrent feature of language development. I will illustrate this argument with a few examples in the next sections, which takes us back to the study of school-children.

Language learning: one process or many?

For a time, some developmental psycholinguists (psychologists and/or linguists who study language development) were sufficiently impressed by the linguistic achievements of pre-school children to suggest that the acquisition of grammar was all but completed before children start formal schooling. However, while they are impressive, the pre-school child's achievements fall far short of mature linguistic competence. The development of communication skills and grammatical knowledge continues at least into adolescence.

Because language is changing and developing over such a long period of time, it seems unreasonable to suppose that the process of language acquisition and/or language learning is a single, continuous one. It would be surprising if the processes involved in language development in children aged nine, say, were not to prove different in some important ways from those of children aged two. Establishing the nature of such differences and how they come about is not easy. But the issues involved are important. They will lead us, for example, to consider the importance of *literacy* as an influence on the development of 'clear speaking' and verbal reasoning. It has been suggested, for example, that the ability to reason *rationally* about abstract phenomena is a direct product of literacy and the educational experiences that teach children how to read fluently. Thus, the issue of language development (acquisition and/or learning) is intimately involved with a range of important educational questions concerning both the teaching and consequences of literacy.

We have already met and discussed some of the evidence that points to changes in children's intellectual abilities between the ages of five and seven years. Now we examine other studies and observations which suggest that the same holds true of linguistic development. The nature of any discontinuities and the way in which they come about are a matter for debate. To what extent are developments after the age of five years attributable to school experience, say, or to changes in stage of intellectual development? Attempts to answer these questions will involve us in (at least) a three-cornered fight. Before entering battle, let us consider some of the changes in the child's understanding and use of language that occur during the first two to three years of schooling.

Listening and talking

Do children understand more than they can say? Put another way, are they able to comprehend utterances which they cannot form themselves? If they can, a number of things might follow. In the first place, it would imply that because a child cannot produce a particular type of utterance (say, for instance, a passive construction like 'The dog was scratched by the cat') it does not necessarily follow that she will not understand it when she hears it spoken. If so, it may be important that we do not underestimate what children can be told and are able to grasp by assuming that they only understand language structures that they are able to say. More important, an ability to understand what they themselves cannot yet produce might provide children with a basis for the development of spoken language. Knowing what 'sounds right', a child is in a position to *evaluate* her own speech. She will know when she has said something that sounds 'odd', perhaps. If she is able to recognize whether or not what she is trying to say sounds right, she may not need anyone to *tell* her that some of the things she says are not linguistically well formed. She may school herself in the complexities of language use. This question is educationally interesting because it provides some measure of the importance of 'teaching' in language development. There are, in fact, several lines of evidence to support the view that children *are* able to understand more than they can say in this sense. Their *receptive* language ability (ability to listen and understand) is often in advance of their *productive* language (speech). Let me illustrate the argument.

I have already drawn attention to the fact that infants take some time to discover the fact that many words which sound like single units of meaning actually encapsulate more than one element. It seems unlikely that anyone in any simple or direct sense 'teaches' them this fact. Rather, what seems to happen is far more a matter of the child's biology, how the hearing system works, than a case for instruction. Studies of the *sequence* in which infants master different systems of prefixes and suffixes, for example, help to illustrate this claim. Consider the suffixes '-ing' and '-ed'. These are used to 'mark' the fact that a particular activity (walk, watch) is in progress (walking, watching) or has been perfected (walked, watched). Children usually master the progressive form before they crack the perfective. Why? Is it because they find it easier to relate a sound ('ing') to an *ongoing* event than they do to relate one ('ed') to an activity that has *stopped* and hence has to be remembered? Or does the answer lie in the way that adults talk to children? Perhaps we speak to infants more about events in progress than those that have been completed. If so, the order of acquisition would reflect frequency of exposure and might be an example of 'indirect' instruction.

It seems, however, that the sequence of acquisition is not determined by the relative difficulty of the *ideas* involved in different verb forms nor by frequency of exposure. Rather, because 'ing' is usually more acoustically *stressed* in speech than is 'ed', infants find it more *salient*. In other words, they become aware of the progressive use of verbs first and begin to use them in their own speech before they master the 'ed' form because the suffix involved is more 'audible'. Studies of language development in children acquiring other languages (e.g. Serbo-Croatian and Turkish) offer further evidence for this conclusion (Gleitman and Wanner, 1982).

On the basis of this evidence, one might conclude that infants acquire language 'naturally'. The fact that many children show a similar sequence of development which seems to rest on the way in which speech is structured (for example, where stress is found) is evidence favouring a Chomskian interpretation of language *acquisition*. Children's acquisition of language is paced by the way in which they hear – a biological phenomenon that has little to do with instruction, informal or otherwise.

Now let us consider some examples of language development in older children. When do children understand what the words 'this' and 'that' mean? Well, first consider how we might express the meaning of 'this' and 'that'. We might define 'here' as 'The region of space occupied by the current speaker ("I")' and 'there' as 'The region of space occupied by the current listener(s) ("you"). Of course, when the speaker in a conversational exchange 'hands over' to her listener, 'here' becomes 'there' and 'there' becomes 'here'. Similarly, we might define 'this' as 'an object in the "here" of the current "I" ' and 'that' as 'an object in the "there" of the current "you" '. When 'I' becomes 'you', 'this' becomes 'that'. The use of such terms, of course, is not restricted to situations involving only two people. For example, if 'we' are talking about 'him', then 'there' may be where 'he' is along with 'that'. However, should 'he' start to address 'us' ('he' becoming 'I'), then both 'this' and 'here' are where 'he' (who, recall, is currently 'I') is located. If 'we' are in the same room as 'him', then 'there' is likely to be a region of space nearer to 'him' than 'us', when one of 'us' is currently 'I', that is. However, should 'he' be talking to 'us' over the telephone, say, then 'this' may well be something far removed, since 'here', when 'he' is 'I', is likely to be at the other end of the phone – in another country, perhaps.

Answering the question 'When do children understand "here" and "there" or "this" and "that"?' is not easy. In some situations, understanding and the use of such words comes very early in life. For example, a three-year-old says 'Give me that' or 'I don't want to go there'. A father says to his infant daughter 'Come to me', and she complies. The pre-school child, in some contexts, seems both to understand and use such words. However, when confronted with an experimenter across a table who says 'Will you give me this pencil' (as opposed to one located near the child), some children aged five years are likely to offer the pencil located nearest to 'them', apparently assuming that 'this' is located near where they themselves are. Reliable understanding of 'this' and 'that' in such circumstances appears at around five to six years (Clark, 1978).

On several occasions I have drawn attention to similar discrepancies between the ages at which children use and understand utterances and solve problems in 'natural' everyday contexts as opposed to formal experimental situations. I have suggested that everyday interactions between adults and children are different in developmentally important ways from those in formal teaching and testing encounters. In everyday discourse, but not in such experiments, the *situation* shared by speakers and hearers provides several avenues for the achievement of mutual understanding. When we talk about 'this' and 'that' in spontaneous encounters, for example, we are likely to *look* at the thing being referred to. A child asked 'Will you give me that, please?' and presented with an outstretched hand, is likely to understand what 'that' is for a number of possible reasons. Non-verbal 'cues' to meaning plus the fact that she may, say, have something that does not belong to her, or which is in some way taboo, probably leave little room for doubt about what the speaker is referring to. 'Will you hand me this, please' is a little more unusual. Perhaps the person making the request is unable to move for some reason or has their hands full. The utterance also seems to imply that some other objects (other possible 'thats') exist and 'this' is something closer to the speaker than any potential 'that'. It also suggests that 'this' is closer to the speaker than the child being asked to hand it over. Put another way, there is likely to be some interpretable explanation or *reason* for the speaker's request and there may well be other cues (nods, points, eye movements) which indicate what 'this' is.

In the experimental situation, however, such reasons and cues are deliberately avoided to test the child's understanding of 'language' itself. The reason why children seem to understand the 'same' words in some situations but not in others is not, then, all that straightforward. I am suggesting, as I did in discussing tests of children's 'logic', that experimental encounters devoid of interpretable *reasons* or obvious *justifications* and which are stripped of many cues that normally make meaning and communication relatively 'transparent' confront young children with unusual demands. Although 'similar' forms of *words* are being used the marked differences in available clues to meaning and the presence or absence of intelligible reasons for utterances show that such apparent similarities are misleading. Logical tasks, and utterances which look and sound 'identical', often differ in *kind*.

Deixis: words that 'point'

A psycholinguist, Eve Clark, has undertaken a range of experiments to investigate children's understanding of terms like 'here and there', 'this and that' and 'come and go'. Such terms are referred to as 'deictic' forms. Deixis, from the Greek verb meaning 'to point', refers to words and to non-verbal features of communication like nods and gestures, which serve to point to or in some way to identify people, times, places and objects in the course of discourse. Pronouns like 'I' and 'you', for instance, unlike nouns, do not refer to members of specific categories of things like 'cat', 'dog' or 'chair'. Their meaning, who or what they refer to, is determined in *use*, so 'I' might be defined as 'the current speaker' and 'you' as 'the current listener'. As we have seen, 'here' can be defined with reference to who is speaking. 'This' and 'that' 'point to' things that are 'here or there', and so on. Clark's experimental studies reveal a developmental *sequence* that children pass through in mastering such terms (again, in formal contexts lacking many 'natural' clues to meaning). 'I' and 'you' are mastered before 'here and there', followed by 'this and that'. 'Come and go' come later. 'Come' in a given encounter might imply 'you cease being an object in the "there" of the current "you" and become an object closer to the "here" of the current "I".'

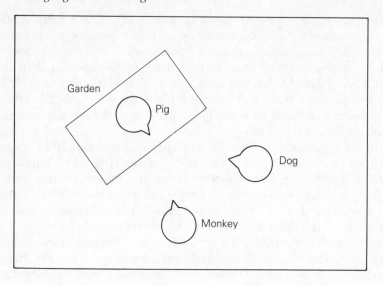

Figure 4.1 Testing deictic contrasts: positions of the three animals, all facing each other, with one inside a specific location and the other two outside facing in

Alternatively, if 'I' is talking about 'us' it might imply 'Let "us" cease to be objects in the "here" of the current "we" to take up residence over "there".' Children's understanding of verbs like 'come and go' and 'bring and take' develops up to the age of about nine years. When we consider the complexity of some of the ways in which these verbs are used, we can see in a reasonably concrete way how the *learning* of language (I use the term deliberately) shades into verbal *reasoning*.

By way of illustration, examine the task shown in figure 4.1. When eight-year-old children are asked to work out problems like 'The monkey says "Go into the garden". Which animal is he talking to?', few children below the age of eight years six months were likely to give 'adult' answers. Although children are using the verb 'to go' quite early in life (e.g. "Can I go out to play?'), their use and understanding of this and many other linguistic terms develops through into adolescence. While the 'same' verb is employed in many different circumstances, the nature of its *meaning* and the intellectual demands involved in working this out vary enormously from one context to another. This is why it is difficult, if not impossible, to give a simple, general answer to questions like 'When do children understand the verb "to go"?' The answer depends upon the *use* to which the verb is being put and upon the *situation* in which communication is taking place.

The evidence suggesting that language *acquisition* in infancy is strongly constrained by natural features of speech, such as acoustic stress, is persuasive. Infants, as many Chomskians have argued, seem to acquire their understanding of language 'naturally' without any teaching or instruction from the more mature. However, when we consider language development in later years, it becomes difficult if not impossible to disentangle language from reasoning and problem-solving. Children have to think about and to *work* at language in order to fathom its meaning. What may seem at first sight to be an issue of language learning, turns out on more detailed consideration to involve *intellectual* development generally. Learning how to put ideas into words (or print) and working out what others mean by what they say (and write) is not a single, *continuous* process but one that changes with age and, perhaps, stage of development.

Teach yourself language?

Clark's experimental studies illustrate and chart the long developmental history involved in children's acquisition and mastery of deictic uses of language. She also observes, however, that outside of contrived experimental situations, it is extremely difficult to detect any 'errors' in children's use of words like 'this', 'that', 'come' and 'go'. This observation raises some important issues. For example, if children do not make errors, or if any errors they make are hard to detect, it seems unlikely that they are 'taught' how to understand and use such linguistic devices by 'correction'. If adults trained in linguistics who have looked specifically for examples of children's errors in everyday talk cannot find them, it seems unlikely to suppose that parents are responsible for teaching their children about these aspects of language by correcting their speech.

A similar conclusion emerges from the findings of Karmiloff-Smith (1979), whose studies of children's use and understanding of determiners (e.g. 'a' and 'the') I referred to in chapter 2. Let me say a little more about her findings. Some of her experiments involved young French-speaking children. The structure of the determiner system in French differs in some respects from that of English. For instance, reference to *singular* and *plural* objects in French involves not only the use of bound morphemes (e.g. '-s') to mark plurality (e.g. voiture, voitures) but also modifications to the determiner as well (e.g. la voiture, les voitures). Indeed, as Karmiloff-Smith points out, the '-s' marker in French is often impossible to 'hear', i.e. it is often non-articulated or unstressed, unlike its counterpart in English (e.g. cat/cats). French children must, then, learn to use and understand plural *determiners* to make and comprehend distinctions between singular and plural references.

As with English children's grasp of words like 'come and go',

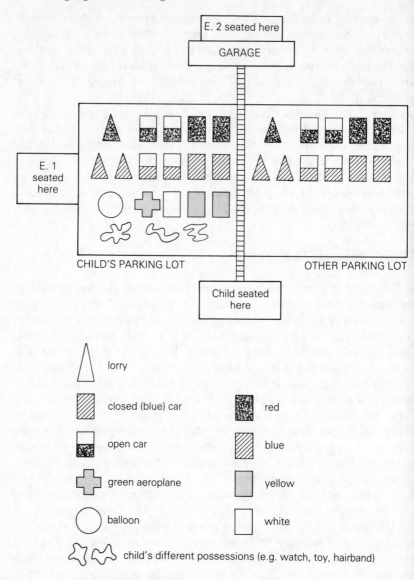

Figure 4.2 The child is asked by E1 to tell E2 to put, say, all the child's lorries in the garage

young French children use and understand singular and plural determiners in everyday discourse without obvious problems. Yet they experience significant difficulties with them in experiments. Part of the explanation for this now familiar (apparent) discrepancy between performance in natural and contrived interactions stems from the fact that words like 'le' and 'les' have several related but *different* means in French depending upon the circumstances of their use. They are, in Karmiloff-Smith's terms, 'pluri-functional'. For instance, four-year-old children face no problems in either saying or understanding the different meanings of expressions like 'Observez le chien' and 'Observez les chiens'. Pre-school children appreciate that the first makes reference to a single dog and the second to more than one. Compare this with the quite different though related meaning of 'les' when, in the experimental setup illustrated in figure 4.2, the child is asked to tell another person that they must take *all* the cars shown and put them somewhere else (in the garage, say). In French, the expression 'Mettez au garage *les* voitures' would be a perfectly adequate instruction. 'Les', used in this context, does not simply mean 'more than one car' but *all* of the cars. Put another way, it refers not only to *plurality* but at the same time to *totality*, to the whole *set* of relevant objects (cars).

The use of 'les' by French children to refer to plurality and totality *simultaneously* emerges at somewhere around eight years of age (again, in this type of situation). Younger children who have not yet mastered the dual function of 'les' manage to get their message across to their listener by saying things like 'Toutes les voitures' (All of the cars). By 'adding' words which to the mature French ear are 'redundant', the child manages to convey the appropriate meaning. Consequently, it cannot be the case that the child fails to grasp the communication needs of her listener, nor is it the case that she does not understand the concept of 'totality'. Her 'problem' is a *linguistic* one.

When I discussed the infant's understanding of 'multi-morpheme' words like 'walking' and 'walked', I suggested that they pass through a stage when such words are understood as *single* elements of meaning. Karmiloff-Smith's studies suggest an analogous state of affairs in relation to words that serve several *functions*. Thus, French children below the age of eight understand and use 'les' to refer to two or more objects but do *not* realize that in some circumstances it can serve *two* functions at the same time. Consider other examples. When children (still in the situation illustrated in figure 4.2) are asked to tell someone to place all the lorries in the garage, a child aged 10 years 11 months said 'Tous les camions . . . ou bien on peut dire *les* camions' which translates as "All the lorries . . . or you can say *the* lorries' (the child stressed the word 'les'). Faced with the same task, a child aged 4 years 7 months said 'Mettez au garage les camions . . . les camions bleus, le camion rouge et les camions bleus' (Put into the garage the lorries . . . the blue lorries, the red lorry and the blue lorries). This child attempted to *describe* or list all the relevant objects. What he or she did not say, however, was where the lorries were to be found. The child also overlooked one of the red lorries (recall what was said about children's powers of attention in chapter 3). This child used 'les' to refer to 'more than one' but did not appreciate that the single expression 'les camions' can be used to refer to the total *set* of objects he or she was attempting to describe.

A child aged 5 years 2 months managed to get the message across saying 'Tous mes camions, un camion rouge à moi, deux camions bleus à moi et tous vos camions, deux camions bleus à vous . . .' (All my lorries, one red lorry of mine, two blue lorries of mine and all your lorries, two blue lorries of yours . . .). Note how this child, by employing *personal* pronouns, conveyed information about the *location* of the objects being described. But, as with the plural form 'les', he or she adds 'tous' to mark the fact that *all* the lorries are implicated (although 'mes' alone would suffice for a mature speaker). The child then proceeds to *list* the groups of objects which make up the *total* set. Eventually, he or she will learn how to refer to this set using the 'simple' utterance, 'les camions'.

I have gone into some detail about this experiment in an attempt to illustrate a number of important aspects of language development. In fact, there are at least eight points worth underlining, some of which we have already met in relation to other studies.

1 Single, seemingly simple, grammatical morphemes serve more than one function. Thus, words like 'mine', say, may simply refer to an object or objects that one possesses (my watch, my toys etc.), or at one and the same time to *totalities* of objects, like 'my cars' or 'my vehicles'. In figure 4.2, for example, the word 'my' can serve both to specify *which* set of objects are being referred to and to signal the fact that all members of this set are involved.
2 Children first employ such words for limited, uni-functional purposes and only after a considerable number of years do they acquire the *system* of interrelated functions that these words also serve. Ten-year-olds may still be grappling with the task of achieving clear, efficient and 'mature' ways of referring to things.
3 The problems that children face in such situations cannot be explained in terms of an inadequate grasp of concepts to do with sets and subsets or by an insensitivity to their listeners' needs. The fact that children find other means of expressing their intended meaning some years before they master 'adult' conventions for making reference shows that they appreciate *what* they need to do. In such situations, development consists in working out the *linguistic* means to achieve efficient communication of their intended meaning. Language acquisition, then, cannot be explained simply in terms of cognitive development nor can communication problems be attributed entirely to a child's insensitivity to other people's communicative needs. Whilst cognition and communicative competence do constrain

what a child can understand and communicate, there are specifically linguistic problems that the child must also solve. It follows that we should be cautious when trying to explain a child's communication 'problems'. We cannot assume that all features of communication or every misunderstanding is a product of intellectual or social factors. Language development itself takes time and effort and may result in unexpected failures of mutual comprehension.

4 Experimental studies of the kind I have been discussing help to reveal aspects of language use which present challenges for children. These are not made obvious in everyday talk. Such problems are not trivial, nor are they simple 'artefacts' of experiments. Children have to learn how to talk in certain ways in order to make sense of many tasks they will face in formal learning situations. I take this issue up in the next two chapters.

5 So far as we can tell, children learn how to make themselves understood without frequent 'error correction' by adults. Indeed, in everyday situations errors may not often arise to be corrected. The young child's limited understanding of adult talk is not revealed by casual observation: its discovery may demand careful and detailed study of the child in 'artificial' situations. If the child's linguistic limitations are not obvious to the naked ear, it seems highly unlikely that we would know *what* to teach the child in everyday interactions. Children do not often 'reveal' their limited grasp of language features that they have yet to master.

6 Before children achieve mastery of mature ways of expressing themselves, they appear to pass through a stage or phase of *self-correction*. I have provided a number of examples. The finding, so common, that children correct themselves yet seem seldom to be corrected by others, suggests that they 'teach themselves' how to use and understand complex aspects of language structure. If social and educational experiences play any important role in helping children to teach themselves, that role must have little to do with overt correction or direct instruction.

7 Children are usually taught how to read some years before the learning processes that we have been discussing have run their course. This raises a number of questions. First, do children face unrecognized language problems in learning to read and write because, while they seem to 'know' and understand things like determiners, pronouns and 'deictic' words, they only use them for a limited range of purposes? Perhaps learning to read and write, like experiments and tests, confronts children with novel intellectual, communicative and linguistic demands. How far does the experience of learning to read and write itself help children to discover and master aspects of their mother tongue? We take up these issues in the next two chapters.

8 Finally, Karmiloff-Smith notes how children who show signs of self-correction often *improved* their performance in her experiments. Their instructions became more economical and 'mature' in form as they took part in tasks. This raises a new set of questions. Whilst I think we can reject the notion that children learn the aspects of language we have been discussing through instruction or 'feedback', it may be the case that providing children with certain tasks, projects, problems and experiences may help them to teach themselves. Similarly, it may follow that children who seldom experience such tasks and demands may have little need or opportunity for self-instruction. These questions are explored in the next chapter.

Educability: some first thoughts

The concept of linguistic deprivation and the explanation for the connection between school achievement and social background that it offered have not withstood the test of time and observation. So the view, echoed in President Johnson's speech quoted earlier, that children are 'taught' how to speak, and the related assertion that some fail to learn how to talk at home because they do not receive appropriate instruction, seem untenable. Children may come to school speaking different dialects but such linguistic variations are not to be taken as evidence that some exhibit 'defective' language. Yet, the fact remains that social background is one of the most reliable predictors of a child's likely performance in school. How these two things are related is still open to question and debate.

A number of alternative accounts have been offered to explain the relationship. One, for example, places the responsibility for differences in children's levels of performance at the door of educationalists and their attitudes. Teachers, the argument proceeds, perceive children who do not talk using 'received pronunciation' and the 'standard' form of their language as less able or less well motivated than children whose talk corresponds more closely to that of the currently 'dominant' dialect. Making (perhaps implicit or unconscious) judgements about children's educational potential on the basis of how they talk, teachers set up self-fulfilling prophesies which lead to the anticipated differences in levels of achievement. Crudely, because teachers expect less of children from some social backgrounds, these children are taught and learn less.

The view that teacher *expectations* influence the way in which they teach and the amount that children learn is often supported by appeals to studies performed some years ago by Rosenthal and Jacobson (1968). The basic design of these studies is as follows:

teachers are told that they are to instruct groups of children who are either very able or somewhat slow. In reality, however, the groups of children involved are 'matched' on the basis of assessments of their learning abilities. Thus, while teachers are led to *believe* that they are to teach either able or less able pupils, they are actually given classes of similar levels of (estimated) ability. The performance of the two groups of children are monitored over time to see if their achievements differ.

The first studies of this type suggested that children whose teachers had been led to believe that they were relatively able learnt more than those labelled less able. So the conclusion was drawn that teacher perceptions and *expectations* exert a direct, *causal* influence on how much children learn in school. Add to such conclusions the theory that teachers view some children as less able because of the way in which they talk, and an alternative explanation for the effects of social background on educational performance emerges: one based on teachers' differential expectations (or prejudices).

More recent attempts to reproduce this so-called 'Rosenthal effect' have, however, failed to produce the same results (Pilling and Pringle, 1978). Nor have such studies provided much by way of insight into the actual teaching *practices* that might lead to differences in children's achievements. Whilst it may prove to be the case that teachers do have expectations of children that are based on social stereotypes and that these do lead to the achievement of self-fulfilling prophesies, the evidence to date is not compelling.

Among other explanations given to account for the effect of social background and language variation on educational performance is the view that different social groupings within modern societies have different values, attitudes and aspirations. Children from different backgrounds are socialized into, come to embody, and carry into schools different world views, to find that they coincide to a greater or less extent with those implicit in the value systems of formal education. To the extent that the values of home and school do coincide, children are likely to fare well. Where there are marked discrepancies between the two systems, however, children may be confused, bored or become antagonistic. Such analyses lead on to a radically different perspective on 'relevance' in education to those we have explored so far. They ask educators to examine their own values and their own views on what education is *for* and to measure these against those held by children and their families.

Another possible line of explanation seeks its power in terms of the quality and ease of communication between teachers and children from different backgrounds. Where children share a dialect with their teachers, communication between them is likely to be relatively easy, but where marked differences exist, the establishment and maintenance of rapport and mutual comprehension may be more difficult to achieve thus inhibiting the transmission of knowledge and understanding.

We will be exploring this and other points of view in the remaining chapters. Be forewarned, however, that the situation is more complex than the suggestion I have just outlined implies. We will find ourselves questioning the view that language in school is in any useful sense the 'same' for (some) children as that experienced at home or in the community. There are marked and important differences in the nature and purposes of communication at home and school and these result in children's exposure to new functions and structures of language that present challenges and special problems. While it may be true that some children are better prepared than others to meet and master these demands, it does not seem to be the case that children from some backgrounds experience *continuity* of linguistic experience when they go to school whilst others experience discontinuity. Rather, I suggest, it is a question of *degree* of continuity.

Language development continues throughout the years of schooling. Children must learn new ways of communicating if they are to learn what it is schools seek to teach. By the same token, teachers also face special linguistic and communicative demands in school which require resources and expertise that are special to the process of education. Perhaps when we have explored some of what we know about the character of communicative development in the first years of schooling, we will be in a better position to discuss and evaluate competing claims about the relationship between children's educability and their social backgrounds.

Summary

The experiments and observations I have just outlined represent only a tiny fraction of a vast literature on language development. However, the points I have just made are, I believe, consistent with the more general picture that has emerged from that literature. The assertion implicit in the quotation attributed to President Johnson, that children must be 'taught' how to speak, and that some children cannot *talk* because they have not been taught 'properly' if at all, is untenable. The allied notion that some dialects or creoles only permit relatively inarticulate, ill-formed and non-grammatical communication must also be laid to rest. While differences in dialect and social background are demonstrably correlated with school achievement we cannot, I suggest, explain the relationship in terms of early linguistic deprivation.

Chomskians argue that children acquire language naturally and that they are born with neurological equipment which enables them to appreciate and analyse the structure of speech. This point of view has proved difficult both to describe and to evaluate. The achievements of infants – their seemingly inborn sensitivity to the human voice and the way in which they respond to features of speech such as acoustic stress and word-like elements in streams of speech sounds – are consistent with this general position. Attempts to program computers to 'parse' and analyse human speech into its meaningful segments or units have encountered tremendous problems and no one, to date, has effectively solved these. The fact that speech is so difficult to analyse mechanically demonstrates the fact that the natural capacities of babies are not 'trivial' and must involve complex, neurological abilities that make the acquisition of language possible.

If learning how to understand and use speech rests on such natural capacities, can we conclude that the more mature, whether parents, older peers or teachers, play an important role in *facilitating* the child's mastery of language? If we accept that children are able to teach themselves, developing and correcting their own 'theories' about the structure of language, can we divest ourselves of all responsibility for the course of a child's linguistic development and achievements? I think not. As Peter Robinson (1981) has pointed out, accepting the now compelling findings showing that children generate, test and refine their own hypotheses about language and its working does not entail the complete abdication by the more mature of any teaching or enabling roles. Simply because the child is active, constructive and generative in her re-creation of language (and knowledge generally) it does not follow that others cannot be more or less helpful and facilitative, or unhelpful and inhibiting, along the way. It is self-evident that children acquire the dialect(s) and the ways of talking and communicating to which they are exposed. Some students of child language seem to argue that mere 'exposure' to a language is all that is needed for its acquisition. We have examined studies which demonstrate that young infants are naturally equipped to learn language and which imply that children perfect certain features of language without frequent exposure to external correction or instruction. But, I suggest, such evidence does not provide sufficient grounds for a *general* conclusion that interpersonal experiences play no formative role in the development of language and communication.

Teaching can be construed in many ways, and instruction by explicit correction is only one potential candidate for a theory of what it involves. In the next chapter, we look in more detail and from a different perspective at the nature of social and linguistic interaction to construct a somewhat different view of what teaching is. Bear in mind, though, that this or any other theory of what teaching entails will have to accommodate a view of the child learner as an active, constructive and generative architect of her own language and her own understanding.

When I tried to characterize Chomsky's approach to the theoretical study of language, I pointed out that his aim was not to provide an account of how people *use* language. His is not a theory of *communication* but of an 'ideal' grammar. Some of the studies and experiments I have just outlined reveal the limitations of such a view when we try to use it as a framework for achieving an understanding of language development (in passing, however, recall that this was never Chomsky's intention). The importance of intonation, gesture, and a shared situation in the achievement of mutual understanding (and, as we shall see in the next chapter, in the acquisition of language itself), were underlined by differences found in children's use and understanding of language in natural and contrived situations. Robbed of such important bases for the achievement of mutual understanding, children find incomprehensible a variety of tasks and utterances when these are encountered in unfamiliar experimental or test situations. Chomskian theory is designed to reveal and describe the general *rules* that are implicit in a language, and different utterances are compared and classified in terms of systems of these rules. However, utterances that are classified as 'similar' in structure for a linguist, because they are generated by the 'same' rules, may be quite different for a child (or an adult for that matter). Put another way, language, as an instrument of communication and an interpersonal *activity* involves more than such hypothetical underlying grammatical rules. To understand the nature of language development and the way in which children achieve comprehension in the absence of important clues to meaning such as intonation, stress and situational cues, we need to look beyond 'grammar'.

The studies undertaken by Clark and Karmiloff-Smith help to illustrate the complex connections between language and reasoning. Some early followers of Chomsky seemed to argue that the acquisition of language was a rather rapid, almost automatic affair, that was largely completed in the pre-school years. As we have seen, the process is not particularly rapid nor does it end before schooling. Piaget provided one of the first and most explicit accounts of the way in which the structure of the child's thinking constrains and paces her understanding and use of language. Several of the studies I have described in this chapter, and others I will discuss in the next two, point to important changes in the child's use and comprehension of various aspects of language that coincide with the advent of schooling at around age six or seven. Karmiloff-Smith, for instance, suggest that the phase of self-correction in the use of determiners appears at about seven years of age. Investigations of many other features of children's use and grasp of speech also indicate that important changes are occurring at around the same time. We have seen that seven years of age, the 'age of reason', also marks some important developments in the way children think. Should we not conclude, then, that the coincidence of developmental changes in both language and cognition, as predicted by Piaget, offers support for his theory of stages?

I suggest not. Karmiloff-Smith, for instance, whilst accepting Piaget's insistence on the interdependency of language and thought, provides several lines of evidence which show that learning language involves the child in the solution of problems that are *specific* to language. Five- and six-year-old children often manage to communicate complex instructions some years before they have mastered the detailed structure of their language. The fact they know *how* to get their message across shows both that they understand the requirements of such tasks (are intellectually competent) and possess sufficient communicative competence to make what they say intelligible to their listener, *before* they have reached mature levels of language comprehension and production. Consequently, it cannot be the case that language learning rests only on non-verbal understanding. It presents many problems of its own. If we accept this conclusion then it follows that a child, for purely linguistic reasons, may not understand what she is taught or told and may seem unable to explain what she knows clearly. Failure to understand and explain may occur not because she lacks 'logic' or conceptual understanding, but because she has yet to learn the appropriate linguistic conventions. From this we can argue that language learning in the school years may be a source of problems, misunderstandings and apparent failures to learn. Oracy – a rather ungainly word used to refer to the expertise, skill and knowledge involved in effective verbal communication – should, then, be an important part of the school curriculum. Human nature may ensure that most children learn how to talk. Social experience and schooling, as we shall see, play a central role in determining both what they have to say and how they are able to express what they mean.

Chapter 5

Making sense

We now move on to look in more detail at the development of language and communication during the years of schooling. We look at research designed to identify the communicative demands that children face in school and to evaluate if, when and how children respond to these. We also study explanations as to why some children find it difficult to fulfil these demands and examine classroom research which offers some suggestions about how schools might better serve such children.

Non-verbal and verbal communication

When children first start to speak, what they talk about is almost invariably prompted by that which currently fills their senses. Their first acts of speech are single words. Later comes a stage of two words, followed by a three-word stage, then four, until, around three years of age, the child begins to use simple sentences. Listened to out of context, much of what infants say in the early stages of language acquisition is highly ambiguous and difficult to comprehend – 'mummy sock', 'more train' or 'my teddy' might each be given several interpretations. Indeed, attempts by linguists to discover a set of rules which would enable them to predict the structure of infant talk in the first stages of language development (that is to write a 'grammar' for early language) have, to date, failed (Crystal, 1976). Put another way, we do not have any theory which provides a valid, formal account of what infants mean by what they say.

And yet, for most of the time, parents and other people who are familiar with an infant seem to understand what he says. There may be an element of guess-work involved. Perhaps we fool ourselves into thinking that we understand what young children mean. However, by paying attention to features of the situation and circumstances surrounding infant talk we can usually find additional clues, such as what they are looking at, their facial expression, tone of voice and bodily movements, to help us decide what they are trying to mean. Research over the past few years has revealed the complex nature of the relationship between grammatical aspects of speech and non-verbal 'cues' to meaning, an aspect of what is sometimes termed 'body language'. This research helps us to understand the role of non-verbal communication in the achievement of mutual understanding, as we shall see. We will also consider the nature and function of what linguists call 'paralinguistic' features of speech. This term refers to things like voice intonation, pauses during speaking and the way in which stress is distributed over utterances. Although a detailed exploration of these topics lies outside our current concerns, non-verbal communication and paralinguistic aspects of speech are worth a brief look, since these will help us to understand some of the challenges that face children when they begin to talk to relative strangers in 'public' situations, like school. I will be arguing that the relationships between verbal, non-verbal and paralinguistic dimensions of communication in school differ from those found on home ground. Language at school is not simply an extension of language used at home. It involves some rather 'special' and unique features, with which young children (and their teachers) have to come to terms.

People from some cultures – Italians for instance – are more facially expressive, ready to move and freer with gestures when they talk than are members of other cultures (e.g. the British). Although many gestures and expressive movements of the face are culture-specific and often recognizably so (mentally compare, say, a Japanese and an Italian speaker), there are important aspects of non-verbal communication which as far as we can tell are universal. High speed film techniques make it possible to examine bodily move-ments in great detail using frame-by-frame analysis. The results of such analyses can be compared with the sound track on the film to study the relations between speech and movement. Using such methods, students of 'kinesics' (a term used to refer to the analysis of movement), have discovered common features in the organization of talk and bodily movements displayed by members of many different linguistic cultures (e.g. Condon, 1980).

One finding is that when a gesture accompanies an act of spontaneous speech, its 'peak' (this is difficult to define non-technically but perhaps you can imagine what I mean) tends to occur close in time to the stressed part of what is being said (think of someone saying 'I did *not*' and thumping a table at the same time). Now, the *start* of any such movement or gesture *never* occurs *after* the word that relates to it. It may occur at the same time or, more usually, precedes the word by about ½th of a second. The organization of the movements creating sounds and those creating gestures displays a tight temporal structure. This structure plays an important role in co-ordinating the act of communication. For example, if one compares the movements of a person speaking with those of someone listening to him, a remarkable degree of temporal synchronicity emerges. The listener appears to 'shadow' the movements of the talker and usually responds to the speaker's movements with one of his or her own no later than 20 msec later (Kempton, 1980). What is so remarkable about this rapid synchronization is the fact that no known response mechanism (for example, the speed at which we can react to a visual or auditory stimulus) is *fast enough* to make this feat possible. The only explanation (barring clairvoyance) is that the listener is *anticipating* where the speaker will make a movement before it actually commences. It is often the case that movements accompany those features of what is said that are likely to be *stressed*. In turn, stress signals where new and important information is to be conveyed. So the mutual timing of movements between listener and speaker imply that the listener is also anticipating the important parts of what the speaker is *going* to say. Synchronicity of movement and speech, then, is likely to play an important role in the achievement of mutual understanding.

In a near-literal sense, the speaker and hearer seem to be 'in tune'. Indeed, List (1963) argues that people move together in everyday interactions, exploiting the same ability that allows them to dance or to sing together. Each of these activities is based on shared *rhythmic* abilities. Although no one as yet has discovered all the verbal and/or visual signals which enable this synchronization to take place, it seems certain that some such system must exist. It also seems to be the case that tiny babies respond to the temporal organization of speech and movement in similar ways. Such findings imply that the 'tuning in' of speakers and listeners is rooted in some shared biological rhythmic system. By this I do not mean to imply that movements and gestures are 'mechanically' tied together. The precise form of a movement, its magnitude and duration, vary from speaker to speaker and from language culture to language culture. Nor do the movements of the listener usually imitate those of the speaker – they may be quite different. What seems to be universal is the *synchronization* of mutual movement.

From pre-verbal communication to speech

But why is this of interest to us here? There are a number of reasons. Later in the book I will discuss the way in which such, usually unconscious, aspects of non-verbal communication may serve to create distrust and discomfort when people from different ethnic or linguistic backgrounds communicate with each other. Differences in the form, manner and magnitude of bodily movements found across diverse human groups may lead to a degree of 'mis-timing' or mis-matching of expectations when members of different cultures interact. Given that people are not usually aware of the relations between their verbal and non-verbal movements (whilst these play an important role in mutual adjustment), members of different cultures or cultural groups may experience a diffuse, unlocatable sense of mutual discomfort when together. These and other features of the way in which we interact with each other may, I shall be arguing, provide obstacles to the mutual trust and relaxation which, as we shall see, lie at the heart of effective and efficient communication.

Another reason for introducing the topic of non-verbal features of communication is to outline the important role they play in the achievement of mutual understanding between adults and young children. Let me give another example. Imagine an adult engaged in interaction with a four-month-old infant. At this age, infants are usually taking an active interest in events going on around them. They constantly move their heads, eyes and bodies (when supported) to orient towards and focus upon things and events in the environment. When they do so, it is likely that the adult will monitor where and what they are looking at, following their line of gaze and pattern of attention. If they speak to the baby, then more often than not it will be to talk about what he is looking at. They may say what it is, perhaps, or comment upon its behaviour or nature. More surprisingly, should the adult, looking into the infant's eyes, turn suddenly to look at something else, the infant may well turn to attend to what she is looking at (for more on this, see Butterworth and Cochran, 1980). How babies manage this feat and know *where* to turn their eyes we do not know. The important point for our present purposes, however, is the fact that many occasions are likely to arise on which infant and adult are attending to the *same* thing. What the adult says, therefore, is likely to relate to what fills the infant's attention. They may put his perceived intentions into words 'Do you want . . . ?' or they might warn, reassure, exclaim, comment, or whatever. In so doing, they are bringing together acts of communication with the infant's early investigations of the world about him, relating language to reality.

Now add a few more elements to the story. Infants, from birth, are attracted and react to the sound of the human voice. By the age of two months, their babbling begins to take on some of the 'shape' of the language around them (Menyuk, 1971). Their intonation patterns, even at this age, demonstrate that they have begun to acquire aspects of the sound pattern of speech (sometimes termed 'prosodic' features, which we return to later). Paralleling these developments is the emergence of distinctive *reactions* on the baby's part to different tones of voice. By eight months, for example, the infant's responses to a questioning intonation are visibly different from those to statements (Kaplan, 1969). Similarly, a sudden 'No!' addressed to an eight-month-old may cause him to stop what he is doing. Consequently, when the infant begins his visual exploration of the world, he is already becoming sensitive to the 'mood music' supplied by human vocalizations. Such sounds enable an adult, say, to warn or reassure the baby about something he is looking at well before he begins to understand and use the words they are speaking. By making what they say and do *contingent* upon the infant's own attentions and activities, then, adults help to ensure communication before the advent of speech. Such communication also provides the baby with the means to *discover* what utterances (and their emotional effects) imply and, ultimately, to discover what speech sounds themselves refer to (Bruner, 1983). Verbal communication is deeply rooted in patterns of pre-verbal communication. Whilst words and longer utterances are destined to emerge from this matrix they are never, as we shall see, totally divorced from it. Although the 'distance' or 'gap' between the social, emotional, non-verbal and paralinguistic aspects of communication, on the one hand, and speech, on the other, may in some sense widen with development, the two never totally part company.

The linguist may be hard put to write a grammar for an infant, but one who knows that child may experience little difficulty or confusion in understanding him because what he says is embedded in a rich, supporting communicative system. Non-verbal and paralinguistic dimensions of interaction, coupled with a personal knowledge of the child (e.g. knowing the things he knows, those he has never seen before; the things that interest, attract or frighten him), enrich anything he might say to enable others to work out what he (probably) intends to mean. In this way, more mature individuals take the major responsibility for working out what the young child intends to communicate. Attending to his attentions, gestures, facial expressions, bodily posture and so on, they interpret what the infant probably means by any sounds he makes. As the child develops and, literally, becomes more articulate, the balance of responsibility for the achievement of shared understanding gradually shifts towards more equal partnership as the child plays an increasingly intelligible role in communication and takes greater responsibility for making what he says comprehensible. By three or four years of age, many children are able to talk to relative strangers with a reasonable chance of being understood.

As I said at the beginning of this chapter, when infants are passing through the early stages of language acquisition, what they talk about is likely to be what fills their senses: what grasps their attention, reminds them of their past or provokes desires for the (immediate) future. Recordings of adult speech to infants in different countries suggest that what is *said* to infants in many different societies is very similar (although there are some cultures which adopt very different practices in communications with their infants). Not surprisingly, talk usually revolves around everyday events – about what the parent is doing with the baby and comments on what he may be feeling or thinking. Talk to young children tends to be stimulated by and contingent upon, the child's perceived level of understanding and interest. At the same time, speech to young children has some special properties. In comparison to talk between adults, it tends to be slower, more repetitive, exaggerated in intonation, simpler in grammatical structure and limited in vocabulary. In this way, adults help to maximize the probability that what they *say* will be within the reach of the child's mind and ear. Indeed, should such adjustments not be made (say when two adults talk together in the child's company) the child will soon 'tune out' (or demand attention). The child selects and attends to talk that is within reach of his comprehension and ignores that which is not. At home such 'inattentiveness' may not be perceived as a problem, but in school it may well be attributed to idleness, lack of interest or boredom. To the extent that a child experiences communication problems in class, we must be aware of the possibility that any 'tuning out' and inattentiveness may be a natural and inevitable feature of such problems.

The pre-school child's experience of language, then, is often tailored to his needs. Other people take the major responsibility for ensuring mutual understanding both by working out what the child means and by making what they say comprehensible to him. Although we are not usually aware of the complex interplay between speech and our other bodily movements, there are occasions when our attention is drawn to them. Irony, sarcasm and teasing, for example, usually, perhaps invariably, involve some *disruption* or deliberate manipulation of the conventional relations between acts of speech and other movements of the body. When teasing an infant, for instance, the expression on our face or what we do with our body may communicate a very different message to that conveyed by what we say. If the baby does not observe or understand our playful use of such conflicting signals and takes what we say or do *seriously*, tears may result where laughter was sought. However, the very fact that we are often able to play teasing games with quite young children stands as testimony to the fact that even babies are sensitive to, knowledgeable about, and can *play* with, some of the relations between verbal and non-verbal dimensions of communication.

If a listener's movements, gestures or attentions are out of synchrony with our own attempts at communication (say, for instance, they keep looking at a door when we are talking to them about something quite different) it usually acts as a clear signal of distress, boredom, or preoccupations elsewhere. The very fact that such observations and experiences are commonplace also provides evidence that the interplay between verbal and non-verbal aspects of communication continue, throughout life, to play a central role in the achievement and maintenance of mutual understanding.

From home to school: conversation and narrative

I have undertaken this very brief overview of the relations between verbal and non-verbal aspects of communication to establish a basis for identifying and discussing some of the problems that children face when they move out of 'private' domains, like their homes, into more 'public' ones such as the school. In the early years of development, adults take the major responsibility for working out what a child means by what he says and does. In school, where eventually the child must come to function as part of a group, *sitting down* for much of the time, the nature of the process of communication changes in a number of ways to confront the child with many new challenges. Let us now move on to consider some of these before thinking about the influence such experiences exert on the child's social, linguistic and intellectual development.

When young children are involved in conversation with teachers talk sometimes centres on things like past experiences and events, hopes and plans or other people. Observation of teacher–child discourse shows that, in such circumstances, children's contributions are usually brief. Teachers ask questions and children usually attempt to answer them. A child might tell the teacher something or react to something she has said, but long periods of sustained talk in which the child provides a longish *narrative* account of his experiences, say, are quite rare. Where such narratives do occur, however, they illustrate the demands and problems facing the child. Let me present and discuss one example to illustrate the intellectual, social and linguistic hurdles that confront the immature narrator.

This is an exchange between a rising five-year-old and an adult in an English playgroup (Wood, McMahon and Cranstoun, 1980). They are talking about 'ogres' and the topic reminds the child of an experience he had with his father in which they encountered someone dressed up as a 'monster' to advertise a children's cereal. The child produces a 'turn' in the conversation some 46 words in length – a rare occurrence in classroom talk:

Adult Do you know anyone that big?
Child Well, once we . . . once we saw one, but he shouted at us.
Adult You saw an ogre once?

Child   No, not a real one, a pretend one. He kept shouting at us.

Adult   Where was that?

Child   That was in Banbury.

Adult   In Banbury there was a pretend one.

Child   He kept shouting at us.

Adult   What did he (chuckles) shout at you?

Child   I've forgotton now.

Adult   He had a big, loud voice, did he?

Child   Hm . . . and . . . he said 'I shall eat him'. . . Daddy said
. . . our Daddy said . . . hm . . . he . . . he . . . he. 'Oh,
what him!' Daddy said . . . Daddy just said, he said, and
the giant . . . I said 'Would the giant eat us?' and Daddy
said, 'If you make a noise it will'.

Adult   Do you think he would, love? (gently)

Child   He might just bite us.

There are many features of this short episode worthy of comment.
Consider, for example, the child's use of pronouns as in 'we . . .
once we saw one'. Who is 'we'? Later contributions from the child
show that 'we' includes at least himself and his father. In 'mature'
narrative, of course, we would expect the characters to be *identified*
by name before pronominal reference is made 'back' to them. As it
stands, the child's use of 'we' remains, throughout the episode,
somewhat ambiguous. Note, however, that the teacher 'tolerates'
such ambiguity and lets the child carry on. Indeed, such tolerance of
uncertainty and a willingness to wait for a speaker's meaning to
become clear is a *general* feature of conversation, even that between
adults (Wardhaugh, 1985). In conversational encounters, 'getting
things right' and 'telling things as they really are' is not usually a
serious requirement. Indeed, frequent interruptions would be deemed
boorish and would probably lead to a breakdown in the interaction.
We know that teachers who most frequently question their pupils
gain least in terms of questions, long utterances and frequent verbal
contributions back from them. Teachers who are more prepared to *tell*
children things and acknowledge what children say without always
following on with a question, tend to develop discussions with their
pupils in which children play a more active role (Wood and Wood, 1983).

The child talking about ogres *does* have some command of
pronoun usage, however. He says, for instance, 'No, not a real one,
a pretend one. He . . .' But later, when he produces a longer more
narrational stretch of talk, we can literally hear him grappling with
the task of making sensible use of pronouns. His difficulty stems
from the fact that both his father and the ogre are each potential
'He's'. Who, for example, was in danger of being eaten? Who was
the 'he' who said 'Oh, what him!'? Which 'him'?

The child's difficulties go even deeper. Should he wish to refer to things said *between* the two other characters, or want to refer to what one said about the other's likely behaviour towards the child *himself*, then 'he' can also serve to refer to the current 'me' (the speaker). In live encounters, of course, where speakers, hearers and bystanders have visible presence, one can see who says what to whom and is likely to have clear signals about the person being referred to. I suspect that in such situations, this child would have no problems in working out or understanding what is happening. Providing an *account* of such events, on the other hand, creates many problems for the young child, effective and unambiguous use of pronouns being one. Understanding and remembering an event, and providing a clear, smooth, efficient and expert narrative account, may be years apart, developmentally speaking.

In one sense, this child clearly knows what 'he' means. But the *use* of 'he' as a word to refer, on different occasions, to different people, creates problems of *planning* and *sequencing*. The pronoun must be 'located' in talk in such a way that it refers unambiguously to the intended referent. The fact that the child at this age (and this one is very articulate for his age) often fails to 'frame' appropriately what he is going to say – by first setting the scene and explicitly indicating *who* the involved characters are, where they are situated, and so on – also creates problems for him in using pronouns.

The frequent pauses, 'hms', repetitions, backtracking and attempts at self-correction evidenced in the child's talk suggest both that he is aware of, and that he is *working on*, the many problems that he has yet to solve in order to make what he says sensible to another person. Younger or less verbally mature children, as we shall see in more detail later, do not seem to be aware of such problems with pronouns and do not often try to self-correct, as in the following excerpt involving a three-year-old:

Adult   Who is Kerry?
Child   Kerry. He's a girl. She's my friend.

There are other aspects in the ogre episode that serve to illustrate features of the child's developing mastery of, and existing problems in, his use of language. For example, when the teacher says 'Where was that?', the child responds 'That was in . . . Banbury', rather than simply 'In Banbury'. This phenomenon, the use of 'full forms' before they are 'elided' (shortened) as they usually are in mature speech, is also a general and pervasive feature of language development. Children only employ economical, elliptical utterances *after* perfecting the unabridged versions from which these develop, even though the shorter forms are presumably more common in what they hear adults say (Gleitman and Wanner, 1982).

Although, up to this point, I have concentrated mainly on one child's use of pronominal reference, I will argue that this illustrates some general and important features of children's intellectual and linguistic development. We turn next to more controlled and extensive analyses of children's powers and problems as narrators. These illustrate in more detail the sizeable gap that can exist for children between what they may *know*, *remember* or *understand* and their ability to *account* for what they know.

Telling stories: four to ten

In a series of studies, Hickman (1985) has examined in detail some of the changes that occur in children's narrational skills between the ages of four and ten years. Children were asked to do one of two things. Either they were shown a short film and then asked to tell an adult about it, or they were presented with a sequence of pictures, rather like a cartoon strip, and requested to tell a story about the events depicted. Hickman recorded and transcribed everything said by each child (and the adult) and then analysed the narratives to evaluate their clarity, coherence and comprehensibility.

Various details of the children's accounts, such as their use of pronouns and determiners (e.g. 'a', 'the' and 'these') were examined, rather along the lines of the way in which I have just commented on the rising five-year-old's story about his encounter with an ogre. By showing children of different ages the same films and pictures, Hickman was able not only to look at children's command of such linguistic devices but also to etch out age-related changes in their abilities to do so successfully. Although the analysis focused on verbal details like the use of pronouns, Hickman bases it on a more general distinction that is worth introducing and discussing here. It will play an important role in our consideration of reading and its relation to spoken language in the next chapter. Drawing on *functional* approaches to the analysis of language (Halliday and Hasan, 1976) she distinguishes between those usages of words (more technically 'signs') that involve 'deictic indexical relationships' and the use of the same words to establish 'intra-linguistic indexical relationships'. Briefly, deictic indexical signs involve the connection or relationship between a word and its 'extralinguistic' context. So, for instance, the use of 'the' to refer or point to an object in the immediate environment (recall Karmiloff-Smith's work outlined in the last chapter) is deictic, whereas its use to refer *anaphorically*, to a person or thing already mentioned (e.g. 'A man . . . *the* man), is an example of an intralinguistic indexical (i.e. used to 'index', or refer to) use of the word. Used in the second way, such terms generate 'textual cohesion', helping to relate and integrate utterances that occur at different times in discourse (or written text). Pronouns can be looked at in the same way. The use of 'I', 'you', 'him' or 'it' in the course of face-to-face conversation, when the people and objects being referred to are present, involves extralinguistic, deictic reference. The same words can also be employed for intralinguistic purposes as when, for instance, the word 'he' is used to refer back to an (absent) individual who has already been mentioned by name.

Hickman, then, like Karmiloff-Smith, concentrates on the *pluri-functional* nature of these terms and examines their use by children to see how far, at different ages, they are able to exploit them successfully to fulfil their different purposes. More descriptively, a child who is able to use words like 'the' to refer both to objects in the world and to things mentioned in previous discourse will be able to tell a coherent story in which everything he refers to is clear and unambiguous. A child whose command of such words is limited to their context-dependent meanings will find it difficult or impossible to tell a clear and coherent story because, as he lacks effective ways of making explicit who or what he is referring to, what he says will be ambiguous and sound 'egocentric'. Let us consider a few examples from Hickman's studies of American school-children: first, two 'extreme' cases, one of a ten-year-old who is well on the way to expertise in the use of such words and the other, a four-year-old, whose use of them is still largely limited to their more 'primitive', deictic function. Note, however, even in the first story from the ten-year-old, how reference to one of the characters as 'she' creates a little confusion. The adult's contributions to the discourse are given in brackets.

The ten-year-old's story A donkey and a giraffe . . . came out (uh-huh) And . . . the . . . giraffe said 'Hi! Would you like to play with me?' And . . . the donkey said, 'No! I'm mad' (uh-huh) And . . . she said, 'What happened?' . . . and . . . the donkey said, 'Well, I made a box to keep my things in.' (uh-huh) 'And I found a penny. And I put it in the blo-box but now I can't *find* the penny' (uh-huh) . . . and . . . and . . . the . . . giraffe said, 'Well, maybe it's at school! Remember? You took it to school.' And the donkey said '*How* do *you* know? I think *you're* the one that took the penny.' (uh-huh). And . . . the gi-giraffe said . . . um . . . , 'No I didn't.' And . . . oh . . . she said, 'How do *you* know?' He said, 'Well . . . you know, I remember you took it' (uh-huh) And . . . then she thought about it for a while and she s-said . . . 'Well, friends don't steal! I'm sorry I was mad at you! now let's go play.'

The four-year-old's story Penny was in the box (Excuse me?) The penny was in the box (Oh really? Oh good) . . . The next day it wasn't . . . He was mad at the giraffe . . . (uh-huh) . . . 'cause he took the penny (He was mad at the giraffe because he took the penny) Yeah, but he di- bu- but he thought he was *tricking* him . . . (Oh!) see b-because . . . bec-be- he-he-he didn't know that he had the penny (uh-huh) . . . (Very good) They go play. (Hm?) They went to go play.

In the light of our preceding discussions of Karmiloff-Smith's work and the examples outlined above, I hope that the nature of the differences between these two excerpts is now reasonably self-evident. Hickman classified each child's use of referring words and referring expressions (e.g. 'There was a donkey in this film') as 'effective', 'ineffective' or 'mixed'. The four-year-old's story is rich in 'ineffective' referring expressions. The very first utterance, 'Penny was in the box', for example, fails to make clear who or what Penny is. The next utterance, 'The penny was in the box' suggests that she meant 'A penny' but note how 'the box' is introduced. If 'a box' had been mentioned earlier (which it had not) then this expression would have been deemed effective; as it stands, it is not. Recall Karmiloff-Smith's conclusion that young children's use of 'the' is reserved for and limited to deictic purposes. In Hickman's studies too, use of referring expressions by four-year-olds suggests that young children do not often use them to fulfil their other, intralinguistic functions.

Seven-year-olds' narratives provided evidence that they were working on the problem of mastering and using referential expressions for intralinguistic purposes. In consequence, the meaning of what they were trying to say was often easier to work out than was the case with four-year-olds. Here is an example from a seven-year-old: this is typical of the age group, in that it provides several examples of attempts by the child at *self-correction*. Once again, the adult's contributions are in brackets.

An example from a seven-year-old A dog . . . and the- and a frog were . . . were was- were um . . . a fr- a dog was there and looked sad. (uh-huh) An- and then a . . . dog came along and . . . (uh-huh) the frog came along and said 'Hi, today's my birthday.'

Unlike the four-year-olds, who seldom attempted to correct their own ambiguous referring expressions, the seven-year-olds' stories contained many examples of pauses, hazes, false starts, reformulations and repetitions: evidence that the children knew that they had work to do in order to achieve coherent, intelligible narratives. Ten-year-olds also frequently paused, hesitated and attempted to correct what they said (indeed, one suspects that adults would too).

Unlike the seven-year-olds, however, their attempts at self-correction usually resulted in *effective* utterances whereas, more often than not, the seven-year-olds' attempts resulted in ineffective or mixed cases, such as 'This story was about the elephant and a lion'. Here, the child uses a scene-setting clause successfully (This story was about . . .) and also uses the non-determinate form to first mention 'a lion'. However, 'the elephant' had not been mentioned before and, to be judged effective, should have been 'an elephant'.

Such mixed cases are informative. They illustrate the complexity of the seven-year-old's task in that a single utterance often contains two or more sources of potential difficulty. Whereas an expert narrator smoothly and seemingly effortlessly manages to co-ordinate all the necessary references in a single utterance, the seven-year-old apprentice usually manages to get one or more parts right but, in so doing, may 'lose hold of' or introduce an error into some other referring expression. He seems unable to attend to and co-ordinate *two or more* demands simultaneously. However, as he works on and perfects his control of each sub-problem or each sub-system (e.g. pronouns and determiners) he is able to handle two or more simultaneously, and eventually integrates them into effective, complex referring expressions.

Before moving on to discuss the more general educational implications of these studies, another finding is worth noting. The examples I have just given were taken from the 'film' condition in which the child first saw and then talked about what he had seen. When the children were asked to describe sets of pictures that remained in view while they told their stories, the performances of the seven- and ten-year-olds were not markedly different from the film narratives. The four-year-olds, however, behaved differently. In the cartoon strip situation, they made more frequent use of deictic expressions like 'This cat . . .', 'That dog . . .', 'Like him . . .', than they did when talking about the (absent) film. Looked at in one way, this increased use of such expressions when the person present can also *see* what one is talking about seems reasonable (note, in passing, the resemblance to Bernstein's notion of 'restricted code' speech). However, the fact that only the four-year-olds, not older children, made more frequent use of such devices raises some interesting questions and suggests some important observations.

First, it supports Karmiloff-Smith's contention that children below age six or seven usually employ determiners (and pronouns) to refer to things in the shared environment, not intralinguistically. Secondly, the fact that the older children did *not* talk in this way suggests that they appreciate the nature of the task, telling a story, in the same way as the people who set up the experiment. In other words, they realized that in order to 'tell a story' one uses language in a particular way to produce 'text-like' accounts. Put another way, they appreciate and to some extent have learned the conventions that are implied in the request to tell stories. The four-year-olds either did not understand such conventions and/or did not possess the linguistic means to realize them. I will take this line of thought further when we discuss the impact of literacy on children's thinking and talking.

Language and cognition (again!)

Piaget was one of the first students of child development to draw our attention to the young child's problems in providing verbal explanations and accounts. He suggested that children entering the concrete operational stage, around age seven, are able to appreciate and begin to anticipate their listeners' needs when they converse with and explain things to other people. This happens because they are able to de-centre and can begin to construe events from other people's points of view. Piaget, then, would not be surprised to find that younger children do not and cannot use or understand 'intralinguistic devices'. They lack the *intellectual* ability to appreciate the fact that when they say things like 'Penny was in the box' their meaning is not self-apparent. Being egocentric, they assume that people share their perceptions, thoughts and memories. The seven-year-old, freeing himself of this assumption, begins to work out how intralinguistic devices operate and can then start to learn how to make what he says understandable to others who do not share his perspective. Such linguistic developments, looked at in this way, are possible only when the child has de-centred himself sufficiently well in order to 'take on the role' of another person.

As we saw in the last chapter, however, it is possible to explain the child's problems and both the reasons and causes of development in other terms. Until a child has mastered and become reasonably confident and expert in using language to refer to ongoing events and situations, he will not be able to use language to refer to *other linguistic expressions*, which is what intralinguistic devices demand. We could argue that there is a natural sequence involved, in which the use of language to refer to events in the immediate environment is a *necessary* foundation for working out how utterances which refer and relate to each other can be constructed. In this view, the young child may not be structurally egocentric, but simply lacking in the verbal means to express clearly and unambiguously what he knows and understands.

Vygotsky's approach, which motivated Hickman's studies, differs from Piaget's in its emphasis on the *formative* nature of verbal interactions. In this view, it is through talking to and with others that the child is exposed to the communicative *functions* of language.

It is through conversation with others that he discovers how to realize different functions in his own speech. As I have already said, Piaget did not deny that social interaction and communication help to facilitate cognitive (and hence linguistic) development. They do so by creating conflict and disequilibrium. Self-constructed *cognitive* changes pre-date and make the appreciation of conflicts and discrepancies possible and provide the basis for the assimilation of linguistic meanings. For Vygotsky and Bruner, however, acquiring the *means* to communicate clearly is what *creates* cognitive and linguistic progress (which are viewed as two sides of the developmental coin). These different points of view have far-reaching implications for education and the role of teaching, since one demands far more involvement from 'experts' in helping a child to acquire expertise than the other. But how are we to adjudicate between them?

Well, we have already considered several lines of evidence relating to this issue in earlier chapters. I do not intend to rehearse all the arguments here except to draw attention to the findings which suggested that children much younger than six or seven can, in some circumstances, reason rationally. They can also, in some situations, transcend their own immediate perspective to appreciate what the world looks like from another point of view. Such evidence can be interpreted as showing that young children are neither incapable of making rational inferences nor are they invariably egocentric. If this is so, we might decide to reject Piaget's interpretation of the young child's problems in giving accounts of what he knows in favour of the view that such problems stem from communication and linguistic demands that he has yet to encounter and master.

There have been studies of pre-school children's communication abilities which can also be interpreted as evidence against a stage of universal egocentrism. These explore the child's understanding of other people's attempts at communication and their ability to make judgements about the clarity or adequacy of what people say. We have just been considering experiments designed to find out how children *use* certain features of language. But what do children themselves know about other people's use of language? Can they judge, for example, whether or not what other people say to each other is clear or unclear? Can they put themselves in the shoes of a person who is being given verbal instructions, to decide whether or not what that person has been told is explicit enough to enable them to do what they are being asked to do?

The basic situation used to try to answer such questions is set up as follows: a child is asked to look on and observe two people involved in a communication game. One of these people has been given the task of telling the other which picture to select from a set of alternatives. The pictures are designed in such a way that incomplete descriptions can be formulated. For instance, imagine that the pictures include examples of boys and girls, some with and some without hats. The hats are also of different shapes and colours. An adequate description of the picture the instructor has in mind demands attention to gender and to the shape and colour of any hats involved. Suppose an incomplete message is given – say the person giving the instructions fails to mention colour and, in so doing, leaves the listener with an ambiguous description that fits two or more of the pictures. What do four-year-olds make of such a situation? Do they realize that what is said is incomplete and therefore ambiguous? Or are they so egocentric that they cannot understand the nature of the listener's dilemma?

It seems that most four-year-olds do not appreciate the listener's problems. In fact they tend to 'blame' him or her for any failures of understanding. They seem to assume that 'to speak is to be understood' and that the person who is talking and who intends to *tell* the other person what to do does just that. At this point, we might conclude that the pre-schooler does not have the intellectual ability to imagine what the problem is like from the listener's point of view. He does not really appreciate what the speaker is trying to do either and assumes that what people say is a direct and unproblematic reflection of the way things are.

The situation is not so clear-cut as this interpretation suggests. Some four-year-olds are able to appreciate the fact that people do not always say enough or say the right things to enable others to understand what they mean. In other words, they appreciate the listener's dilemma and realize that what the speaker says is not necessarily a complete or comprehensible account of what they want the other person to do. Left like this, with the observation that some four-year-olds can do things that other children will only manage to do when they are older, such evidence cannot be used to justify any particular point of view. Perhaps some children are mentally or linguistically precocious. However, two other discoveries suggest that the reason why some children are able to appreciate the listener's dilemma is not simply a product of something 'in' the child but a consequence of his experience.

In the first place, children who are competent at judging the adequacy of what the informer tells his listener are more likely than those children who can't do so to have had rather specific communicative experience at home when talking to their parents. Let me illustrate with an example. A child says something to his mother which she finds ambiguous or unclear. How does she respond? Well, she might *ask* the child 'Which one . . .?' or 'Do you mean x or y?' In other words, she asks questions to try to clarify what the child had said. Or, she might say 'I don't understand. I don't know whether you want me to do x or y'. To a mature ear, such grammatical variations in the *way* parents signal their uncertainty to children might seem equivalent. However, evidence collected by Robinson and Robinson (who used the language samples collected by Gordon Wells and his colleagues in Bristol (Robinson, 1986)) suggests that they are quite different in their effects on children's language development. Those children who were most likely to be given an *explicit account* by their mothers of how and why they found what the child said unclear, were most likely to appreciate the listener's dilemma in communication games. Children whose parents employed *questions* to clarify and 'repair' what they said were less competent in judging the adequacy of communication and more likely to simply blame the listener.

The discovery of relationships between the way in which parents talk to their children and aspects of those same children's linguistic development does not necessarily imply, of course, that one phenomenon *causes* the other. It is conceivable, for example, that children who are verbally precocious solicit ways of talking from their parents that differ from those solicited by other children. Further evidence, however, strengthens the view that parents do influence their children's communicative competence and demonstrates that it is possible to teach young children to improve their so-called 'metalinguistic awareness' (that is, their knowledge *about* language in contrast to their ability to *use* it).

The Robinsons involved nursery school children as participants in the kinds of communication game outlined above. Different methods were employed in response to any ambiguous or incomplete description given by different groups of children. When the children in one of these groups gave such messages, the 'teacher' responded by explicitly *telling* the child about the nature of their uncertainty. In other words, she would say something like 'I don't know what you mean. I don't know whether you mean x or y.'

After a few teaching sessions, children from each of the groups were asked to listen to two other people playing a similar communication game and to explain why a listener sometimes faced problems. Children from the group who had, when they played the game, been told explicitly about any inadequacies in their own messages were less likely than those in other groups to blame the listener. They were more often able to articulate the nature of the listener's dilemma. This evidence, taken in conjunction with that from the home observations, provides strong support for the view that young children are not inevitably egocentric in such situations and that they can be taught how to make explicit judgements about the adequacy or otherwise of what people say (at least, in some contexts).

Vygotsky, recall, argued that intellectual and linguistic development proceed from the external, social plane to become personal, mental activity by a process of 'internalization'. Children's verbal reasoning, for example, represents 'inner speech' and 'inner dialogue'. Talking to others and being addressed by them are destined to become mental activity as the child 'takes on the role' of others and holds inner dialogues with himself. The *form* that this dialogue takes depends upon the characteristic ways in which the child talks to and controls others and in turn is talked to and controlled by them. Those of a Vygotskian persuasion could argue, then, that the findings from the Robinsons' studies support Vygotsky's view and demonstrate that social interaction and such experiences as talking to, informing, explaining, being talked to, informed and having things explained, structure not only the child's immediate activities but also help to form the *processes* of reasoning and learning themselves. The child inherits not only 'local knowledge' about given tasks but, gradually, internalizes the *instructional process* itself. Thus, he learns how to learn, reason and regulate his own physical and mental activities. More about this later.

On a more mundane level, these studies demonstrate that it is possible to teach young children to learn quite difficult communication skills which seem to involve the ability to 'de-centre'. Being relatively inexperienced and lacking expertise in the task of analysing and evaluating their own and other people's verbal communication, most young children assume that failures of communication are necessarily the fault of whoever is listening. Perhaps this assumption is the most consistent with their own, everyday experience? As I have already said, adults talking to young children usually take the major responsibility for working out what they mean and it may well be the case that the child's assumption that 'to speak is to be understood' is a reasonably fair reflection of what usually happens in their communications with others. However, in the Robinsons' teaching experiment, many children quickly revised this assumption when they were given *explicit* insights into other people's states of mind in response to their own attempts to instruct. They made progress in learning how to analyse and evaluate linguistic instructions.

In the final chapter of the book, I will return to a discussion of the Robinsons' and other studies to ask what they have to tell us about the nature of effective *instruction*. Note that the Robinsons also found and used other methods to teach children, and that these proved less effective than the one I have described. There are many other ways we might think of to teach children how to analyse and evaluate informative speech (e.g. simply telling them what the correct way to do it is and hoping for 'imitation' to lead to learning). How and why different teaching methods work in various contexts should help us to understand not only the nature of instruction but also more about the processes of learning.

Information-giving

The finding that young children can be helped to increase their 'metalinguistic' understanding adds some weight to the argument that linguistic and intellectual development are, in part at least, facilitated by specific social experiences. This is not to say that children are usually taught how to talk and how to make what they say meaningful and informative in any direct or explicit way. We have encountered many examples of *self-correction* by children which provide strong evidence that self-instruction plays an important and central role in learning. Even so, this does not mean that others more expert than the child exert no influence upon his learning and development. The seven-year-olds in Hickman's studies, for example, were not explicitly *told* that their use of referring expressions was often ambiguous. They seemed to realize when what they were saying did not 'sound right', and themselves worked on the problem of finding the right way to make what they said comprehensible. We are obliged, I suggest, to assume that children often know a great deal about what they cannot yet do successfully. One way of expressing this is to say that they often *understand* and can *recognize* as correct what they cannot yet themselves *produce*. Given this state of affairs (which as we shall see is more widespread in development than the examples I have given to date), the child is in a position to *construct* and to *perfect* his own performance through problem-solving. Recognizing, for example, what 'sounds right' he has a goal or target against which he can measure and evaluate his own performance. He can assess when he has 'got it'.

The image of the child as a problem-solver and architect of his own knowledge and understanding is, of course, compatible with Piaget's views. It is also consistent with those implicit in several other theories of learning and development. Bruner, for example, describes the child as a problem-solver and views the process of instruction as one of helping the child to *discover* manageable problems. But accepting the child's 'natural' problem solving and self-instructional abilities does not *necessarily* imply that his inter-actions and encounters with others exert no formative influence on what and how he learns. Before looking more analytically at the nature of such influences, let me discuss further evidence relating to the nature of children's capacities to make sense to others. This, from studies of adolescents, paints a far less rosy picture of children's 'natural' linguistic and intellectual abilities. It also suggests that educational experience plays an important role in determining how far and to what extent children are able to perfect their own expertise in using language as an instrument of explanation, instruction and 'other-regulation'.

In an extensive investigation of adolescent communication skills, Brown and her colleagues (1984) worked with 500 14- to 17-year-old Scottish school children. Three hundred of these pupils were judged, by their schools, to represent the lower 'third' of their year in academic ability and were considered unlikely to leave school with any formal academic qualifications.

Underlying this research is a distinction between what Brown et al. term 'chat' and 'information-giving speech', the latter being the main subject of their investigations. Chat is what we have been referring to as conversation. It is a highly interactive affair in which all participants share the responsibility for ensuring mutual understanding and for developing topics of talk. Observed chatting to each other in pairs, the pupils were talkative, often witty and seemed to suffer no problems of communication. Though a little more reticent with an unfamiliar adult interviewer, they were able to engage them in intelligible conversation. However, even relatively minor increases in demands on communication produced noticeable impairments in their performance. For example, simply asking a child to 'talk' to a friend into a tape recorder led to speech that was more hesitant, not so articulate and less coherent than that found in face-to-face conversation. Even such a relatively minor degree of 'disembedding' of the process of communication led to measurable deterioration in performance. The absence of a 'live' partner, and the non-verbal, paralinguistic and interactional support they would have offered, had marked effects on these pupils' ability to make what they tried to say accessible. When demands were further increased, and children were asked to give detailed instructions and explanations, performance deteriorated to an even greater extent. Before discussing the studies of information-giving, however, let me pause to say a little more about the nature of conversation and the important differences that exist between, say, relaxed talk with a friend and more stressful interactions with teachers.

In a very readable and informative book, Wardhaugh (1985) considers in detail the many social practices and values that are implicated in conversation. He points out that conversation is, by its very nature, typically and literally mundane. It is about everyday experiences and events. It is important that one does not delve too deeply or react too analytically to the conversational talk of others. People have the right to remain silent if they wish and there are implicit conventions that inhibit us from going 'too far' in probing people's motives, proclivities, behaviour and beliefs. Privacy has to be respected and we must be aware of the bounds over which we should not pass. These bounds, of course, vary according to our relationship and degree of intimacy with the person with whom we are talking. Insistence upon 'the total truth', upon absolutely clear and unambiguous utterances and full disclosure, is threatening, disruptive and rude.

These seemingly self-evident observations take on an important significance when we consider the differences between the child's everyday experiences of conversation and the use of language in school. Schooling is about imparting, sharing, discussing, analysing and evaluating knowledge and skill, among other things. The 'search for truth', accuracy, clarity, for *evidence* of knowledge and understanding are part and parcel of the process of education. Reflecting these differences in the underlying *purposes* of talk in the community and school are marked differences in the nature of the relationship between people involved in discourse and different aspects of their use of language. For example, in school it is quite legitimate (if not always desirable, as we shall find) for the teacher to ask all the questions. In everyday discourse, questions perform a variety of functions. Most obvious is the search for information. People usually ask questions of others in order to find out things that they do not know and need to know. Such questions are 'legitimate' if the person asked can understand *why* his questioner wants to know and if disclosure of the information asked for has no implied negative consequences for the answerer. If it does, then the usual process is to *negotiate* the conditions under which an answer will be provided. Imagine, for instance, being asked a question about how much you earn by a visitor to your doorstep.

Questions are also used to frame requests, to ask for help or permission. Here too, gaining an answer is not only a *linguistic* issue but a moral one. Does the person have the *right* to make such requests? Have they taken proper account of what compliance would entail for the person asked? If, say, the loss of time, prestige or rights that will be experienced by the answerer is far greater than the relative benefit that will accrue to the questioner, then the request is likely to be deemed unreasonable at best. Questions are also used to display courtesy, interest and to cement relationships. They are a way of being polite (Goody, 1978). Showing concern about and interest in another person by asking them to tell you things is a commonplace but often delicate activity. As I said above, knowing how far it is permissible and polite to go in probing a person without causing offence involves knowledge of the cultural values of the person being asked. I will return to this point when we discuss interactions between people from very different social and cultural backgrounds.

Questions asked in school 'violate' many of these normal conventions. Teachers are licensed by our society (like policemen, doctors and lawyers) to ask questions with the expectation that they will receive answers, even though these often transgress everyday conventions. There are, of course, still limits on what can legitimately be asked about, but teachers are allowed, even expected, to ask questions to which they know the answers. Although parents of pre-schoolers often address what Wells calls 'display' questions to their children, that are also designed to solicit known answers (often known to both parent and child), any failure to comply by a pre-schooler with a home audience is likely to have a very different significance from failure by a school-aged child in the classroom. Failure for the older child in school is likely to be more serious and personally threatening. Teachers may also ask children to justify, prove or in some way demonstrate the basis for, and rationality of, anything they say. Getting things 'right' in class may be at a premium in a way that it is not in informal chat. The child, on entering school, has to discover and comply with a range of conventions, rights and obligations that constitute the roles of pupil and teacher. Implicated in these conventions are important differences in the functions of language.

Chat between teachers and children, though founded in different conventions to those governing other social encounters, is still typified by shared responsibility for the achievement of mutual understanding (in which, as we shall see, teachers usually play the leading role). Information-giving acts of speech, as their label implies, are concerned with things like providing clear instructions, directions and explanations. When Brown et al. tested their academically less able pupils' ability to use speech for information-giving purposes, they discovered that these pupils were usually incapable of providing coherent, comprehensible, informative narratives. Even when asked to tell an interviewer about events or experiences that were familiar to the child, their performance was frequently uninformative and difficult to understand. The following extract, in which a pupil tries to tell the interviewer about the film *Jaws* (the child had also read the book), illustrates the listener's difficulties (each plus sign indicates a pause of a few seconds).

Interviewer	Is the book like the film?
Pupil	+ + A wee bit.
Interviewer	Hmm + + What's different in the book?
Pupil	In the book + + + Hooper dies in the film but he never dies but he went in a cage down + to see if he could see the fish + and like + + + + and trying to get in + the fish + but he couldn't + + the fish turned er the cage over but then he went away and Hooper just went and swum out and hid behind a rock and + in the book he said that he died.

Did Hooper die in the book or the film?

Brown and her colleagues went further than simple observation, however. They designed a range of co-operative tasks of varying levels of complexity and difficulty which they used with some of the pupils to help to foster their skills in giving information and instructions. Some were communication games in which one child had to tell another how to perform a task. Others involved creating narratives.

A variety of techniques were used to introduce these different activities into the classroom in co-operation with teachers. A detailed account of the study is not possible here, but a number of its main findings are worth noting. The researchers developed a range of assessment procedures that involved teachers in evaluating children's language. These included attention to things like the presence or absence of critical information, and the extent to which information was provided in an appropriate rational sequence. Also examined was the child's use of referring expressions involving terms like determiners and pronouns to see if it was clear, from the child's narrative, who or what these referred to. The assessments revealed considerable progress as children participated in the activities. Later, follow-up studies demonstrated that the pupils *remembered* what they had learned and were able to *generalize* what they had learned in one task to improve their performances on others. Use of referring expressions also became more explicit, accurate and intelligible.

Another finding, one that I will elaborate upon in the next chapter, was that the children who first played the role of *listener* were significantly more articulate and informative when it came to their turn to play the role of speaker than were children who first acted as speakers. Brown suggests that the experience of trying to *comply* with instructions sensitizes the child to the problems of being on the receiving end of less than informative instruction. The children obviously learned how to solve some of these problems, how to make what they said less 'egocentric' and ambiguous, by playing the seemingly 'passive' role of listener. Provided, then, that the child has to act upon what he is told, *listening*, at least in some contexts, is a more powerful vehicle for learning how to *talk* informatively than is exclusive experience as a speaker.

Classroom 'registers': means to ends

These findings give rise to a number of implications and questions. They demonstrate, perhaps unsurprisingly, that the potential for the development of communicative competence (or what now seems to be referred to as 'oracy') extends throughout the years of schooling. In so doing, they pose a question and raise some issues: why were these children, many of whom were about to leave school, so inarticulate and poor at giving information, directions and explanations before participating in the study? The fact that they could be helped to improve these skills shows that they did not lack the necessary *competence* to learn. Why, then, had they not learned in the normal course of their education?

A number of very different explanations might be advanced in response to this question. We might argue that the development of such communication skills is not part of the business of schooling, but such an argument is difficult to sustain. Lacking the ability to plan, organize, regulate and express what they know in order to inform others, these children are surely likely to be handicapped in their vocational choices and in their personal lives. Even if the ability to inform and explain did not influence other aspects of the child's educational achievements (and I will argue in the next two chapters that it does), an inability to present oneself as articulate and informative must surely act as a barrier to competence in many situations – not least in interviews for jobs.

Note that what is at issue here is not whether a child speaks using the 'Standard English' dialect. Rather, it is his ability to *exploit* his own linguistic resources to achieve certain communicative ends: to use certain 'registers' of language. This research was not intended to 'remediate' speech nor to 'teach' children to speak a dialect different from their own. Its goal was to help them to learn how to make sense and give a good *account* of themselves. If we can accept that the development of 'oracy' is a legitimate goal of education, as the UK's Bullock report recommends (Department of Education and Science, 1975), why is its achievement seemingly so elusive for many children?

Brown and her colleagues suggest that at least part of the answer to this question lies in the typical 'registers' of classroom discourse: the way in which teachers typically talk to pupils. Let me outline (and elaborate upon) this line of argument. Many studies of classroom discourse in different parts of the world have found that the most dominant feature of teacher–pupil interaction is the question–answer–acknowledgement exchange. Teachers ask nearly all the questions. By way of illustration, in two studies, one of English pre-school children in playgroups and nursery schools and the other focused upon American high school students (aged 17), the frequency of teacher questions as a proportion of all their utterances was 47 per cent and 43 per cent respectively. For the pupils, the incidence of questions was 4 per cent and 8 per cent (Wood and Wood, in press). The more questions the teachers asked, the less children had to say. The pupils were also less likely to elaborate on the topic of talk, ask questions or to talk to each other when teacher questions were frequent.

There is an extensive and argumentative literature on the topic of questions and their role in teaching. Here, I can do no more than select and discuss fragments of research that are most relevant to our present concerns. Some educationalists (e.g. Blank, Rose and Berlin, 1978) argue that teacher questions are powerful tools for encouraging pupils and students to *listen* and to *think*. To be effective, however, a teacher's questions must be of the appropriate kind and at the right 'level of demand' if pupils are to profit by them. Blank has developed an elaborate scheme for classifying questions that she offers as a way of analysing and evaluating teaching talk with pre-school and young school-children. Some questions (for example, 'What do we call this?', asked in relation to a common object) are concerned with relatively 'low level' demands and permit a very restricted range of answers, perhaps only a single word. Others, e.g. 'Why did that happen?', may call for more thought and explanation. Yet others, 'What do you think about . . . ?' may have no obvious, correct answer but call for analytical reasoning and informed judgement.

Observations of teacher questions addressed to children of widely different ages and in a variety of disciplines have led to the conclusion that teacher questions are more often of the 'closed' type with known right answers. The responses to such questions by pupils are likely to be terse and simply correct or incorrect. When pupils answer a teacher's questions, they usually say no more and stop talking. Consequently, where such specific, closed questions are frequent, children will say little. Now, if the goal of asking questions is *only* to ascertain whether or not a child knows a particular fact or name, one can argue that such results are defensible. However, if other goals are also being sought – for example, encouraging children to reason out loud, to ask questions of their own, to state their own opinions, ideas and uncertainties, or to *narrate* – then the frequent use of specific, closed questions will not bring about the desired ends.

In one extensive study of teachers' use of questions in a number of disciplines, including natural history and physics lessons, Nuthall and Church (1973) investigated the impact of different types of questions on pupil performance. They compared lessons in which teachers used a preponderance of closed questions demanding specific factual answers with those in which they employed more open-ended questions designed to encourage reasoning, discussion and speculation. They found that the children taught through specific questions tended to do better when tested for retention of factual information. Those who were asked open-ended questions did indeed speculate, hypothesize and discuss more (though they did not learn so many specific facts per unit of teaching time). This finding may not seem surprising. It does, however, suggest that what and how children think and learn can be influenced by the way in which the teacher conducts his or her lesson!

Schools are expected to achieve a variety of different, often conflicting, goals with their children. Teachers may find some of these goals, say teaching a body of facts, to be in 'competition' with others, like fostering the development of skills in narration, self-presentation and informing others. The hope that each of these objectives can be met with the same 'register' and approach to teaching, typically the question–answer exchange in which the teacher asks almost all the questions, seems a vain one. It is not my task to try to define what the objectives of a school or teacher should be. However, the findings that have emerged from studies of classroom interaction offer teachers some practical suggestions as to how instructional means and learning outcomes might best be married. Frequent, specific questions tend to generate relatively silent children and to inhibit any discussion between them. Telling children things, giving an opinion, view, speculation or idea, stimulates more talk, questions and ideas from pupils and generates discussion between them.

If all this sounds obvious, then explain why so many studies have found that classroom talk is dominated by teacher questions.

Although Nuthall and Church found that teachers' use of specific questions led to more rapid learning of factual information by their pupils, an examination of longer-term effects of different questioning 'regimes' suggests that pupil achievement is higher when they encounter more demanding, open-ended questions (Redfield and Rousseau, 1981). Further support for this conclusion comes from a study of the questions that *parents* characteristically employ with their children. Here too, more demanding, open-ended questions from parents were found to be predictive of a number of measures of children's educational achievement (Sigel and McGillicuddy-Delisi, in press). Sigel argues that such questions facilitate the development of educability in children because they invite them to 'distance' themselves from the immediate, short-term consequences of their experiences. In so doing, the child is enjoined to decentre, think about and reflect upon his own activities and, in consequence, becomes more analytic, less impulsive and achieves more effective control of his own learning. As we shall see in the final chapter, the notion that children 'internalize' the processes of control to which they are exposed in order to regulate their own learning and thinking emerges from a variety of research studies.

Other studies have shown that teachers can be helped to modify their own teaching styles to adopt different questioning techniques. Some of these illustrate the difficulties involved and relate back to our previous discussion of the relationship between verbal and non-verbal dimensions of communication. When teachers ask pupils questions, they tend to leave about a second of silence, on average, before they resume talking (if the children have not responded). In a study of the effects of different teacher 'wait times' on children's responses, teachers were provided with a buzzer (which only they could hear) and were asked, having posed a question, to wait until this was sounded before going on. The buzzer was controlled by an observer, who waited for three seconds after each question before activating it (again, if no response was forthcoming from the class). The increased 'wait time' allowed to children resulted in more frequent, relevant, thoughtful and 'high level' responses to the teachers' questions (Rowe, 1974; Swift and Gooding, 1983).

In face-to-face conversation, as I have already said, the *synchronization* of communication is finely tuned. Perhaps, when a teacher is faced with a group of pupils, the cues that enable such synchronization to emerge are destroyed or in some way inhibited, so that a teacher's timing is out of synchrony and sympathy with the pupils' responses (which are likely to vary from child to child anyway). Perhaps increasing the time allowed after a question has been asked enables most or all of the pupils to formulate their thoughts? Such results illustrate how specific features of discourse exert an important influence on the process of classroom communication. One suspects that it would prove a difficult task for teachers to sustain control over such normally spontaneous features of their classroom talk as time after questions, however.

In the book by Wardhaugh mentioned earlier, he says (p. 71):

> Teaching is not only a special form of conversing with others – it is an especially difficult form, if for no other reason than that the teacher must 'converse' with a large heterogeneous group of listeners. Good teaching requires one to be good at a particular kind of conversation; it is a skill not easily acquired because of the special demands it makes, and it is not a skill one can readily practise outside the classroom, since it is very rarely appropriate to any other circumstance.

The studies we have just been discussing lend considerable weight to his argument.

Classroom discourse is typically controlled by teacher questions that often demand quick, terse, factual answers and leave little time for children to respond, elaborate or reason out loud. Perhaps this explains, in part at least, why some children do not learn how to express their ideas, formulate their thoughts or say what they know. Furthermore, if the teacher asks all the questions, then he or she dictates the course of events; what will be thought about and when. We have to ask ourselves whether this provides the *pupils* with opportunities to plan, regulate, reason and explain themselves.

Brown and her co-workers suggest that many children need more involvement in activities designed to help them to learn how to listen to and use language informatively and thoughtfully. Their evidence demonstrates that children *can* improve their own levels of performance. What the longer term effects on such children's educational performance might be we discuss in the final two chapters. The researchers provide examples of the kind of materials that can be used to make this possible and show how teachers can analyse and evaluate their children's performance to monitor progress. Offering more opportunities for linguistic initiative to the child is not an abdication of teacher responsibility if and when the activities are structured carefully, managed effectively and evaluated properly.

Summary

In this chapter I have been exploring the special communication demands that face both teachers and children in classrooms. Throughout the years of schooling, children's use and expertise in various functions of language develop. These developments can be detected in fine-grained and important changes in the way in which they use a variety of linguistic processes that are involved in producing sustained, coherent narratives and in both giving and understanding information. We should expect to find that a child's ability to employ determiners, pronouns and a variety of linguistic devices improves through a stage of hesitant disfluency and self-correction to smooth, well organized and comprehensible creation of verbal text.

We have examined evidence which demonstrates that some, probably many, children do not achieve such fluency and, outside of relaxed and relatively undemanding conversation, face considerable difficulties in trying to explain themselves or instruct others. Such findings rule out any supposition that these aspects of linguistic function come about 'naturally' or inevitably. They demand specific types of experience. The fact that a significant proportion of adolescents are poor at giving a good account of themselves when asked to inform and explain suggests that schools need to do more, if they are not to see children leave their gates for the last time unable to exploit their communicative resources to the full. Classroom-based studies show that children and adolescents can be helped to become more articulate, fluent and confident in their powers of self-expression.

We have also considered the challenges that communication in the classroom creates for *teachers*. What appears to be the dominant teaching register, involving frequent teacher-directed questions, may be effective in achieving certain managerial and instructional ends, but it seems unlikely to provide good conditions for developing children's powers as narrators, informants and, perhaps, self-regulating learners. The challenges confronting the teacher are far from trivial and demand considerable expertise in what are very special forms of communication.

I have already drawn attention to the implications of special linguistic problems for our discussions of children's learning and thinking. Language and cognition are fused in verbal reasoning. Comprehension problems, which arise because children have yet to master specific features of language use and structure, act as a barrier to learning and understanding. Lacking expertise in the processes of creating coherent, 'disembedded' or 'decontextualized' accounts of what they know and understand, children may appear intellectually incompetent when, in reality, they are still grappling with the problem of making sense to other people. This process takes time and creates many challenges for both pupils and teachers.

In the next chapter, we explore more fully the proposition that in 'learning how to mean' (to borrow a phrase from Halliday, 1975) children not only advance their expressive linguistic abilities but also discover how to regulate, plan, evaluate and monitor their own intellectual activities. If sound, this proposition implies that the nature and quality of classroom discourse plays a vital role in developing a child's ability to learn and to reason analytically. Our attention shifts from talking and listening to consider the development of reading and writing. Though obviously related, in that literacy is 'parasitic' on the spoken word, there are many important differences between these two modes of communication. Learning to read and write promises more benefits than access to new ways of learning, instruction and recreation. As we shall see.

Chapter 6

The literate mind

In the UK children usually move from primary into secondary schools at around eleven years of age. When they make the move, they begin their preparations for public examinations. The curriculum in secondary schools is usually quite different from that followed in the primary school. It is expected that most if not all children will have learned to read well enough in the primary school to begin reading to learn in the secondary years, for example. Facility with the written word becomes increasingly important as secondary schooling proceeds. Some children over the age of eleven still find writing and reading difficult, however. We explore some of the reasons as to how and why these children find the achievement of literacy difficult.

Some psychologists and anthropologists believe that the development of literacy, both in the individual and in a society, leads to marked, stage-like changes in linguistic and intellectual abilities. We explore evidence for such changes in this chapter. We consider the proposal that children's thinking undergoes an important change at around the age of thirteen. We also explore the relations between these changes and developments in children's linguistic abilities which seem to occur at around the same time. This leads us on to discuss the effects of poor literary skills on children's thinking and academic prospects. Hence the title, 'The literate mind'.

We begin the chapter with an exploration of Piaget's view that the onset of adolescence usually sees a change in the nature of children's intelligence. More specifically, we examine his theory about the relation between logic and thinking. This topic, difficult and controversial though it is, is important to us because it holds out strong implications for the issue of when we should start to teach formal disciplines in school.

What is logical thinking?

Let us start with Piaget's views on the nature of mature, logical thinking. These are not easy to summarize or to evaluate. Why bother? Why should we concern ourselves with an issue, namely the relation between logic and everyday thinking, that has taxed the minds of philosophers and psychologists for many years yet still remains unresolved? Well, as I hope to show, it is not really possible to evaluate Piaget's theory or its educational implications without some sense of where, in Piaget's view, the developing structure of the mind *culminates*. In his theory, intellectual development has an ultimate destiny or destination. Cognitive structures are driven towards a specific, structural end point, a state of ultimate stability and *equilibrium*, which involves the achievement of a sense of logical necessity. The natural direction followed in intellectual development leads to the stages and structures that we have already considered. If we decide that Piaget's account of the nature of mature, logical thinking is unacceptable, then we must be prepared to reject or revise both his account of children's thinking and the constraints imposed by the proposed stages of intelligence upon the nature of learning and understanding, teaching and explaining.

Evaluation of the theory is difficult for a number of reasons. First, Piaget never suggested that adults *typically* reason in logical terms. A good deal of everyday thinking is practical and intuitive, not formal and logical. Consequently, as we see later, though there are several lines of evidence which show that even highly educated people (including those trained in logic) find it very *difficult* to think in formal logical terms, Piagetians might argue that this does not refute the theory. Piaget never implied that logical thought was easy, as far as I am aware.

A second source of problems comes from the fact that Piaget appeared to modify his own theory about the formal operational stage of development. He seems to accept that this stage, unlike the earlier ones, may not emerge from self-directed, everyday interactions in the world but from specific *educational* experiences. For instance, the study of mathematics and learning how to plan and conduct scientific *experiments* may provide the cognitive demands and intellectual problems that foster the emergence of formal, deductive reasoning. Therefore evidence which shows that people from some parts of the world seem unable to solve problems involving hypothetical, propositional reasoning (I will give examples later) cannot be used to reject the theory (Piaget, 1971, pp. 94–6). Like several other major theorists, including Vygotsky, Bruner and Donaldson, Piaget accepts the importance of a fluent, articulate command of *language* to foster the transition from concrete to formal operational thinking. Although he argues that logic arises from action, not language, he accepts that verbal reasoning is a major *vehicle* or medium upon which logical *operations* operate. Thus, evidence demonstrating the importance of linguistic abilities (like the capacity to read and write fluently) in the development of logical reasoning also leaves the theory untouched.

There are relations between the ability to reason in hypothetical, logical terms and literacy. For example, those people from non-literate cultures who have been studied to date fail to give evidence of formal reasoning. Most very deaf children, those who are born deaf or become deaf before learning to talk, eventually solve concrete operational problems but not formal operational ones – that is, problems which involve abstract or hypothetical ideas. I will give some examples of such problems later. The vast majority of them also fail to achieve functional literacy (Wood, Wood, Griffiths and Howarth, 1976).

Such empirical relations between literacy and logical reasoning have led some theorists, like David Olson (1977), to conclude that learning to read and write fluently is what makes *possible* the achievement of deductive logic, both in the individual and in a culture. Piagetians, I suppose, might counter that experiences gained in the course of doing science and mathematics are as important, if not more so, than literacy. Perhaps the achievement of logical thinking is what makes fluent reading and writing *possible*?

Finally, one source of my difficulty in trying to write this chapter stems from the status of the educational implications that we have been drawing from the theory. As I mentioned in the opening chapter, Piaget wrote little, and that reluctantly, about such educational implications. Many of the recommended applications of the theory have been left to others (e.g. Schwebel and Raph, 1974). I will be arguing in this chapter and the next that the competence, knowledge and skills that we seek to pass on to children through education have little or nothing to do with helping them to learn how to reason in formal, logical terms. Being a competent, intelligent, moral, creative and adaptive member of our culture does not rest on a capacity to think as a logician. But this may not be incompatible with Piaget's theory of mind. Perhaps he would agree that, in everyday social life, logical operations and a sense of logical necessity are not often brought into play. Many people in other cultures lead adaptive, competent lives even though they fail to solve problems involving formal logic. Perhaps the very limited scope of the theory, judged in relation to what is involved in competent everyday activity and reasoning, is why Piaget wrote so little about education? I don't know.

A detailed examination of research into adult reasoning (e.g. Johnson-Laird, 1983), coupled with recent theoretical analyses by philosophers concerning the relation between formal logic and reasoning (Boden, 1979) seem, to my mind, to demonstrate that Piaget's use of formal logic as a framework for analysing rational human thought is of limited value. Trying to describe, assess and foster intellectual competence in children, adolescents and adults has little or nothing to do with helping them to construct or discover general-purpose logical operations. Others, of course, are free to reach their own conclusions.

In the next few pages, we look at the issue of 'logicism' in two ways. We ask if, measured against the rules of (one variety of) formal logic, adults emerge as 'sloppy logicians'. More positively, we explore some reasons why our everyday talk and thought should not be measured against logic at all but studied and described in quite different terms.

Thinking in childhood and adolescence

In the UK children move into secondary schools at eleven years of age and most begin 'serious' preparation for public examinations two years later. Is this timing purely arbitrary, or are the educational demands placed on children changed at this age because the child is in some way 'ready' to meet new intellectual challenges? As we have seen, children's powers of concentration, their ability to study, pay attention, memorize and think analytically, to talk informatively and listen critically, all develop throughout the early school years (and beyond). Most children in the UK leaving primary school should have achieved a grasp of the foundations of literacy and mathematics and will have developed some ability to listen, as members of a group, to sustained episodes of narrative and explanation. Perhaps, then, most children are prepared for the study of a wider, more formal curriculum.

There are several lines of evidence, which I consider later, that point to some important 'discontinuities' in the linguistic, communicative and intellectual abilities of children between the ages of eleven and thirteen years. We have already explored evidence for and against the view that an important change in cognitive abilities occurs between the ages of five and seven years. Allied to this were discussions of the issue of 'readiness' for learning and different theoretical perspectives on it. The same set of questions emerges again in this chapter in relation to a proposed change in stage of development that usually occurs in early adolescence. If we decide that adolescents think in different ways from younger children, then it follows that the nature of the educational demands we make of them might quite properly be different in kind.

We must also explore the influences that might lead to the different levels of competence in the child at eleven and thirteen, and ask how far these are part and parcel of the general stream of development or a direct and specific product of education. This will bring us, eventually, to a consideration of the impact of literacy on intellectual abilities. Reading has served, traditionally, as a major avenue for gaining access to information – that is, we read in order to learn, to be informed and entertained. Perhaps the advent of other means of mass communication, like film and video-recordings, promises to obviate the need for text or to render literacy less educationally important than it has been in the past. Or does the ability to read help to foster intellectual abilities and ways of thinking that cannot readily be developed in other ways? That is the question we consider later in this chapter. First, however, we explore the view that changes in the ability to learn, think and communicate occur as 'natural' developments accompanying the onset of puberty.

Another shift at age 13?

As I have tried to explain in earlier chapters, according to Piaget the patterns, regularities and implicit structures that are discovered by the child as she acts on the world lead to the construction of concrete operations. The infant and child, like all of us, is naturally intolerant of ambiguity and paradox. We cannot live comfortably with conflicting ideas about the same phenomenon, nor can we perform two mutually exclusive actions at the same time. Consequently, we are driven to create ever more all-embracing and internally consistent intellectual schemes. Thus, eventually, we construct and understand logic. The adolescent is in the business of constructing a more abstract logic than she entertained during the concrete operational stage – one founded in *formal* operations which permit the application of logic to *propositions* about the world and not simply to 'reality' itself. Thus, the thinking of the adolescent differs from that of the younger child in a number of important respects. Let me cite a few examples to illustrate the main differences between concrete and formal ways of thinking.

An often used example of a problem whose understanding demands the exercise of formal operational thinking involves the workings of the humble beam balance. If children aged, say, nine or ten years of age are asked to discover and formulate the principles which dictate the workings of such a balance, they will probably discover the fact that adding weights to one side of a balanced beam will cause it to tilt. They are also likely to discover, through experiment, that balance can be destroyed by moving a weight on one side further from the fulcrum or by moving one closer to it. When they achieve formal operational thinking, they will appreciate the fact that weight and distance *interact* in very specific ways (according to 'laws') to dictate the phenomenon of balance. They will discover how to calculate and comprehend the *abstract* concept that physicists have chosen to call the 'moment'.

But concrete operationalists, though not devoid of intuitions and hypotheses about how beams balance, are not intellectually equipped to discover or grasp such abstract hypothetical concepts. They will appreciate, for example, that reversing a concrete operation annuls any change it brought about; so they are able to restore balance, say, by replacing a weight previously taken off or by moving one back to a position that previously ensured balance. What they *cannot* do, according to Piaget, is discover how to *co-ordinate* the effects of the two *systems* of concrete operations, i.e. one dictating the effects of weight and the other the effects of distance. Each of these systems has *observable* consequences on the behaviour of the balance. But to appreciate how they interact in order to grasp the abstract concept of a force requires a different *form* of reasoning.

Suppose we attempt to teach this concept to concrete operational children by using mathematical procedures. We might introduce them to the concept of 'commutativity'. So we show them, say, that five units of weight (all objects used are of the same weight for the purposes of this experiment) on one side of the beam create a balance with one unit of weight which is five times the distance from the fulcrum to that occupied by the five weights. Thus we show them that 5(weight) × 1(distance) = 1(weight) × 5(distance). In essence, what we are trying to teach them is that the (constant) *units*, weight and distance, are commutative.

We proceed to show them, using equations, that a numerical equivalence of the sums of products which represent the state of affairs on the two sides of the beam (e.g. (2 × 3) + (4 × 1) = (2 × 5)) always ensures balance, while any non-equivalence revealed will turn out not to balance. At this point, if they understand, children need not resort to further experiment. Having discovered the *principles* governing the phenomena in question, they realize that mathematics can be used, with certainty, to predict what *would* and *must* happen were they to test out any predicted outcomes. In so doing they are also beginning to grasp the concept of an 'equation' and its relation to nature.

Understanding the concept of the 'moment' and the relation between the behaviour of the beam balance and mathematical equations demands *formal operational* thinking. A moment cannot be 'seen', it must be *constructed*. It is not a direct product of observation, nor the visible result of concrete actions (like adding weights or changing distances) but an intellectual construct which, when grasped, enables us to *understand* the 'deeper' or more abstract workings of nature. We are driven to create abstract concepts because we cannot make sense of natural phenomena without them. Nature 'obliges' us to construct abstract concepts and formal operations when we seek to understand and control it.

I will return to the issue of teaching abstract concepts in the next chapter. For the moment, I hope that this example serves to convey some sense of how and why Piaget distinguishes between concrete and formal operations. The former relate directly to perceived and tangible changes that occur as a product of specific actions, while the latter operate on and yield *abstract* concepts like the moment. This example also illustrates another general feature of Piaget's analysis of development. Intellectual demands that children have faced and mastered at one stage of development resurface in a different form at the next stage. For instance, recall the example used in chapter 2 to illustrate the relation between concepts of number and the activity of counting. Numerical symbols and mathematical procedures only have meaning for a child when she has constructed the concepts to which they refer. Similarly, whilst we may be able to teach children under eleven years of age to manipulate equations to produce the 'right' answers, we should not assume that this means that they *understand* the phenomena that such procedures are designed to 'explain', model or predict. The child has to abstract, co-ordinate and construct in order to appreciate the ways in which such procedures serve to represent reality.

The intellectual divide between *procedural knowledge*, like knowing how to 'solve' equations, and *conceptual understanding*, such as that needed to grasp the connections between equations and physical phenomena, is surely real and important. How many times have we ourselves experienced the phenomenon of manipulating symbols without knowing what it is they really mean? Concepts of 'force', 'mass', 'acceleration', the quadratic function, differentiation and integration; how many children are 'taught' how to do sums and experiments which implicate such concepts without grasping what they mean on *earth*?

More is at stake, however, than agreement over the distinction between procedural skills and conceptual understanding. If one accepts Piaget's analysis, then it follows not only that the pre-adolescent cannot be schooled in the mathematics of physics but also that his or her stage of development militates against all forms of *hypothetical* formal reasoning. Consider, for instance, abstract concepts like 'money', 'profit', 'honesty', 'fairness', 'time', 'socialization', or 'rights' and 'obligations'. Some terms like these probably possess some meaning for primary school children. In some sense they know what it means to be 'honest' or 'fair'. They can grasp some sense of history and the fact that people in different countries live in different ways. But a *formal* and abstract understanding of such concepts, by definition, demands an ability to transcend 'common experience' and the construction of concepts that, while 'embodied' in everyday experiences, like a pound coin or sharing sweets, are not visibly *present* in them. An abstract understanding of economics, for example, involves the realization that our own notion of 'money' is part of only one system whereby people manage to co-ordinate and distribute the fruits, products and costs of their individual labour. Barter, cattle, members of one sex, may all serve the same 'purpose' in different economic systems. The notion that all societies encounter common needs and have to fulfil similar functions in order to survive and reproduce is an intellectual construction, not a 'visible' phenomenon. There may be little in common between the currencies of different lands, but their *equivalence*, in terms of the role they play in social organization, may be grasped if one can think abstractly in terms of certain *propositions* about how societies operate. What is at stake here is not simply whether one believes or subscribes to a particular theory of economics but the intellectual capacity to entertain abstract, hypothetical propositions about the subject which can be reasoned about in a disciplined and logical way.

If one accepts such views on the differences between adolescent and child thinking, it follows that many lessons, whether in economics, sociology, history, geography, psychology or whatever, will be closed to pre-adolescent children whenever they demand an ability to grasp formal notions of equivalence, such as an abstract concept of 'money' that embraces many different fiscal systems. The emergence of such concepts is made possible by the development of abstract, hypothetical and *formal* systems of reasoning.

Logicism

The elegance and power of Piaget's theory stem, in part, from his view that the structure of intelligence develops towards increasing levels of abstraction, generality and stability. Once a given phenomenon can be represented in formal, logical terms, its conclusions are irresistible and enduring. This does not mean, of course, that learning, creativity, new ideas and fresh insights terminate with the development of formal operations. Logic is, arguably at least, not the source of most of our insights. Further, an argument might well be logically compelling yet still prove wrong because the premises or assumptions upon which it is based, from which inferences are drawn, may be at variance with reality. A new discovery or observation, a novel way of looking at a phenomenon (like Newton's perception of the significance of the fact that apples fall from tree to ground, or Archimedes' supposed insight in his bath) may lead to changes in assumptions about the nature of the world and lead, eventually, to the displacement (sorry, Archimedes) of a previously held theory. That theory may have been logically compelling, but its explanatory power limited because it was based on an assumption or a set of assumptions that neglect what are discovered to be important aspects of the phenomena the theory seeks to explain.

Piaget's view of adolescent intelligence illustrates the divide between logic and reality. Although the adolescent's thinking is *structurally* completed with the achievement of formal operations, it does not follow that learning is at an end, nor does it mean that they understand the world in the same way as more mature members of their society. However, the *form* of adolescent learning is different in kind from that of younger children. The 'task' of the adolescent is, so to speak, to 'play' with logic, to deduce the conclusions that are implicit in her 'theories' of the world and to test these against reality. In this way, she comes to resemble the scientist, who tests the hypotheses and deductions that he draws, logically, from the structure of his theory. Piaget's portrayal of adolescents seems somewhat harsh. In 1940, for example, he wrote

Adolescent egocentricity is manifested by belief in the omnipotence of reflection, as though the world should submit itself to idealistic schemes rather than to systems of reality. It is the metaphysical age *par excellence*; the self is strong enough to reconstruct the universe and big enough to incorporate it.

I think this quotation illustrates a number of features of Piaget's thinking about the relation between formal reasoning and reality. In the first place, the fact that he says 'the world should submit itself to idealistic systems of reality' demonstrates that while his view is that intelligence is pushed towards the construction of formal operations, it does not follow that it guarantees the discovery of real-world 'truth'. Logical proof (demonstrating that an argument is coherent and compelling) and the demonstration of empirical or real-world validity (does the same argument work in practice?) are not the same thing. However, formal operations endow the adolescent with the competence to *investigate* the implications and practical value of her ideas. The idealism of adolescents, in this view, is a natural consequence of intellectual development. The task of the adolescent is to recognize that a view of the world that might be true 'ideally' may turn out, on further reflection, observation and experiment, to be 'unrealistic' and unworkable. So Piaget offers us a particular 'image' of adolescents and, perhaps, helps us to understand why, to more mature minds, they often appear over-idealistic and hypercritical of the adult world.

If we accept Piaget's theory of development, one embraces not only his description of what children and adolescents can and cannot do, but also the very important argument that the course of intellectual development is constrained by the construction and emergence of logical operations. So, to evaluate the theory, we must question the view that children are developing towards logical competence and the implication that mature thinking can be

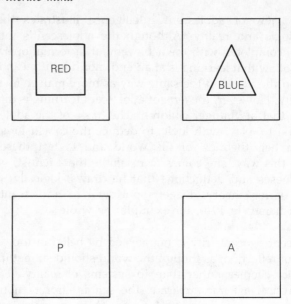

Figure 6.1   Wason's card-turning experiment

analysed in terms of formal logical operations. Let me explore this very difficult question with a few examples.

One might accept the 'logic' of the following chain of reasoning yet know full well that the conclusion it entails does not make 'sense': 'All blue whales have pink feet. This is a blue whale. Therefore, it has pink feet.' To employ an argument analogous to that used by Chomsky when demonstrating the 'independence' of grammar from meaning, one could say that such examples show that 'logic' and a sense of logical necessity (i.e. given certain assumptions, certain inferences must follow) on the one hand, and what we might call 'common sense certainties' on the other, are different things. There are surely many good zoological and linguistic reasons why whales cannot have feet and still be called whales, and I doubt if any of us have ever seen a 'real' whale with pink feet. But this lack of 'sense' does not detract from the 'logic' of the argument. Logic, then, is not synonymous with making 'sense' and cannot be 'reduced' to it.

Other 'logical' conclusions are not, however, so easily evaluated (Wason and Johnson-Laird, 1972). For example, look at the four symbols in figure 6.1. You are shown four cards, displaying a red square, a blue triangle, a consonant and a vowel. You are also informed that each card shown has a geometric shape on one side and a letter on the other. You are told that if a card has a *red* square on one side, then it must have a *vowel* on the other. Which cards need to be turned over in order to test this rule? First, note in passing that in everyday problem situations one would probably find it much easier and more efficient to turn over the lot than to spend time thinking about the 'logic' of the problem!

Suppose I say that you must turn over the card bearing the square and that bearing the vowel. Is that recommendation logically sound? No. Although most adults who have been tested with this problem say that this *is* the correct answer, they are, logically speaking, wrong. Why and how? Well, the rule does *not* imply that all vowels must bear a red square on their obverse side. Consider, for example, the statement that 'If a man is a Texan then he is tall.' Does it follow that any tall man must be a Texan? No. Nor does it follow that if you are told that a red square has a vowel on the other side then it must be the case that a card bearing a vowel must bear a red square. However, if a red square *must* have a vowel on its obverse side, then it follows that a card bearing a consonant must *not* have a red square on its other side. If it did, we would have discovered a red square which did *not* accompany a vowel, and this would violate the rule. So, we must turn over both the card bearing a red square (no consonant on the other side) and the one bearing a consonant (no red square on the other side).

Given that the vast majority of adults (some of them trained logicians!) who have been tested with this problem get it wrong, does it follow that most of us are 'illogical', at least some of the time? Does it also mean that Piaget's analysis of the destination of intellectual development is indefensible? These, as I have already said, are hard questions.

First, let us not lose sight of the fact that adults not only get logical problems 'wrong' but that they usually give the *same* logically incorrect answers. If most of us agree in our conclusions, does it not seem plausible to suppose that our verbal reasoning is governed by certain 'rules' and that these are different from those implicated in formal logic? *Why* do we answer such questions in the way that we do? This is a difficult and controversial issue and I do not intend to spend a great deal of time on it. However, let me consider a few possibilities which suggest that we are not 'obliged' to assume that logic provides a good 'theory' of how people normally think. Let me illustrate this argument with evidence drawn from studies of formal reasoning undertaken with the help of people from non-schooled, non-literate societies.

In a very extensive study of the Kpelle, a Liberian tribe, Cole and his colleagues (Cole et al., 1971) posed verbal problems of the following type to adults.

Experimenter   At one time spider went to a feast. He was told to answer this question before he could eat any of the food. The question is: Spider and black deer always

	eat together. Spider is eating. Is black deer eating?
Subject	Were they in the bush?
E	Yes.
S	They were eating together?
E	Spider and black deer always eat together. Spider is eating. Is black deer eating?
S	But I was not there. How can I answer such a question?

(some time later, after the question had been repeated)

S	Oh, oh black deer was eating.
E	Black deer was eating?
S	Yes.
E	What is your reason for saying that black deer was eating?
S	The reason is that black deer always walks about all day eating green leaves in the bush. When it rests for a while it gets up again and goes to eat.

The answers given by the adult Kpelle to this and other 'logical' problems suggest that drawing 'logically compelling' conclusions, seemingly so 'obvious' to mature members of our sort of society, is not a common practice for the Kpelle. On first sight, one might argue that the Kpelle are 'illogical' or unable to reason rationally (indeed, many early anthropologists reached such conclusions about 'primitive' minds). However, a more serious analysis of what the Kpelle are doing in trying to 'make sense' of this, for them, curious social encounter with a foreigner, together with a consideration of our own 'failures of logic' such as those just illustrated, sheds a different light on the issue.

First, as Cole and his colleagues point out, the Kpelle assess the plausibility of what is said and, eventually, agree to give an answer to the (repeated) questions by testing them against their 'common sense' knowledge. They do not see the problem in 'formal' terms, to be tested against some rules of logic, but as a description of an (implausible) event or situation whose *plausibility* is to be assessed. The conclusions reached reflect the *rationality* of what is said measured against what is likely to happen in Kpelle experience. Looked at in this way, the Kpelle way of reasoning is not totally dissimilar from our own. Perhaps the question about 'tall Texans' posed above did not lead us to draw inferences that are at variance with the rules of logic because 'common sense' told us that many tall people are not Texans. However, when we are given 'abstract' problems, like the one with vowels and shapes, our conclusions tend to depart from the dictates of logic. But why?

There are a number of possible reasons. First, consider the so-called 'fallacy of affirming the consequent', the phrase used to describe the 'mistake' of assuming that 'if p then q, it follows that if q then p'. If I say to a friend 'If it rains, I will go to the cinema' (if p then q) will he or she assume 'naturally' that if they see me in the cinema it must be raining (q then p)? I suggest that they would. Why would I *bother* to talk about my plans with reference to the weather otherwise? I suggest that *implicit* in my statement is a presupposition, shared by my friend, that if it does *not* rain, I will not go to the cinema (not-p then not-q – a logically invalid inference, given only that p implies q). Imagine the likely reaction of my friend should he see me in the cinema and say 'Oh, it's raining then', only to be told, 'No – because p then q (rain, then cinema) it does not follow that q then p (cinema, then rain)'. I doubt if he would welcome the logic of my argument! Rather, an *explanation* as to why I had 'changed my mind' would be more legitimate. Similarly, when I say to him 'If it rains (etc.)' and he asks 'What will you do if it is fine?' and I say 'Go to the cinema', he may not question my logic but he might well doubt my sanity!

It is possible to argue, that, like children confronted with 'logical' tasks, adults also draw upon practices and presuppositions derived from everyday social experiences when they try to solve abstract, formal problems. Perhaps they assume that 'If a red square then a vowel' 'A vowel then a red square' because such assumptions are implicated in the way people usually talk to each other? Whatever the reason there are clear differences between the inferences that people draw from verbal statements and the conclusions that logicians reach when they *treat* such statements as *formal propositions*.

When we are set logical problems like the card-turning one, the logician characterizes that problem in terms like 'p' and 'q'. The 'values' of these symbols are derived from the problem set. So p is the set of red squares and not-p is what is left over, the set of blue triangles. Similarly, q is the set of vowels, and not-q the set of consonants. The relations between these sets of things are *fully determined* by the 'syntax' of the problem. Everything you know about shapes and sounds and all the things you presuppose about verbal statements that people use to talk about their plans and intentions and the conditions that these are contingent upon, are *irrelevant* to the 'logic' of the problem. Put another way, the logician's 'interpretation' of the statements given is 'closed' and 'fully determined'. When we talk about our plans in everyday life using similar forms of words our listeners are unlikely to take what we say so 'literally'.

This very brief and non-technical account of possible differences between logical discourse and everyday communication points to one direction in which we might look for an explanation for our so-called 'failures of logic'. Comparing our performances with the rules of logic may be a very misleading way of trying to understand how we actually think. Logical inferences are not synonymous with the *implications* that we draw from what is said in everyday discourse. We do something different. This, coupled with the very different stance or attitude taken by logicians and non-logicians when they analyse the 'meaning' of language, might help us to understand why we don't talk and think like logicians. Thinking in formal logical terms demands explicit training and familiarity with the conventions that logicians abide by. Looked at in this way, logic is a special *system* of thinking that, like mathematics, helps to perform certain tasks. Later, we take up the question of how and why formal logic itself was invented.

As I have said already, Piaget never implied that everyday communication is governed by formal operations (though there were times when he seemed to come close to it). I have presented these examples to demonstrate the limitations of formal logical operations as a 'model' to describe how people draw inferences from verbal statements. Education, if concerned at all with helping children to develop formal, logical thinking, has many more important objectives to pursue. We could still argue, of course, that when we investigate *nature* we are 'forced' to accept logic. Other people may 'agree' with our interpretations of causal statements involving 'if . . . then', but nature will not tolerate such assumptions and will force us to discover and to abide by the rules of formal logic. I do not intend to pursue this argument further here save to say that studies of scientific and mathematical thinking (explored in the next chapter) do not provide support for the view that *scientific* thinking rests on the rules of formal logic (Lunzer, 1973). As we shall see, mathematical 'discourse' *is* based on special ways of thinking and talking, but these do not seem to abide by the rules of formal logic either.

Let me conclude this difficult and in many ways unsatisfactory excursion into the turbulent and muddy waters of logicism with two observations. First, even if we accept the view that some form of logical reasoning is needed to construct workable, abstract theories about the natural world, as Piaget argued, I believe it would be educationally dangerous to assume that the capacity to do such things is what 'drives' and 'constrains' most of our thinking. People's thinking involves much more than this and it would be inadvisable to base an education on the implicit or explicit assumption that the development of 'logic' is the only or even a primary goal of schooling. I will say more about this later. Second, Piaget couched his analysis of logic in terms of a particular system of formal rules that logicians had constructed when he was developing his theory. Since that time, several different systems of logic have been invented. Some people working on the construction of 'intelligent machines', for example, still believe that one of these logics will provide a good general theory of how we think. Perhaps we will one day discover a 'logic' that explains how children, adults and people from different cultures reason, though I doubt it. Or perhaps we will find time and time again that every such 'logic' is only a 'special' tool, a particular way of thinking that helps us to solve certain sorts of problems (like programming intelligent computers). I see no reason for trying to best-guess the future on these issues. However, given the evidence we have already examined from the study of children's thinking, together with what I have presented here on adult reasoning, I suggest it is reasonable to conclude that Piaget's characterization of what it is children develop *towards*, i.e. formal operations, can be rejected. Some of us *can* think using the rules that Piaget felt were the natural culmination of all intellectual development, but most of the time we think in quite different ways, and we should not regard such thinking either as 'sloppy logic' or as an immature form of logic. Rather, the assumptions we make, the implications we draw, the 'models' of the world we construct and the way in which we *communicate* ideas and understanding are quite different in nature to formal logical thinking. Let me now look in more detail at other ways of thinking about the nature and development of rational thinking.

Language in talk and text

Piaget's description of the course of intellectual development in terms of the construction of logical operations, though unique in scope and detail, represents only one of several attempts to use logic as a framework for the analysis of reasoning. Opposed to this general approach, as we have seen, is the view that formal logic is not the destination or 'pinnacle' of development. Rather, it represents a special way of thinking that has been developed, over many generations, as have mathematics and science, to perform certain functions and to handle specific types of problem. Logic, for instance, may be viewed as a special way of 'checking' a series of propositions and inferences for internal consistency of a particular type, and has nothing to do with the intellectual processes that were involved in the *creation* of the ideas involved.

Other students of child development, as we have seen in preceding chapters, emphasize the role of language and schooling in the formation of abstract reasoning. In chapter 1 we saw that Vygotsky argued that schooling and instruction involve the trans-mission of scientific ways of thinking, and inculcate in children the development of 'self-regulation'. He also argued that learning to *read* leads to important and far-reaching changes in the *nature* of children's knowledge and use of language. In becoming literate, children do not simply learn 'another way' of communicating or a new 'code' for representing speech. Rather, writing and reading make novel demands on children and involve them in learning how to exploit new *functions* of language. Text is not simply speech written down, nor is writing merely the substitution of visible symbols for acoustic ones. Both reading and writing involve ways of communicating that transform the nature of children's knowledge of language and lead to more analytical ways of thinking.

Let me outline, briefly, the main aspects of Vygotsky's argument in the light of recent studies of children learning to read and write. In chapter 4 I introduced and tried to illustrate the way in which linguists traditionally analyse the nature of language. The term 'phoneme' refers to the theoretical 'units' of speech sounds which form the building blocks of languages. Morphemes are units of meaning comprising one or more phonemes. Some morphemes, recall, like 'dog', 'cat', 'green', are termed 'free' in that they can stand alone and still convey meaning, whilst others, like verb inflexions and markers of plurality, are only meaningful when combined with free morphemes.

The analysis of 'prosodic' features of speech drew our attention to phenomena, like stress, intonation patterns and pauses, that help to convey emotion and emphasis, to differentiate questions from statements, commands from requests and to convey attitudes like sarcasm, irony and secrecy. The rules that govern how morphemes and words are structured to form grammatical utterances are labelled rules of syntax. Semantics and pragmatics refer to the analysis of linguistic meaning. They include, among other things, the study of how the meaning of utterances is influenced by factors like the relationship between the speaker and hearer and the social context they are in.

Although, as far as I am aware, Vygotsky did not undertake his analysis of the differences between spoken and written language in this terminology, I don't think it will do any marked injustice to his views to reformulate them in such terms. This strategy also has the advantage of allowing me to relate his pioneering analysis to contemporary studies of literacy and its development.

Literacy and decontextualization

When two or more people are engaged in face-to-face conversation, communication between them rests on much more than the words they use and any grammatical rules they exploit, as we saw in the last chapter. When children begin to write, they are likely to find the process difficult and demanding, not only because writing makes unusual demands on their bodily control, manual dexterity and powers of perception and attention – though such things in themselves are difficult enough. They also face a new range of *intellectual* challenges. Unlike face-to-face conversations, where responsibility for mutual understanding is *shared* between speakers and listeners, solitary writing requires children to bear all the burden of responsibility for making what they are trying to mean intelligible and accessible to their reader(s). When they talk with others, they know *who* it is that they must make sense to. If what they say is ambiguous, unclear or unintelligible, then the person or people they are talking to may ask questions, seek clarification or ask for elaboration. Writing on her own, however, the child must learn how to *anticipate* likely sources of misunderstanding and take them into account, when she may not know *who* it is she is writing to or for.

Looked at in this way, the effective writer must act both as the presenter and the receiver of communication. It should come as no surprise to find, then, that children who *modify and correct* what they write as they go along usually write more intelligibly and grammatically than children who do not edit their own work. Self-correction, as I have argued before, is evidence of the fact that children are involved in self-instruction towards the achievement of goals. They realize that what they write may not necessarily be comprehensible or readable. They do not assume that because *they* themselves know what they mean by what they write, other people will. They are 'de-centring' or 'disembedding' their ideas as they read what they write to evaluate its accuracy and accessibility.

Externalizing our ideas, imaginings, thoughts and feelings in such a way that they are put into a verbal context, sequenced in an understandable way and expressed unambiguously in a written medium is *not* a simple extension of what we do when we participate in conversations. In the last chapter, I outlined some of the problems that children face when they are asked to narrate their experiences and views. In these circumstances, children have to 'take on the role of the listener', decentre or decontextualize their thinking. We might expect, therefore, that such experiences provide a bridge into literacy. This idea has been put forward by a number of students of child language and literacy (e.g. Perera, 1984; Romaine, 1984). The work of Brown and her colleagues referred to at the end of the last chapter also offers some indirect evidence for this view. Children who were poor at information-giving, a special and demanding form of narrative, were academically weak and, one suspects, not reading well. As far as I am aware, however, no strong evidence exists to prove that skill in producing and understanding coherent and intelligible narratives predicts levels of literacy. So the proposed connection between the two remains speculative.

Even in situations that demand giving and listening to extended narratives, however, the people involved are visible and audible to each other. A listener's reactions, both verbal and non-verbal, serve as feedback regarding her understanding of what is being said. Writing is a far more demanding occupation, since such feedback is non-existent. The absence of an audience, then, and the responsibilities this confers on the writer, make the task of learning how to write rather difficult for children. But the divide between spoken and written language is much deeper than differences in the nature of the audience involved.

The written and the spoken word: learning to read

Everything written in English can ultimately be 'de-composed' into the twenty-six letters of its alphabet. Analysing spoken English into its constituent phonemes, a more difficult and uncertain business, reveals forty-four elements (Perera, 1984). Clearly, then, there can be no simple relationship between English as it is written and spoken. Consequently, when learning to read, children are not simply uncovering a simple code for translating speech into print. In fact, the relation between elements of speech (phonemes) and their 'corresponding' elements in written language (so-called 'graphemes') is considerably more complex than this suggests. Imagine the same word being spoken by a person with a Welsh, Yorkshire or Cockney accent; by a young girl or a grown man. Each asked to write the word (given that they are literate enough) will produce the same pattern of letters. But the nature of the *sounds* they make in producing the same word will differ considerably.

We do not normally speak in mechanical, clearly articulated words. The 'same' word in the context of different utterances even when spoken by the same person may *sound* quite different, yet it looks the same in print. Put another way, while the 'same' phoneme may sound very different when produced in different contexts by the same speaker or by different speakers saying the same thing, a corresponding *written* account of what they say may be 'identical'.

It is clear, then, that the task of reading and writing differs from speaking and listening in that literary forms are more uniform and less context-sensitive than speech. Indeed, as Perera points out, the 'neutrality' and the greater uniformity of the written word renders it less prone to 'prejudice'. Imagine the same words written by an Englishman, a Scotsman and an Irishman. Does their writing betray their dialect? Similarly, a thing written many years ago may still be readable today even if the way in which words are pronounced has changed. But from the child's point of view, learning to read may present many challenges and surprises since the uniformity of written text is bought at the cost of a rather poor 'fit' with speech.

Although this is not an appropriate place to discuss how our 'commonplace' conceptions of things like words, sentences and language itself have come about, it is interesting to note that some linguists argue that modern 'theories' of language are based on experiences with *written* language and, as such, are *not* the proper place to start thinking about the nature and structure of *speech*. When we help children to learn to read we are doing more than teaching a new and neutral 'code' for representing what they already do with and know about speech. Rather, we are introducing them to radically new ways of thinking about *language* itself.

Written English is 'irregular' in many respects. Put another way, how things said are written down does not always follow general rules: there are many exceptions, as Perera illustrates. So, for instance, the 'same' sounds may be written differently (plain and plane; an ice cream, a nice cream; attacks on buildings, a tax on buildings). Words like 'the' which, as we have seen serve several different linguistic functions, sound and are known to the mature, literate ear as the 'same' word that performs 'different' functions. Karmiloff-Smith suggests that for young children, the different uses of words such as 'the' may seem, like 'plane' and 'plain', to be two words that happen to *sound* similar but have different meanings. There are certainly enough 'homophones' in English (words that sound the same but are written differently) to reinforce such an assumption. It is possible, then, that children's discovery of the fact that the same word has several functions is *facilitated* by learning to read and write.

When one considers the way in which different accents and dialects treat many words, it also becomes apparent that speech sounds that are very similar in some dialects may be pronounced differently in others. Consequently, children who use different dialects may face a different set of 'puzzles' as they learn to read depending upon the nature of the 'matches' and 'mismatches' between their dialect and the written form (Perera, 1984, pp. 212–15).

Learning to write and read confronts children with challenges because they have to take greater responsibility than they do in conversation for making what they communicate intelligible and understandable outside of a shared *context*. It also demands that they discover a range of often irregular relations between the nature of speech and the structure of written text. Literacy, Vygotsky argues, leads children to develop more explicit and objective 'theories' of language and helps to develop their self-regulatory abilities as they learn how to plan, monitor and evaluate their writing. Being able to write well demands the capacity to take other people's perspectives and states of mind into consideration and the ability to set up, in language, situations that, in conversational exchanges, may be 'given' and 'taken for granted'. The cost is a good deal of hard work.

The story does not end here. There are several other ways in which spoken and written language present quite different challenges to children. Let me consider some of these, briefly, before returning to the issue of the relation between literacy and intellectual development.

Prosody and punctuation

Written text provides a very poor and weak representation of features of spoken language such as intonation, stress and pause patterns which, as we saw in the last chapter, play an important role in verbal communication. Using written symbols like full-stops, commas and colons, writers can provide some guidance to their readers about how they intend their text to be organized and read. But the repertoire of symbols available to them is limited. Other punctuational tactics, like the use of underlining, italics or upper-case letters, can be used to give some sense of where the writer's intended *emphasis* lies and how he intends a sentence to be 'parsed' (analysed) and interpreted. Consider, for instance, the effect of simply inserting a comma into 'I wasn't shopping seriously' to create 'I wasn't shopping, seriously'.

In comparison with the many subtleties of meaning and emotions that prosody carries in speech, however, punctuation is a blunt tool. Becoming literate must involve more than learning how to 'translate' written symbols into spoken ones. Reading demands *interpretation*. Similarly, a well-written text demands a sense of how the strategic use of words, grammar and punctuation is likely to affect a reader's interpretation of what is being written. As Perera points out, the fact that many features of tone of voice and manner of speaking cannot be conveyed by prosodic means in print has led to the evolution, largely for literary purposes, of an enlarged vocabulary for describing and conveying manner of speech. When we hear talk, we know whether a person is shouting, whispering, insinuating, implying, hinting, or whatever. Even when we listen to verbal accounts of what other people have said in conversation and narrative, the speaker can convey *how* something was spoken by imitating the tone of voice used. In text, however, we must use special *words* (like 'whispered') to get such messages across. The reader must make inferences about how a written text should be analysed to reveal its structure and has to decide where stress and emphasis should be laid. Expert readers usually perform these functions 'automatically' and without conscious awareness of how they do so. But children have to learn *how* to 'interact' with text in order to interpret its writer's intended meaning.

As we delve more deeply into the nature of the expertise needed to read and write fluently, we will explore the view that it is by developing the ability to analyse and interpret written text that children acquire special linguistic and intellectual skills. These, I will argue, are often called upon in psychological tests of children's intellectual, linguistic and communicative abilities. They are also demanded by teachers when they confront children with lessons involving descriptions, explanations and questions about abstract, unfamiliar and hypothetical topics. First, however, we need to look in more detail at the different demands placed on children by the spoken and written word. What else, in addition to new vocabulary, skill in interpretation and a more 'objective' knowledge of their own language, do children learn in the process of becoming literate?

Consider what is involved in deciding on the meaning of what look like 'simple' written sentences such as 'John was washing the car'. As I will explain in more detail later, a reader, reading this sentence in isolation, is likely to 'sense' an emphasis on the 'clause-final' element (the car). However, imagine this sentence being *spoken* in a number of ways, with a different word being stressed in each case. Suppose, for instance, stress is laid on the word 'John'. Here, we could imagine the utterance serving as a *denial* of a previous utterance, such as 'Peter was washing the car'. Now suppose stress is laid on the word 'was'. This might imply the denial of another assertion – one which suggested that John was *not* washing the car. Emphasize 'washing' and we can imagine the utterance serving to deny yet another suggestion, perhaps that John was servicing it. Repeat the exercise with the addition of a single symbol, a question mark, 'John was washing the car?', and another range of possible meanings can be constructed.

As expert readers, we are able to construct or imagine a variety of spoken versions of what, in print, is an identical piece of text. In connected text, of course, such sentences would be embedded in longer sequences of written utterances which might lead one 'naturally' to a particular interpretation. An example might be 'Mary had said that because Peter was washing the car, he couldn't help her with the dishes. But Alice said that she had been duped. Peter was sitting in the garden, sunning himself. John was washing the car.

Hardly riveting narrative, and as we shall see stylistically poor written text, but I hope it serves to illustrate a number of aspects of the reading process. Only when a reader is able to take in and memorize relatively long stretches of text does it become possible to estimate where any intended and important *stress* might lie. Expert readers seem to fomulate such interpretations 'naturally' and, like the chess Grand Masters discussed in chapter 3, they are not usually aware of the processes that underlie their expertise.

When skilled readers encounter a particularly difficult text, they may resort to reading aloud or may start to talk themselves through the text. In so doing, they can try out various interpretations, perhaps experimenting with different prosodic possibilities to see what they 'sound like' and mean when location of stress is varied. Usually, however, skilled reading takes place at a rate of about 300 words per minute, approximately twice the speed of normal speech. It seems unlikely, then, that expert readers usually read by 'talking' to themselves. Precisely what they *do* do when they read is still not clear. It seems reasonably certain, however, that they do not convert visual symbols into sub-vocal speech (Underwood, 1979). Rather, their interpretation and understanding of what they read seems to involve so-called *direct* processes – that is, they seem to pass 'straight' from visual symbols to construct an interpretation of the meaning of what they are reading.

Writing, planning and self-regulation

I have just considered some of the problems and demands reading and writing create because the written word is a poor medium for representing prosodic information. However, the expert writer, by employing a number of techniques special to the creation of coherent written texts, can overcome these limitations. Similarly, an expert reader can, so to speak, 'reverse' these writing techniques and conventions to reconstruct a writer's intended meaning. Both the reader and the writer, as I have said, are usually unaware of the nature of their expertise. Systematic analysis and research are needed to help to articulate what it is that they *do* yet cannot describe. By making *explicit* what is implicit in their performance, we gain an objective understanding of the tasks, demands and problems that children have to face when we try to teach them to read and write fluently. Perhaps, following Vygotsky, such knowledge may also help to make us better teachers.

Competent speakers of English are strongly predisposed (without realizing it) to lay stress on the final element in a clause, what linguists refer to as 'end focus' (Perera, 1984, pp. 193–5). So in 'I went to the village on the *hill*' or 'I gave my daughter a *ball*' or 'Houses are so *expensive*', stress is normally placed on the words in italics. Of course, the 'rules' governing the distribution of stress, as we have seen, are waived or changed in some contexts. So, for instance, if the second statement was said in response to the 'You gave your son a ball for his birthday' stress, in the sentence above, would probably fall on the word 'daughter'. Note, however, how stilted or pedantic such a response would seem. Far more likely, I suspect, would be something like 'No, not my son, my *daughter*'.

A writer, confronted with the task of 'communicating' a stress on adverbials, objects and complements, can capitalize on the fact that, in English, these parts of speech occur clause-finally. For example, 'I gave Daddy a sweet' (stress on the direct object) or 'I gave a sweet to Daddy' (stress on the indirect object), 'I went to town yesterday' (stress on an adverb of time), 'Flowers are so beautiful' (stress on a subject complement). The writer, wanting to stress such words, can 'rely' on the natural tendency of a reader to 'read in' stress at the appropriate places, and so needs no 'special' tactics to get her prosodic message across. But as Perera points out, when writers wish to stress other features of what they wish to write – specifically words which form grammatical *subjects* or *verbs* – then they face problems (in English, that is: other languages have different rules and, no doubt, create a different set of literary problems).

When we speak, we can draw attention to nouns, pronouns, verbs or any word in an utterance by *stressing* them, making them relatively louder or longer, say: 'The *queen* gave him a pen', 'Someone really *ransacked* the house'. Underlining, bold type, italics can be used to convey the fact that the conventional foci of stress (i.e. the object 'pen' and the object 'house') are not the words to be stressed. However, there are also *syntactic* techniques for achieving the same ends. For example, if we write something like 'He was given a pen by the queen' or 'Last night, the house was really ransacked', the desired emphasis is achieved by ensuring that the final clause element is the word to be stressed.

Perera also demonstrates how, by including 'interrupting constructions' into a sentence, a writer can highlight a key word that might otherwise appear unstressed. For instance, if instead of writing 'The students' results were outstanding' we write 'The students' results, to their surprise and delight, were outstanding', we achieve stress on the word 'results' as well as on the final word 'outstanding'. So the way in which our 'habits' of speech lead us to place stress on a very specific element of the structure of utterances (i.e. clausal position) produces challenges to the writer and demands the 'invention' and fluent control over a variety of structural literacy devices. These help to ensure that the organization of what is written corresponds to what the writer wishes to communicate. To appreciate and comprehend the message, of course, readers also have to have command of the 'conventions' involved.

Let us consider a specific example of a linguistic structure that is 'special' to the written medium. Some forms of the passive voice are very rare in speech and seldom addressed to children – utterances like 'Mary was kissed by John' or 'He was given a pen by the queen', for example. Mastery of such structures appears late in language development. When I was at school, I was told that one employs the passive voice in 'science' writing in order to depersonalize written narrative and to make it more 'objective' (e.g. 'A bunsen

burner was placed under the retort'). However, linguistic constructions like the passive voice (there are many other examples) serve a
much more general and important function than this. They enable a
writer to make her reader's task easier. She can construct her
sentences in such a way that her intended stress lies where her
reader tacitly 'expects' to find it. In the examples just given, the use
of a passive construction serves to highlight 'John' and 'the queen',
enabling the writer to lay stress on words that, in 'active' sentences
like 'The queen gave him a pen', would not be read as stressed.
Thus the use of a passive construction enables a writer to emphasize
words that would not stand out if she were to use more common,
spoken forms.

The phenomenon of 'end focus', the term given to our tendency
to emphasize final clause elements, coupled with the absence of rich
prosodic cues in written language, create a need for a range of
grammatical devices in print that are not necessary in speech. The
fact that young children do not often use or readily understand
certain grammatical forms (like agented passives) should, then,
come as no great surprise. Such constructions only become really
functional when the child becomes *literate*.

Another general 'principle' governing the way in which we talk
and write to good effect is the tendency to 'save the best until last'.
The major 'theme' or most important or dramatic idea to be written
should come as close to the end of what is said as possible.
Contrast, for instance, 'The weary refugees dragged their precious
burden onward towards the tiny light' with 'Onward, towards the
tiny light, the weary refugees dragged their precious burden'. If the
thing to be highlighted, the theme, is the precious burden, then the
second version, where it appears at the end of the utterance, brings
it into focus more dramatically than the first version, which better
serves the purpose of highlighting the 'tiny light' towards which the
refugees are moving. In speech, dramatic effect and highlights can
be achieved by many verbal and non-verbal means. The listener,
moving in rhythm with the speaker, can be caught up in the flow of
words and actions to anticipate and share any drama. The writer,
however, often needs to employ grammatical structures, punctuation
and ways of sequencing ideas which, though rare in speech, offer
the means for the achievement of her literary ends. If you are
anything like me, you will now start to analyse this text to discover
that some of your problems of comprehension can be attributed to
my writing. (I think that's where I intended to place the stress.)

The 11 to 13 shift: a linguistic perspective

By the time they reach their thirteenth birthday, many children are
using grammatical forms in writing that are structurally more

complex than those typically found in their speech. For the majority of younger children, the opposite holds true: their speech is grammatically more complex than what they write. As children develop and learn through adolescence, the efficiency and accuracy with which they can absorb information from the written word progressively exceeds what they can take in from listening to speech. For example, shown a videotape of a discussion between two students and verbatim written accounts of the same events, sixteen-year-olds recall more if they read than if they watch. More interesting, perhaps, is the finding that the written word was superior for all the children tested, regardless of their reading ability (Walker, in Perera, 1984, p. 163).

Studies of the development of spoken language reveal the emergence, during the years of schooling, of a range of complex grammatical constructions that are also involved in the creation of effective and dramatic writing. As she learns to read and write, the child's speech begins to 'inherit' structures encountered in written text. Consider, by way of an illustration, four 'stages' that have been discovered in children's attempts to utter complex sentences. I have taken this example from Romaine (1984).

This guy he owns the hotel he went to B.
This guy that he owns the hotel he went to B.
This guy that owns the hotel he went to B.
This guy that owns the hotel went to B.

Note too, as Karmiloff-Smith discovered with children's emerging command of determiners, how children again pass through a period of dysfluency and 'over marking' (in this case, with the 'redundant' use of pronouns) before they perfect the mature form of words.

In the last chapter, we considered various lines of evidence which suggested that children's developing skills as narrators and inform-ants emerge through the years of schooling. The child who is fortunate enough to achieve fluent levels of literacy has at her disposal a whole new range of words, linguistic structures and skills in planning which enable her to create interesting, informative, dramatic and *coherent* narrative. Such a child may draw upon and exploit two powerful bodies of expertise. On the one hand, she has her *voice*, perhaps the most versatile of musical instruments, rich in prosodic melody and embedded in bodily movements that help to orchestrate her interactions with her listeners. On the other, she has command over a range of literacy devices and structures that can be exploited in speech to make what she says dramatic, flexible, variable, versatile and, should she so wish, fast and efficient.

No matter what accent or dialect a child happens to speak, the achievement of fluent literacy, powers of narration and the ability to use language informatively offer her the same rewards. Speech that is, so to speak, parasitic on written language should not be dismissed as merely 'posh'. It provides children with a range of skills to help make what they say clear, interesting and informative.

Once functional levels of literacy are achieved, a reader is able to read text at a much faster rate than she normally hears speech. The grammatical structures in written language tend to be more 'compressed' (and, therefore, structurally more complex), and more varied than those of speech. The amount of 'redundancy' in written text (such as the frequency with which the same idea is repeated or paraphrased, for example) is usually lower than it is in speech. Unlike a listener, who is likely to be subjected to the frequent pauses, hesitations and false starts in verbal communication that provide the *time* that she needs to comprehend, the expert reader may proceed at her own pace. She may review, anticipate and skip, consulting, if she chooses, paragraphs, pages or chapters in advance of where she has read in order to get some sense of where the writer is 'going' (in academic texts, I always read the index and bibliography first). All these features of reading provide opportunities for greater efficiency and autonomy for a reader than a listener.

But what of children who do not reach levels of literacy that are deemed functional? Surveys of the levels of literacy in the USA suggest that around eighteen million American adults have reading ages below nine years. The Bullock report (commissioned by the UK Government) estimated that two million people in England and Wales are unable to read beyond this level. In practical terms, these figures give some measure of functional illiteracy – of adults who are unable, for example, to read tabloid newspapers, recipes and other everyday aids to communication and social adjustment. People who leave school with reading ages of eleven years or less have not made the 'shift' we have just been discussing. It would be interesting to know what consequences this has on their language and communication skills. Are they, like the children in Brown's studies, likely to face problems in narration and in information-giving situations? I don't believe we have the necessary evidence to reach such a conclusion, but it seems a fair bet.

The reasons for this state of affairs, for illiteracy, are, of course, the subject of heated debate. I do not intend to consider the issues involved in detail here. Many articles and books have been dedicated to the subject (Perera provides an excellent source of information) and there is not sufficient space to rehearse all the evidence and arguments here. However, I hope that the studies of language, communication and literacy that we have considered in this book will help to provide a psychological perspective on and a framework for thinking about such issues. Let me point out briefly how the ideas and findings we have been discussing can be used as a guide to help evaluate various theories of reading difficulties.

Why do some children find learning to read so difficult?

We have seen that learning to read involves a number of linguistic, social-communicative and intellectual demands. It seems reasonable to suppose that difficulty in meeting one or all of these might explain why some children have problems in learning to read and write. In view of the fact that the written code relates, albeit by a complex set of rules, to speech, we would predict that children who have problems either in hearing or in analysing the sound patterns of speech will face reading problems because they lack the necessary basis for learning how to 'encode' written symbols into speech sounds. Because written language does not map on to speech in any simple or direct way, we might also expect that these children will find it hard to use the written form in order to 'learn' about the structure of speech and language because the relations between the two forms of communication are too complex. Deaf children, as I have already said, face enormous problems in learning to read and only a tiny minority reach the eleven-year-old level when they leave school.

We have to remind ourselves that 'analysing' our own speech into the 'elements' that make possible the creation of a readable visual code is an intellectual achievement, not simply a 'natural' product of the ability to talk. Speech is an activity which fulfils purposes and needs, like informing, asking, refusing, explaining, negotiating and so on. The activity of speaking is, for most people most of the time, an automatic affair. In learning to read, language becomes an *object of attention or study* and, I have suggested, becoming literate changes the nature of our language and our conceptions of it. In learning how to write and read, children have to think 'objectively' about speech and learn how to analyse and, in writing, to represent it.

By this, I do not mean to imply that pre-literate children or non-literate peoples lack an explicit knowledge of their own language! Children's intuitive sense of the nature of language, though no doubt influenced and made more explicit by learning to read, probably comes about by quite different developmental routes, such as nursery rhymes, stories, word play and language games. For example, as part of a wide-ranging study of British children's play and folklore, the Opies (1959) documented a variety of children's play on words. Participation in these activities demands a subtle sense of the structure, functions and ambiguities present in language at a number of levels. Consider the following examples and reflect on what they imply about young children's implicit knowledge of language.

> Masculine, Feminine, Neuter,
> I went for a ride on my scooter.
> I bumped into the Queen
> And said, Sorry old bean,
> I forgot to toot-toot on my tooter.

> Sir is kind and sir is gentle.
> Sir is strong and sir is mental.

> Adam and Eve and Nipmewell
> Went in a boat to sea.
> Adam and Eve fell out,
> Who was left?

Although I have been stressing the role of literacy in the development of children's objective awareness of language, such widespread and sometimes ingenious word games demonstrate that children's knowledge of the sounds, structures and functions of language arise as a product of playful, everyday activity. Reading may help to sharpen, extend, develop and discipline their knowledge and use of language, but such word games, puns and the like suggest that most children are aware of the music of sound and the many possibilities (usually somewhat vindictive in intent) afforded by the rich ambiguity inherent in language and communication. Anthropologists have observed children in non-literate cultures playing games which also derive their fun and their sting from a play on words or from 'abuses' of language's more 'serious' functions (e.g. Schwartzman, 1978, p. 383). These observations, coupled with studies of word and sound play in babies and pre-school children, suggest that becoming aware of and exploiting the humorous possibilities offered by the ambiguous and metaphorical nature of speech is not simply a product of learning to read. Rather, an awareness of the various 'levels' and functions of language revealed in children's word play may be an important preparation for the achievement of literacy itself.

Some credibility for this view comes from several lines of research showing that some children who find learning to read very difficult are unable to do things like pick the 'odd man out' from triplets like 'fun, bun, man' (Bryant and Bradley, 1985). Perhaps, then, word play and language games perform an important role in laying the foundations for literacy (though I am not implying that this is their *purpose*, of course).

Several times throughout this book I have drawn attention to the way in which expertise in an activity is reflected in processes of attention, perceptual organization and memorization. What an expert is able to perceive as she observes an event that draws on her expertise is more organized, memorable and meaningful than that experienced by a novice. Put in other terms, the expert's 'speed of encoding' is faster than that of the novice. Basically, this term refers to the time taken by an individual to perceive, analyse and respond in some task-appropriate way to a perceptual event. So, the 'speed of encoding' of Grand Masters confronted by a chess configuration is faster than that of novices. As I said in chapter 3, Grand Masters do not have formidable general powers of perception and memory: their faster and more accurate reactions in such situations are attributable to special knowledge.

Slow encoding speeds when novices try, say, to read a word, take in a mathematical problem or even attempt to 'count' the number of objects in a small set, place limits on how much the novice can assimilate and memorize. The capacity to *perceive* and the ability to *perform* are, in such tasks, two aspects of a single process – one which, so to speak, follows a 'spiral path' in development. As the child becomes practised in acting upon some component or components of the task, her actions become increasingly automatic (though it has to be admitted that we do not yet understand the biological processes that make this possible). However, developing 'automaticity' means that the child no longer has to consciously *attend* to the practised elements of her task activity. 'Automated' actions may be performed without the need for constant monitoring or awareness. As some aspect of the developing skill is automated, the learner is left free to pay attention to some other aspect of the task at hand. She 'perceives' more and can concentrate on perfecting some other feature of her performance. So the metaphorical spiral grows in diameter as expertise develops.

The problems of novices may bemuse an expert. Grand Masters cannot empathize with the beginner's problems and do not understand why the novice is unable to *see* and recall what is, for them, so obvious. Similarly, the problems facing children when asked to attend, to 'see' and hold in mind what they read may be difficult to grasp by someone who is an expert reader. As we would expect, children who read well are able to 'encode' and comprehend the written word *faster* than poor readers. What we do not understand (though several *theories* exist) is why some children, despite instruction and practice, remain slow encoders. Many reading schemes exist to try to overcome such problems and there is a great deal of controversy, both about the origins of these problems and possible solutions to them.

We might expect to find other sources of difficulty for children at 'higher levels' of textual organization. The various demands – at the level of vocabulary, syntax, use of 'interlinguistic' processes, together with the problems of planning and organizing text – that we have been discussing may create several different barriers to the achievement of literary expertise. What is still unclear is whether the reason why some children do not discover and *learn* how to write and read text, say, beyond the level achieved by the average eleven-year-old, lies with their 'encoding' abilities. As I have said, slow encoding acts as a barrier to higher levels of expertise. Or is it the case, as some students of reading believe, that their problems stem from the fact that they have had insufficient experience or exposure to the more complex uses and structures of language involved in more advanced text? I asked in the last chapter, for example, if poorly developed skills in creating narrative and speaking informatively inhibit the development of literacy. I don't think we know.

Structure and purpose in written language

Perera demonstrates in some detail how the structural complexity of written language varies according to the specific communicative purpose it serves. Who is a text written for and what are its readers intended to gain from it?

There are marked differences in the organization and structure of text written for different *purposes*. The style and grammatical structure that are relevant to the creation of an aide memoire written to remind oneself, a letter written to a friend, a novel or historical text, or a worksheet outlining a scientific procedure, differ in many features, gross and fine. Similarly, the intellectual demands involved in reading and writing such very different texts vary. How stringent are the requirements made on the writer's ability to envisage and take account of her intended audience in each case? What background knowledge will a reader need to possess in order to make sense of what is written?

Perera suggests that many children find reading and writing difficult in more demanding contexts because they lack the relevant experiences that help them to understand both the reasons *why* different types of writing exist and the way in which these variations in the purpose of the intended communication lead to demands for different styles of writing and, in consequence, entail a knowledge of special linguistic devices. Whereas children may understand some of these purposes (e.g. writing to a friend) and may draw upon their everyday experiences to make sense of the demands involved, they may not have listened to a historical text or episodes of scientific discourse, nor realize why and how people write about such things. Evidence about the effects of home circumstances on children's reading development demonstrates that access to books at home and the experience of being regularly *read to* are positive indicators of likely progress – more about this in the final chapter. Perhaps the fact that we do not typically read *academic* texts to children means that they do not develop any intuitive sense of what such things *sound* like. Perhaps if they did, processes of self-instruction, working towards a goal that is intuitively recognizable, might be set in motion.

A somewhat similar line of thought has motivated recent attempts to help children with reading and writing problems in the United States (Palinscar and Brown, 1984). This work, motivated by Vygotsky's theory of development and by his writings on literacy, starts from the assumption that some children fail to advance beyond the initial stages of reading because they do not know how to 'interact' with text – i.e. they do not become actively engaged in attempts to *interpret* what they read. Briefly, the intervention techniques used involve bringing into the open, making public and 'audible', ways of interacting with text that skilled readers usually undertake automatically and soundlessly. So, for instance, the teacher discusses a text with a child, asking aloud the sorts of questions a sentence or paragraph might provoke (though not necessarily asking the *child* questions at this stage). The teacher might speculate aloud about what is likely to come later in the text or puzzle over an ambiguity and ask how it might be resolved. The child is later encouraged to play the 'teacher's role' and to work alongside and discuss texts with other children. Children taught in this way made marked progress over a handful of formal teaching sessions. They were in the seventh grade (this probably means they were aged around 12 to 13 years) and were described by their teachers as having severe problems of reading comprehension.

At the beginning of the study, the children involved were found, on tests of reading comprehension, to be in the bottom 7 per cent of their year. After the study, their success rate on independent tests of comprehension rose from 10 per cent to 85 per cent success, near average for their grade level. How far and to what extent such methods might work for all children with reading problems we do not know. It is important to note that these children were described by the researchers as having 'decoding skills' (or 'word-attack' skills) that were normal for their grade. Whether the same teaching techniques would work for children with problems of decoding we must doubt. However, it is worth noting that even though the children were able to decode, their *teachers* persisted, before the study, in attempts to teach these skills. The teachers were not attempting to work on the *real* problems facing the child. Their implicit theory of what literacy entails, and hence their views on the nature of reading problems, presumably did not extend to the processes we have been discussing in this chapter.

The argument underlying these studies is that children who find difficulty in learning how to 'interact' with text can learn how to do so if these normally unobservable processes are made an *explicit* part of what is taught. Following Vygotsky, the argument is that the children in this study progressively 'internalized' self-regulatory activities until these became an automatic part of their own reading. This is why their own performance, both on tests and in class, improved. Put in other terms, these children were exposed to processes implicated in *expert* performance that are usually invisible and inaudible. By attempting specifically to *teach* these activities, children who were not learning them as a 'natural' response to teaching and self-instruction were helped to discover and master them. There are now many educators and researchers, including those involved in teaching both reading and mathematics, who are currently emphasizing the need for teachers to lay greater stress in their teaching on the activities involved in skilled self-regulation. The hope is that by making what are usually *implicit* aspects of writing, reading and thinking more *explicit* they can be communicated to the would-be learner.

If heeded, the demands such pleas make on teachers are formidable. I will explore some of the justifications for making such demands, and the implications they have for the process of education, in the remaining chapters.

Summary

We began this chapter by discussing logic and its relation to the study of reasoning. We have ended it with a brief discussion of reading problems. The juxtaposition of these two seemingly very different topics was motivated by claims about the impact of schooling and literacy on learning and thinking. I have tried to identify some of the intellectual, linguistic and interpersonal demands involved in learning to read and write. Children must learn how to perfect a range of intellectual abilities; to plan, self-regulate, edit and self-correct in order to write coherent text. They must be able to anticipate the needs of a reader and this, as we have seen, leads to a range of very specific *linguistic* demands. The vocabulary, grammar and organization of well-written text differ in important ways from those involved in verbal communication. Earlier in the chapter, I mentioned Olson's view that the achievement of literacy, both in a culture and an individual, is what makes possible the emergence of formal, logical thinking (recall, too, my comments on the limited import of such special ways of thinking).

Briefly, non-technically, and with apologies to Olson for a rather rough treatment of his thesis, the argument proceeds as follows. In learning to read, children have to *reflect upon* the structures of language. Their knowledge of words, syntax and the process of communication becomes more 'objective' as a result. They read about things that they have never experienced, which may be hypothetical, imaginary and abstract. To achieve this end, they must be able to use and understand language without many of the contextual bases for achieving mutual comprehension that exist in speech. Their attention, in short, is drawn to the *syntax* of language. Because the written word endures, and permits review, analysis and comparisons between ideas that may have been written down at very different times, any *inconsistencies* implicit in text – contradictions, for example – are more likely to come to light than they are from speech which is fleeting and not memorized *literally*. The increased powers of memory and the greater opportunity for detailed *analysis* of language afforded by written text enables the literate culture to reflect upon and evaluate its competing ideas, histories, opportunities, experiences and so on.

So an explicit awareness of the formal *structure* of language, an *analytic* attitude to communication, fostered by the written word, combine to produce a stage-like change in thinking. The tests, rules and practices implicit in practical logic, what Piagetians refer to as concrete operational thinking, may now be applied to (hypothetical) propositions found in text. Statements about events or things that have never been directly *experienced* can be tested for consistency or conflict with other statements. Statements thus become *propositions*. Grammatical syntax enables the generation of 'non-sensical ideas' (like 'Whales with pink feet'). Such ideas can be tested against each other to see if they are mutually compatible (for instance, do they lead to very different predictions for action?). If, say, two propositions, 'Man is an animal', 'Animals have four feet', lead to contradiction, then the reasons may be sought and the scientific investigation of the logic of linguistic classification begins.

When psychologists pose strange, 'logical' problems to members of other cultures or to functionally illiterate children, they demand a degree of 'decontextualization' and *analytic* attention to language that are not normally found in everyday, verbal communication. In this view, then, literacy (though I would also add narrative, autonomous speech and information-giving) 'explains' phenomena associated with formal logic and the 11 to 13 shift.

I hope that I have now managed to convey some sense as to why many students of children's thinking and learning place so much stress on terms like 'disembedding', 'decontextualization' and 'decentration' as important landmarks charting the course of intellectual development. As children's experience of communication moves from talk at home, through stories, classroom conversation, to educational narrative, information-giving, question-answering, and into reading and writing, they are enjoined to rely increasingly on the content and structure of language. While they do, as we have seen, meet a wide variety of special *linguistic* problems as they make this journey, many of the demands they face are also *intellectual* in nature. As they learn how to plan, evaluate and regulate their own attempts to learn and inform through both the spoken and written word, they are exposed to, and if they are lucky, they assimilate, a range of interpersonal and cognitive abilities. Many children fall by the wayside. Some possible reasons for this are discussed more fully in the final chapter.

Chapter 7

The mathematical mind

We now look at some of the common misconceptions that children entertain about mathematics, and examine these in the light of the theories of intellectual development that have been the focus of earlier chapters. In particular, we consider what is involved in teaching and learning aspects of 'abstract' mathematics. We also discuss how and why many children seem to make slow progress in learning mathematics and leave school barely numerate. This leads us on to a discussion of the 'relevance' of mathematics to everyday life and to a consideration of motivation for learning. We also compare and contrast early linguistic development with mathematics learning to identify some of the factors that make mathematics hard to master. Finally, we consider the role of discussion in teaching the foundations of mathematical reasoning.

Teaching and learning mathematics

In the preceding three chapters, we have been considering a range of issues revolving around the development of language and communication. But language is only one of the systems of symbols that provide tools for thought. Piaget, as we know, considers action and the operations that are constructed through it, not language, as central to the development of intelligence. Vygotsky adopts a somewhat different stance: as we saw in chapter 1, he argued that the developmental origins of language and thought are separate. Although he agreed with Piaget's stress on the importance of activity as the basis for practical intelligence he argued that, around the third year of life, language intersects with non-verbal thought to form the foundations for the development of verbal reasoning and self-regulation. From this time on, language starts to play a fundamental, formative role in intellectual development. However, non-verbal thinking remains. Not all symbolic activity requires language. Art, arithmetic, skill in sport and many other activities may proceed adaptively and intelligently without the involvement of verbal thought. Consider, for example, Einstein's views on the relations between language and creativity revealed in the following quotation. The distrust of premature attempts to *verbalize* new thoughts which he expresses is echoed in the writings of many creative individuals (e.g. Ghiselin, 1952):

> The words or the language, as they are written or spoken, do not seem to play any role in my mechanism of thought . . . in thought are certain signs and more or less clear images which can be 'voluntarily' reproduced and combined . . . the elements are, in my case, visual and some of muscular type . . . conventional signs and words have to be sought for laboriously only in a secondary stage.

The fact that some forms of activity, including some ways of thinking, do not implicate language does not necessarily imply that they are not influenced by communication and teaching, however. In considering the relation between *communication* and the development of knowledge, we have to discuss more than the issue of speech and its role in thinking. For example, some deaf children with a very limited command of spoken and written language perform as well as the best of their hearing peers on tests of mathematical ability (provided that the tests used are not couched in complex written language). Even so, the average deaf child leaves school in the UK performing in mathematics at a level typical of twelve-year-old hearing children (Wood et al., 1984). Although there is evidence showing that deaf children do not seem to require 'inner speech' or verbal reasoning to do very well in mathematics, the vast majority lag well behind their hearing peers. They find learning more difficult because the process of *communication* with their teachers is difficult. Their acquisition of *knowledge* is consequently impeded (Wood, *in press*). However, even with hearing children there is reason to suppose that communications with *their* teachers also generate considerable though less severe problems in lessons on mathematics, as we shall see.

Statements of discontent with the standards achieved in mathematics have been voiced in many tongues. The following quotation, from a Dutch scholar (Wolters, 1986), echoes sentiments expressed by people in many other countries.

> At the present time there is no teacher who can actually say that all is well with the teaching of arithmetic.
> There are far too many children who dislike arthimetic or worse, children who think it is a 'stupid' school subject. With

relatively few exceptions, this situation is quite general and has to be taken for granted.

Mathematics is difficult to learn and hard to teach. Perhaps one of the reasons for the popularity of Piaget's views on intellectual development was the reassurance it seemed to offer in identifying children's 'natural' capacities to construct the fundamental conceptual basis for mathematical thinking. The objection, that instruction too often involves attention to procedures and a neglect of conceptual understanding, can be seen as a criticism of many approaches to the teaching of mathematics. But it also inspires some hope that better methods can be invented. Piaget's emphasis on the importance of relevant activity and self-directed problem-solving as the proper developmental basis for more abstract conceptual understanding is shared by many students of child development, educational theorists and teachers. Where agreement ends, and argument begins, is on the importance of instruction, both informal and formal, at home and in school, in helping children to make mathematical *sense* of their experiences. How active should teachers be, for example, in aiding a child in his problem-solving and his conceptual constructions? Very active, as we shall see.

Bruner (1966a, 1966b, 1971) argues that instruction is a necessary requirement if a child's spontaneous activities are to be transformed into symbolic, rational thinking. He shares Piaget's view that action is the starting place for the formation of abstract, symbolic thinking (like that involved in solving mathematical equations, for example) but does not agree with the notion that the child is *unable* to grasp the conceptual relations between practical activity and more abstract levels of thinking before a particular stage is reached. Rejecting Piaget's emphasis on logical operations and, with this, the view that the evolution of symbolic thinking is constrained by stages of development, Bruner offers a different perspective on both the process of coming to *know* and the nature of learning. He distinguishes between three 'modes' in which knowledge is expressed or 'represented'. He labels his three modes of representation 'enactive', 'iconic' and 'symbolic'. Enactive representation is similar to Piaget's notion of practical intelligence. For example, a child who can group sets of objects according to one or more criteria, say by size, colour or shape, is displaying *enactively* a level of understanding of classification. If children can imagine or draw pictures that *depict* the outcome of sets of actions, then they are using *iconic* representations. Basically, the defining characteristic of this form of 'knowledge representation' is that the representation created must bear a *one-to-one* correspondence with the event or activity that it depicts. I will give some concrete examples later.

Numbers themselves, verbal and written symbols, do not bear a *one-to-one* relationship with the entities they depict. Similarly, symbols like '+' '×' and '−' do not, in themselves, bear any *perceptual* resemblance to the operations to which they refer. And, like function words in language, they possess several different meanings as mathematical symbols, depending upon the sort of problem (e.g. dividing whole numbers or dividing fractions) involved (Skemp, 1971). Like Piaget, Bruner conceptualizes the development of knowledge in terms of growing 'abstraction' and arbitrariness in the symbolic content of thought, but he does not share Piaget's view that different modes of representation only become available to children at specific stages. So, for instance, whereas Piagetian theory implies that children will only be able to perform tasks involving the use of abstract hypothetical propositions or algebraic notation when they reach the stage of formal operations, Bruner argues that much younger children can, given appropriate instruction, learn how to both perform and understand such intellectual activities.

In the last chapter, I used the concept of the 'moment' applied to the workings of a beam balance to try to illustrate Piaget's distinction between concrete and formal operations. Bruner and his colleague Kenney (1965), used the same apparatus to show that eight-year-old children can be taught to understand this principle in relation to the quadratic function (the connection, I hope, will become clear in a little while). Let me outline the nature of their experiment and the instructional techniques they employed.

The first materials used with the children (the researchers worked with a class of eight-year-olds in their own school) were wooden blocks in various shapes and sizes, like those illustrated in figure 7.1. One goal was to introduce and exemplify the notion of a 'variable' and a symbolic means to represent it (i.e. 'x'). The children were encouraged first to play with the blocks and to arrange them to produce specific configurations and patterns. The purpose of this was to help them to construct, in action, an *intuitive* understanding of the way in which different physical arrangements of the material serve to create different configurational outcomes, e.g. to find out how they might be arranged to produce squares and rectangles of various sizes. In Bruner's terms, they helped the children to create a wealth of *enactive* representations of action–configuration relations.

The researcher-cum-teacher continued until the children had discovered the fact that *squares* of different sizes could be created by putting sets of four blocks together, as illustrated in figure 7.1. Bruner's view is that through active, protracted, guided manipulation with the material, children were helped to construct *iconic* representations. Diagrams and pictures were also used to help illustrate how particular groupings of blocks could be used, say, to build squares and rectangles of different sizes. The instructor introduces *symbolic* reference to the blocks and configurations. For instance, if we ignore the relative sizes of the blocks being used, we can appreciate the fact that larger 'squares' can always be created with sets of four blocks, provided that these meet certain criteria. There is, so to speak, an 'algebra' which describes the squares so constructed that is independent of the sizes involved. Learning that the relationship between the four constituent blocks holds no matter what sizes are involved is, perhaps, easier to do in reference to *drawings* of the blocks than to the blocks themselves. An iconic representation need not and usually does not render a *faithful* or perfect 'model' of that which it represents, as children of this age can appreciate, since their drawings of cars, people, buildings and other things are not usually the same size as the things they represent. Although in one-to-one correspondence, iconic representations may represent *trans-formations* of some features of the things they depict, difference in absolute size being one example.

The children are asked to entertain the idea that a block, like that depicted in figure 7.1, can be called an '*x*-square'. Similarly, they are asked to think about the small strips as '$x \times 1$' pieces. The small square piece then 'becomes' a square of unit size (1×1). Now, how can the large square be described? Well, it comprises an '$x \times x$' square, two '$x \times 1$' strips and a '1×1' square. What these pieces create is a larger square, each side of which is '$x + 1$' – an $(x + 1)$ square or $(x + 1)^2$. Put into 'conventional' notation, an equation emerges, namely $(x + 1)^2 = x^2 + 2x + 1$. By referring to blocks of different size, it can be shown that this *algebraic* representation holds no matter what value 'x' takes. Providing its chosen value remains

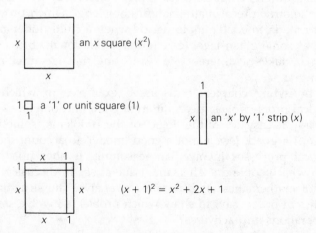

an x square (x^2)

$1\,\square$ a '1' or unit square (1)

an 'x' by '1' strip (x)

$(x + 1)^2 = x^2 + 2x + 1$

Figure 7.1 The quadratic function: $(x + 1)^2 = x^2 + 2x + 1$

constant through the activity of making up one configuration, the equation represents the outcome.

Given time, suitable materials and effective instruction, then, the children were helped to create and solve equations involving the quadratic function. It can be argued, of course, that the children did not really understand the notion of equations, variables and the way in which the quadratic function refers to the growth of the area covered by squares. In fact, this proposition is not easy to evaluate. What we accept as evidence for 'understanding' itself depends on our theory of knowledge. The usual test of understanding is to see if the learner can generalize the *principles* involved. Can he solve different problems which involve the 'same' logic? The problem is, what we accept as the 'same' logic depends upon our theory of what that logic is!

Recall how, in discussions of language development, I argued that questions such as 'At what age do children understand words like "come" and "go"?' are theoretically inadvisable because, involving words and grammatical structures that are pluri-functional, their meanings in different contexts make different demands on children. Such a question lacks a sensible resolution. Rather, one must qualify it with another question, one about the *purpose* for which, and the context in which, words like 'come' and 'go' are being used. One can argue in a similar way about principles in mathematics. An expert mathematician 'sees' common patterns and principles in many phenomena whose *appearances* are very different. The non-expert does not. Differing levels of knowledge and expertise will be revealed by the extent to which individuals are able to 'uncover' and understand such commonalities. In Piagetian terms, knowledge is revealed to the extent that *invariances* and *equivalences* are appreciated despite very different appearances. Piaget offered a very specific theory of the structure of mathematical knowledge which provides one set of criteria to enable us to decide when a child understands the world at some given level (e.g. formal operational). Bruner, as we shall see, takes a different view and one that is rather more difficult to grasp.

In the preceding chapter, I discussed examples in which the 'same' logical problem was given different content. Sometimes that content made it easy to *see* the 'logic' of the problems, sometimes not. Hence, I argued, *logic* is not a good 'model' to account for the psychological processes involved in reasoning. It does not 'map' well on to what people do. The same issue arises in discussions of the 'logic of mathematics'. Is it possible to analyse the structure of mathematics in order, say, to show which problems involve similar mental operations and activities?

What we face, when we compare Piaget and Bruner, is nothing less than two competing theories of knowledge. Let us explore the

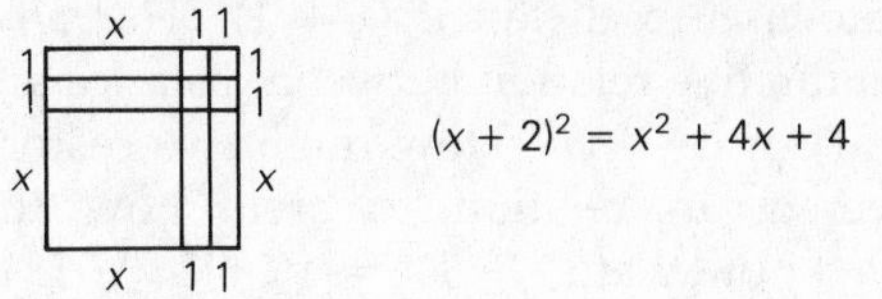

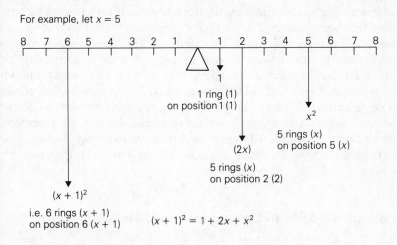

$$(x + 2)^2 = x^2 + 4x + 4$$

Figure 7.2   The quadratic function: $(x + 2)^2 = x^2 + 4x + 4$

issue further with reference to the Bruner and Kenney study of instruction. The quadratic function provides a way of representing, calculating and 'modelling' the effects on the area of a square of unit increase in its dimensions. Add two sets of units, to create an $(x + 2)^2$, and the outcome depicted in figure 7.2 emerges. See what happens when we add three sets of units, then four, and so on. But the quadratic function serves as a model and calculus for other phenomena in nature, including the behaviour of a beam balance.

Examine the situation depicted in figure 7.3. Let $x = 5$. Suppose, before this, we had on each side of the beam, five rings or weights placed together at five units of distance from the fulcrum, then we had $(x \times x)$, i.e. 25, on each side. Clearly, the beam should balance. Then, as depicted in figure 7.3, on the left-hand side of the balance we increase both the weights and the distance of the weights by one unit in each case. We can represent the modification to weight as

For example, let $x = 5$

Figure 7.3   The beam balance. Having discovered with instruction that distance and weight are in a commutative relationship – e.g. that one ring on position 5 balances with five rings (each of equal weight) on position 1, children eventually discover how they apply the quadratic function to this case

$(x + 1)$ and likewise to distance $(x + 1)$. The *product* of the two (recall the commutative relation between distance and weight) yields $(x + 1) \times (x + 1)$ or $(x + 1)^2$. How might we restore balance? Well, having discovered, in relation to area, how to 'unpack' such expressions, we know that $(x + 1)^2 = x^2 + 2x + 1$. Will the equation 'work' for the beam balance? If, say, on the right-hand side we leave the five units of weight where they are (x^2) and create $2x$ by putting five weights at two units from the fulcrum and place one weight at one unit (1×1) what happens? Balance is restored:

$$(x + 1)^2 = x^2 + 2x + 1$$
$$(5 + 1)^2 = 25 + 10 + 1 = 36$$

Having helped children to discover one 'application' of the quadratic function, Bruner and Kenney went on to show that they could be helped to *generalize* what they had learned to a new context. The claim is not that children could immediately 'see' the commonalities (would we?) but that, with relatively little instruction, they could be helped to discover them. The materials used by Bruner and Kenney in this study were invented by a mathematician and teacher, Dienes (e.g. Dienes, 1960; Dienes and Jeeves, 1970). He has created a range of such tasks and activities and an approach to mathematics teaching which involves children working together in groups which are given a fair degree of autonomy.

If one accepts the fact that eight-year-olds can be taught to use abstract, algebraic mathematical procedures and can *understand* how they function (in some contexts), then the view that such lessons are best or properly left until later falls. It may not be considered *worthwhile* to teach such things at eight – other lessons may be judged more important. Teachers may not be sufficiently knowledgeable and well trained to undertake such instruction. But, if one accepts Bruner's theory, the reason *why* children are not taught or do not learn how to use and understand abstract mathematical procedures is not that they are theoretically *incapable* of doing so. Any reason sought must exclude an appeal to their 'natural' abilities.

Procedural skills and conceptual understanding

I have already commented several times on the nature of the divide between an ability to execute procedures and the achievement of a conceptual grasp of the purpose that such procedures serve. Bruner and Piaget are in basic agreement about the fact that procedures must ultimately be grounded in practical activities if they are to be understood. Here I will explore the view that the extent of the divide between these two features of learning in mathematics has proved, for many children, too wide to bridge.

The literature that documents the kinds of mistakes and misconceptions that children make and entertain about mathematics is far too large to review here. Several detailed accounts already exist (e.g. Bell et al., 1983). What I propose to do is to identify some general conclusions that this work has led to before trying to interpret how and why some errors come about on the basis of the different theoretical perspectives on learning that we have been considering. Can we identify and explain the common mistakes that children make? Can we understand how and why these come about? Can we point to aspects of the process of teaching that probably fail, or others that might succeed, in helping children to overcome their problems? These are the questions that concern us in the remainder of the chapter.

The most extensive recent studies that I know of concerning children's understanding of mathematics are the product of two large-scale surveys of mathematical achievement in England and Wales. The main findings of one, undertaken by the Assessment of Performance Unit, are published in six volumes. These list both achievement levels and common errors made by children aged from eleven to fifteen on a large number of different mathematical tasks (Department of Education and Science, 1980–82). The second study, which I will draw on more heavily here, was undertaken by a research team working on 'Concepts in Secondary Mathematics and Science' (CSMS) at Chelsea College, London (see Hart, 1981, for an overview). These surveys enable us to assess the things that children learn or have failed to learn up to eleven years of age. As we shall see, some of the misconceptions that children entertain run very deep and suggest that the early *foundations* of mathematical knowledge are often very shaky.

Mathematical abilities and mathematical misconceptions

In the CSMS study, Hart and her colleagues examined the mathematical achievements of, and the errors made by, some 10,000 children aged from top junior (eleven years of age) to 15-year-old secondary school pupils. The tests used were specially developed by the team. They cover a range of topics including measurement, number operations, place value, decimals and fractions. Not all of the ten areas investigated (e.g. vectors and matrices) involved the youngest groups of children, since such things are not normally taught in British primary schools. I will concentrate here on the topics that are included in the primary school curriculum.

The tests provided a measure of children's levels of performance in the ten mathematical domains studied and revealed many common weaknesses and widespread, persistent problems. Testing was followed up with more intensive work with individual children who were asked to talk about their techniques for solving various problems. These interviews provided insights into the nature of children's understanding and misconceptions and provided a basis for inferences about how and why they find specific aspects of arithmetic and mathematics difficult.

One of the general conclusions to emerge from the study is gloomy but becoming typical. 'The overwhelming impression obtained is that mathematics is a *very difficult* subject for most children.' The investigators also note that the introduction of 'modern mathematics', motivated by a desire to engender greater *conceptual* understanding in children about the 'foundations' of mathematics, has not succeeded. 'It was hoped that a child faced with a new mathematical system might ask "What are the elements; which operations combine those elements; are the commutative, associative and distributive laws applicable etc?" This aim does *not* appear to have been fulfilled.'

The CSMS group developed some rather complex statistical procedures to identify four main stages in children's mathematical achievement. These stages represent different groupings of mathematical tasks and operations that tend to 'go together' in performance. They are not stages in the Piagetian sense, so we cannot say, for example, that children at CSMS stage 1 lack certain operations of mind possessed by children at higher stages. The groupings of the things that children can and cannot do at different ages and levels of achievement 'emerged' from the data. Consequently, it is not possible for me to give a simple, general picture of what the stages are. Instead I will try to illustrate some of the things that children can and cannot do at different levels of performance.

The first two stages, in which approximately half the children remained throughout their years of secondary schooling, were characterized as involving knowledge of a 'form of social arithmetic or mathematical literacy'. Children, about half of whom were 'arrested' at these stages, are able to perform most of the 'basic' operations (i.e. $+$, $-$, $\div$, $\times$) but only on small (1 to 12) whole numbers. Even at this level many still find multiplication difficult (more so than division; which, as the team point out, goes against the received wisdom). These children often 'avoid' multiplication and substitute addition. So, for instance, asked to multiply 5×3, they add five to itself three times. This strategy may be effective with small numbers, but once large integers are involved or the problem involves fractions or decimals, the procedure breaks down. Some children, faced with a fraction, may resort to the simple expedient of adding together all numbers at the top and then adding

The signpost shows that it is 29 miles west to Grange and 58 miles east to Barton.

How do you work out how many miles it is from Grange to Barton?

$29 + 58$	$58 \div 29$	$58 - 29$	29×2
$29 \div 58$	$58 + 29$	58×29	$87 - 29$

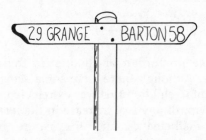

Figure 7.4 The 'signpost' problem

together the numbers at the bottom, so $\frac{3}{4} \times \frac{4}{5}$ yields the 'solution' $\frac{7}{9}$.

About half of the children in the sample displayed, at best, only a tenuous and extremely limited basic understanding of the number system. They did not realize, for instance, that between 1.4 and 2.3, as between any two numbers, there are a theoretically *infinite* number of other numbers. Only children who reach the fourth stage, some 30 per cent of the fifteen-year-olds and a mere 2 per cent of those aged thirteen, display this level of sophistication. Similarly, children in the early stages find it difficult to handle any degree of abstraction and many do not even *recognize* which operations they should perform on a verbally stated problem. For example, one type of problem used shows a signpost displaying the names and distances of two towns that lie in 'opposite' directions. The children are asked to say how far apart the two towns are and shown eight possible solutions to the problem (figure 7.4). They are asked to *identify* the operation that would yield a correct answer. The child in the following sample interview was trying to solve a problem of the type illustrated in figure 7.4, but different distances (18 and 23 miles) were involved.

Tracey (age 11)   Does it mean that is, er, 18 kilometres to Grange and 23 kilometres to, er, Barton, does that mean that it's from the same place?

Interviewer   That's right: from this signpost here. It's 18 miles that way to Grange and 23 miles that way to Barton.

Tracey   Take 18 away from 23 . . . . 5.

The problems that children face when they have not only to do 'sums' but determine what *type* of mathematics a verbally stated problem involves are well documented (Bell et al., 1983). The CSMS data show that, for 'a significant proportion of secondary-aged children, it is not simply the case that they are unable to *generate* a solution. They cannot even *recognize* one.'

For many children, progress in mathematics appears to be a very slow affair. For instance, about 40 per cent of children in the first year of secondary school were unable to solve the problem:

$$2312$$
$$-547$$

About the same proportion of children in the fourth year also failed such items. Although there were some signs of progress, for around 50 per cent of children this was extremely limited. Evidence, amongst this group, of any real increase in the *understanding* of the foundations of mathematics and the nature of number was conspicuous by its rarity.

Mathematical discourse and everyday language

Verbally stated questions not only demand an ability to work out the nature of the problem. Children have to understand what the *words* used mean in mathematical terms! Consider, for example, humble words like 'share', 'bigger' and 'straight'. A problem like '10 sweets are *shared* between two boys so that one has 4 more than the other. How many does each get?' provoked, from one child interviewed, the protest, 'That's wrong, if you *share* they each have 5, so one can't have 4 more'. Similarly, in graphical problems, 'straight' for many children means only a line that is perpendicular to the edge of a page, so a slanting line, by their definition, can't be 'straight'. Terms used in mathematics are often 'parasitic' upon words used in everyday discourse. But they have special and technical mathematical meanings which, if not *negotiated* with children in activity and discourse, cause problems. Children's interpretations of what they mean, based on everyday language, are often at variance with what they mean in mathematical terms. For example, prepositions like 'into' and 'by' should invoke specific procedures when they are implicated in maths problems like '391 *into* 17' and '17 divided *by* 391'. Confusion over the meanings of such terms was common in the CSMS data. Children tend to use these prepositions, for example, as though they have the same meaning as 'shared between'. They did not appreciate the very different *interpretations* of problems that these little words should imply. The 'pluri-functional' nature of many linguistic terms has been discussed in earlier chapters. When used technically, as they are in mathematics and other disciplines, the meanings of many common words expand even more.

Unless the connections between mathematical terms and procedures are firm in children's understanding, they will, quite naturally, fall back on everyday, plausible interpretations of problems which implicate them. Consider how many more times they hear and use such words in everyday discourse, and it is not surprising that they should need considerable experience of their 'concrete' meanings in mathematics to learn and memorize what procedures they should evoke.

A final example of the important relations between everyday language and mathematical discourse would be amusing, if its implications for the (secondary school) child involved were not so serious:

Interviewer Do you know what volume means?
Child Yes.
I. Could you explain to me what it means?
C. Yes, it's what is on the knob of the television set.

Instruction, interview and dialogue

In chapter 3, I discussed instruction viewed as 'the contingent control of learning'. Recall the experiments with the construction task in which we compared and evaluated different ways of teaching. Techniques of instruction, whether employed by mothers or an experimenter, that relied almost exclusively on either *telling* children what to do or simply *showing* them how to do it did not work. Rather, the meaning of verbal instructions – what instructions like 'Get the four biggest blocks' entailed *in practice* – had to be negotiated. By helping children to understand what such expressions and words meant in relation to the specific task at hand, it was possible to teach them how to do it.

In addition to the notion of instructional contingency, I also introduced and illustrated a number of teaching functions such as 'highlighting' critical features of a task that children 'overlook', 'reminding' them about previous relevant experiences, and breaking the problem down into more manageable sub-tasks. The CSMS interviews with children, which were designed to help to explain how and why they make 'common' errors, can also be viewed as a form of *discourse* that shares many similarities with verbal instruction. The interviews can be examined and interpreted as examples of teaching. Consider, for example, that interviews are designed to help people to reveal their knowledge and thoughts. As such, they form a starting place for discovering where the 'learner is at', a crucial basis for effective instruction. Perhaps we would do well to regard expertise in *interview techniques* as an essential aspect of teaching.

There are several examples given in the CSMS publication of children discovering how to solve a problem that, initially, they got wrong. The reasons for their errors were numerous, but the simple expedient of discussing how they were thinking about and trying to solve a problem sometimes cleared up the source of difficulty.

For example, in the following excerpt, the interviewer simply *reminds* a child of a critical 'step' in the problem that she has 'overlooked'. The child is trying to subtract 28 from 51 (another preposition, notice).

Maria	Do you take the top from the bottom? (Tries, and takes one from eight, writing seven in the answer). Can't take five from two – have to take one of these (indicates 1 in 51).
Interviewer	Explain what you did there.
M	Crossed out the one (of 51) and put nought (in its place) and put the one on there (i.e. to the left of five to make 15).
I	What was that to do? Why did you do that?
M	I put one on the tens.
I	OK. Right, now what are you going to do?
M	That's wrong.
I	Why is it wrong?
M	I'm supposed to take 15 from two and not two from fifteen.
I	Can we do it the other way? Can we do it this time so that we take the bottom one from the top one?
M	Is that how we're supposed to do it?
I	That's how you usually do it, yes.

Maria then went on to solve the problem and explained how 'borrowing' of the ten works.

Another child, tackling one of the 'signpost' problems referred to above, was helped to understand the problem by being invited to think about it (represent it to herself) by 'imagining' herself at a cross-road. When this did not work, the interviewer reformulated the problem in 'simpler' terms. By inviting the child to 're-view' the problem in a simplified, more context-dependent, immediate and 'concrete' form, she was led to recognize the *type* of problem she was dealing with and thence to formulate the correct answer to the original, more difficult problem. Note too how the child decides, even before she attempts the problem, that she is likely to fail.

Hilary	Oh no, I'm no good at these . . . you times those two together don't you? . . . No, you can't . . . (long pause)
I	Imagine standing there and you're looking up at the

signpost, OK? Now that way it's 18 kilometres to Grange and that way it's 23 to Barton: we want to know the distance between the two.

H   23

I   23?

H   (Long pause) . . . I'm not very good at doing kilometres . . .

I   Let's try something else. We're sitting right here, right? Say someone said it was three paces to the window and it was five paces to the window that way . . .

H   You'd add them.

I   How far from one window to the other?

H   (Long pause) . . . eight.

I   Yes, what are you doing?

H   Adding them!

Asking a child to *approximate*, to think of the problem in general terms before tackling its procedural complexities, provides, as in the following example, a *sense* of the solution and leads on to effective problem solving. The child is trying to multiply 5.13 by 10:

Billy   You can't put a nought on the end of there as it's a decimal . . . (long pause)

I   How big, roughly?

B   50 . . . 51.3

Children have to *regulate* their own thinking in mathematics, as in any other effective problem solving situation. They have to learn that 'appearances' may be deceptive and that the first answer that happens to 'pop into their head', or the initial conceptualization of the problem's *nature* that comes to mind, may not necessarily be appropriate. Overcoming impulsive first thoughts and *re-viewing* one's initial attempt at solution does not come easily or readily to some children. In the following example, a child (aged 13) had already decided that 8 multiplied by 0.4 yields a larger number than 8 divided by 0.4 (illustrating, in passing, another of children's misconceptions, that 'multiplication makes it bigger'). The child is shown three pairs of sums and asked to 'Ring the one which gives the BIGGER answer'. The sums are:

(a) 8×4 or $8 \div 4$
(b) 8×0.4 or $8 \div 0.4$
(c) 0.8×0.4 or $0.8 \div 0.4$.

Left to her own devices, the child placed rings around all the multiplications. Asked some time later:

I   Why did you choose the others first time?

Fung Mei   'Cos they're times and it always seems more than divide.

I   Why isn't that true here?

F   They've got decimals – in 8 × 0.4 you times by a little, in 8 ÷ 0.4 you share between a little so each person gets more.

I   What if I asked you which was biggest, 0.8 × 1.2 or 0.8 ÷ 1.2?

F   That one (0.8 × 1.2).

I   It's got a decimal, though.

F   'Cos it's got a whole number as well it makes it bigger.

This child clearly has some sophisticated notions about decimals, division and multiplication. Her only 'error' was not to *think carefully* enough about the problems.

Self-regulation and the 'zone of proximal development'

One of Vygotsky's theoretical arguments is that 'self-regulation' is discovered and perfected in the course of social and instructional interactions. Some children may be more 'impulsive' than others, but the ability to regulate one's own thinking and activity, to recognize that first to mind is not always correct, to seek reformulations, simplifications and 'ball park' estimates of likely solutions to a problem, are each, in this view, intellectual *achievements* that arise out of interactions between novices and those more expert.

The examples of 'teaching' that I have just given seem mundane. If they *were* mundane, if such children received such skilled guidance as a regular feature of their mathematical problem-solving, then one suspects that they would become more expert mathematicians.

Brown and Palinscar, whose work on reading I mentioned in chapter 6, also bring a Vygotskian approach to the study of children's self-regulation in problem solving (Brown and Ferrara, 1985). I have not space to go into detail here, so only some of their main insights and findings can be discussed. They developed a method for 'scaling' the amount of help given to children in a variety of problem-solving situations (including IQ test problems). Their system resembles that discussed in chapter 3, in that their scheme ranges from general verbal help (e.g. 'Can you think of another way . . .?') down to demonstrations (e.g. 'Look what happens if I do this'). Working with children drawn from 'low ability' and 'remedial' groups, they discovered that these children were poor in self-regulatory activities.

On the basis of Vygotsky's theory, one would argue that these children lack such skills either because they have had little exposure to people who perform them, or because they need more experience than other children in order to learn how to do them. Self-regulation is usually a private, invisible and inaudible activity. Brown and her colleagues sought to help children discover how to regulate their own problem-solving by *externalizing* the processes of self-regulation such as asking oneself questions, reminding oneself, looking for new evidence, trying to view the problem from a different angle and so on. This they did by *acting out* with the children these sorts of processes in joint problem-solving. Some children (these tended to come from economically poor backgrounds) only needed very *general* and non-specific help in order to improve their immediate problem-solving performance and to *generalize* what they learned to other, similar (sometimes more difficult) problems. In Vygotskian terms, these children had 'wide zones of proximal development'. In other terms, what they could achieve with a little expert *guidance* was far superior to their *unassisted* efforts. They learned a lot with a little help. Other children (who often came from better-off homes) needed more protracted and specific help in order to learn. They have 'narrow zones of proximal development'.

Brown and Ferrara point out, as they did in relation to the teaching of reading, that the children with 'wide zones' were being held back because their teachers expected too little from them. They continued to stress 'low level' demands when, with a little help, some children were able to make relatively rapid progress. These children, they conclude, can and do 'internalize' the help they receive and discover how to regulate their own problem-solving (at least in relation to the types of tasks taught). I will return to a discussion of these ideas in the final chapter.

Mathematical meaning and 'syntax'

In the last chapter, our discussion of 'logicism' drew attention to the *different* meanings that statements used in everyday social life take on when they are regarded as logical propositions. Viewed as logic, our everyday understanding of what people mean by what they say may appear 'illogical'. But everyday utterances, I suggested, are best viewed as serving different *purposes* and entailing different meanings and implications to those that they may entail logically. One of the problems that children face in learning mathematics is of a similar nature, because the 'language of mathematics' entails assumptions and meanings that differ from those implied by the 'same' terms in everyday talk. As many students of mathematics learning and teaching have commented, children find the derivation of *mathematical* procedures from verbally stated problems difficult. One reason for this, as the above examples illustrate, is that many of the words used in mathematics also have more diffuse and less defined everyday meanings and this state of affairs creates problems for many children. The implication is that the mathematical meanings of such terms, what procedures they should imply, have not been *negotiated* as part of the process of teaching. As I said in chapter 3 and in several other places, children will not perceive the meanings of what they are shown or told if they possess insufficient knowledge and understanding to assimilate what they are 'taught'. They may appear 'inattentive' and unable to 'concentrate' for any length of time, not because they possess certain traits of character or personality but because they lack the necessary prior knowledge to 'hear' or 'see' what they are told and shown. Although some children may have genuine problems of inattentiveness, restlessness and overactivity, many, one suspects, find vigilance difficult to maintain because they simply cannot understand what they see and hear.

The CSMS team reach a similar conclusion. 'It is *impossible* to present abstract mathematics to all types of children and expect them to get something out of it. It is much more likely that *half the class* will ignore what is being said because the base upon which the abstraction can be built does not exist. The mathematics must be matched to *each individual* and teaching a mixed ability class as an entity is therefore unprofitable' (p. 210). Later, they recommend 'Perhaps we should get away from "I'll show you" and into "let us discuss what this means" '. Yes, but I would also add that, initially at least, it is also necessary to *work* together so that the meaning of what is *said* can be related to what is to be *done*.

Walkerdine (1982) has examined UK primary school lessons in mathematics from a somewhat similar perspective. She questions the widespread assumption held, she believes, by many teachers that children first develop their *own* conceptual understanding of number, sets and the like and are then 'given' the symbolic means to refer to or to articulate these. Rather, she argues, classroom discourse should be looked at, and evaluated, as a process in which the *nature and meaning* of mathematical symbols themselves are negotiated through a process of shared practical problem-solving. Symbolic representations that emerge from jointly constructed activities, as illustrated by the Bruner and Kenney study, are meaningful to the extent that the relations between mathematical *procedures* that should be evoked by appropriate words and symbols have been worked out in co-operative activity.

Looked at in this way, the seemingly metaphorical term 'mathematical *discourse*' takes on a more literal meaning. As I argued in the last chapter, however, it is a *special* form of discourse rooted in certain assumptions, practices and purposes that differ from those in everyday conversation. Mercer and Edwards (1981) make a similar point and help us to see how 'deep' lie some of the presuppositions and practices that govern mathematical thinking.

For instance, if young children are asked questions like 'If it takes three men two days to dig a hole, how long would it take two men to dig the same hole?', why is it irrelevant to respond with an answer like 'Well, if the hole has already been dug, the earth will be soft' or 'If there are three men, one can have a rest' or 'Have they got different tools?'? If this were a 'real world' problem, such considerations might well be vital. If the earth is like concrete, for example, the effect of the tools used on the time taken might be paramount, not the number of men digging. Making mathematics 'relevant' to children by invoking everyday imagery may serve not to simplify their problems but make them more difficult. References to everyday activities are likely to provoke a whole range of inferences and presuppositions from children that obscure or distort the nature of the problem set. Mathematical discourse rests on its own system of rules. Logical discourse demands the partial *suspension* of everyday common sense, pragmatic knowledge and a rejection of implications that are a 'normal' part of what we say by what we mean in natural discourse. In mathematics too, special and specific things are implied by what is said when a problem is given in words. The 'same' spoken or written statements do not entail what they entail in their everyday meaning. The 'ground rules' for interpretation are changed. Unless the child has some sense of what is relevant to the mathematics and understands why other considerations are irrelevant, how is he to understand the nature of the problem? I suggest that the notion of what 'relevance' means in relation to mathematics is often ill-conceived. Making *mathematical sense* is not synonymous with what makes sense in practical problem-solving – like deciding how long one's garden path is likely to be out of commission because two rather than three men are going to dig it up!

Many of the children in the CSMS study did *not* approach mathematics with a problem-solving frame of mind. They did not, for instance, try to check and correct their answers. Rather, 'Many are just too thankful to have an answer, any answer, to even dare investigate further'. Contrast this state of affairs with what children do with and to their own language. The disposition to correct oneself is not an attribute of personality or ability. When children know, albeit intuitively, what *looks, sounds or feels* right, we have reason to be confident that they will self-correct and self-instruct. Children who do *not* show signs of self-correction, as many do not in mathematics, are, I suggest, offering mute testimony to the fact that they do not know what they are doing or where they are supposed to be going.

Learning and generalizing procedures

Children appear to generalize what they learn in mathematics. The trouble is that what they have learnt or assimilated is often, at best, only partially correct. What they learn may be quite *different* from what the teacher has tried to teach them. Children, as many investigations have revealed, are usually systematic in their mistakes, using what are sometimes referred to as 'buggy algorithms' – procedures that yield consistent (but sometimes wrong) answers. The problem stems from the fact that buggy algorithms may give correct answers to some questions. For instance, some children who are able to solve the following problem '$6 + 2 = x - 5$; what is x?', get the wrong answer when asked to solve '$5 \times 6 = x \times 10$', giving the answer '20'. They seem to have formulated a rule 'When you bring something over from one side of an equation to the other, subtract it from what you find there'. Unfortunately, there are occasions on which this yields the correct answer. So, a child who simply gets 'ticks and crosses' as 'feedback' from his teacher is on a 'partial reinforcement schedule'. Responses or ideas that receive *occasional* confirmation or reinforcement often yield the strongest habits.

Many children invent their own methods for answering maths questions. For mathematically able children, this may confer benefits, since they sometimes invent methods that are faster and more efficient than those taught by their teachers (Resnick, 1976). The CSMS team also give examples of 'esoteric' methods invented by children themselves, that work. For instance, given the problem of adding 38 to 27, one child, aged 13, said 'When I first did it I thought I'd try doing it in my mind – I said 3 and 2 – 30 add 20 is 50, so I went to add 7 and 8 together. I said 8, 9, 10, take 2 off the 7 is 5, and that makes another one, that's 6' (i.e. 65). 'You're supposed to carry but I don't always do that.' He used a similar approach when asked to subtract 28 from 51: '2 from 5 is 30, then I said 8 takes 1 leaves you 7, then I said 7 from 30 leaves 23'.

Children do attempt to develop methods for answering questions and often generalize such methods to produce a form of 'faulty logic'. Again whatever they have been *told* does not get through to all children. The conclusion must be either that such children 'lack something', or that they have not been taught because the teaching methods used do not 'bridge the gap' between practical problem-solving, intuitive understanding and symbolically evoked procedures.

Mathematical 'blocks'

Common reasons often heard (from adults) about why they are 'no good' at maths include reference to natural ability, motivation and not seeing the 'sense' in the subject. We, of course, have just been discussing this *last* explanation. There *is* no sense in learning procedures that do not ultimately relate to activity, as Piaget and others have argued so persuasively.

The CSMS team found, like many other researchers before them, that performance on IQ tests correlates with and predicts likely success in maths (and vice versa). Even if it is the case, however, that some children are naturally endowed with a keener mathematical mind than others, knowing this fact alone helps us little in deciding what we are to do about the situation. Either one assumes that below some (currently unspecified) limit of 'natural ability' children can only learn so much (e.g. only basic mathematical literacy?) or that we are in urgent need of new approaches and fresh resources in mathematics education if many children are not to remain mathematically incompetent.

The issue of 'motivation' and 'de-motivation' of children has received much, often wise, thought (e.g. Holt, 1967) and I do not intend to consider the issue at length here. However, recent research into the development of motivation and its relation to *effort* and performance has shed some new light on the issue. Heckhausen, a German psychologist, has undertaken a series of studies to investigate changes in children's motivation with age and cognitive development (e.g. Heckhausen, 1982). Briefly (I'm fast running out of available space) he argues that up to the age of around eleven years (another shift coming up!) children do not entertain a very clear distinction between *effort* and *ability*. The child at this age, in his view, perceives as equal all who manage to achieve the same goals. The fact that some children do things faster than others does not seem to overly concern them. However, around age eleven, things begin to change. The child now appreciates the fact that two people who put in different amounts of *time and effort* to achieve the same ends must *differ* in some way. The concept that emerges to co-ordinate concepts of effort and achievement is *ability*.

Some children, when this realization dawns upon them, are in a cleft stick. If they work hard to achieve what others seem to find easy then they betray their *low ability*. Since ability is at a premium (at least, in many cultures) the child may experience a desire not to try, to run away, drop out, show a lack of interest and decide that mathematics, say, is 'silly'. In this view, the relation between ability and performance is mediated not simply by the genes but by *self-perception* and a desire to avoid betraying signs of incompetence. One suspects, given the results of David Hargreaves' (1967) study of child 'cultures' in the secondary school, that such children will find others who share their views on mathematics and, indeed, schooling in general.

Another quite different (but not necessarily opposed) perspective on achievement motivation and its origins has emerged from the study of differences in the mathematical development of boys and girls. The British APU surveys revealed small differences, usually favouring boys, in mathematical achievement in the primary school (Department of Education and Science, 1980–82, *Primary Survey Report No. 3*, pp. 118–19). During the years of secondary schooling, however, these differences, still favouring boys, become greater (Department of Education and Science, *Secondary Survey Report No. 1*, pp. 74–7). These surveys also revealed a more negative attitude towards mathematics amongst secondary-aged girls. The reasons for these differences have been, and continue to be, the subject of much debate. Dweck and her colleagues (Dweck et al., 1978), have looked beyond test scores and speculations about innate differences in aptitude to study the *experiences* of boys and girls in mathematics lessons. They provide many insights into the complex dynamics in these lessons, but two of their observations are of interest to us here. Dweck and her group examined the 'feedback' given to boys and girls by their teachers in mathematics lessons. There were some marked differences. Boys, for example, more often received *negative* feedback. But this did not often reflect on their *intellectual* abilities. There was, so to speak, a 'hidden message', which was that if they were not doing well, the reason was not due to mathematical incompetence but to other factors, such as inattentiveness. When the boys received praise, or *positive* feedback, this was likely to focus upon intellectual competence, signalling that they were good at maths. Girls received infrequent negative feedback from their teachers, but when it *did* occur, it was very likely to reflect upon their ability in maths. So for boys criticism is common and by no means a special event. It does not reflect upon their competence. However, if feedback is positive (and this is a special event for boys), it usually reflects well on their mathematical ability. Because negative feedback is rare for girls, when a girl *does* receive it, it forms a notable event and is likely to convey the idea that she is not very good at the subject.

One implication of these observations is that, perhaps unwittingly, teachers create a very different climate in the mathematics classroom for girls and boys. This acts to make 'error' a more serious affair for girls and to induce in them a sense of mathematical incompetence. This would explain why girls do less well and have more negative attitudes towards the subject. Another important finding was that boys who were subjected to a similar pattern of feedback to that met by girls also felt that they lacked ability in maths, supporting the notion that teachers do contribute directly to their pupils' sense of competence (or otherwise).

One of Piaget's central messages to those involved in education must surely be that children are *naturally* motivated to learn (and to self-instruct). If children do not correct their own efforts, lose 'motivation', and find attention, concentration and self-regulation *hard*, as many seem to do in mathematics, then we had best look to factors found in the classroom before we decide to attribute the 'failures' exclusively to characteristics of the child. Let us look at the issue of learning and motivation from another angle. Why, when children seem so competent as learners in some contexts, do they appear to lack motivation and ability in others?

Developing language and learning mathematics

The findings that I have just reviewed, the theoretical explanations offered as to why we found them and the educational implications they suggest, are not new. Neither are they out of date. For many years now, at least since the work of Piaget and Bruner gained a wide readership, emphasis in the teaching of mathematics has been laid on the importance of relevant practical activity, problem-solving and on the need for attention not only to teaching procedures but to fostering conceptual understanding. The invention of 'modern mathematics' reflected these concerns and goals. But there is little evidence that any real progress has been made and few signs that the 'problem-solving' agenda has been fulfilled.

Learning mathematics is hard, and so is teaching it. Why? In an attempt to answer this question, I intend to compare and contrast, briefly, some of the major features of early language development, in which children are usually so *competent*, and then ask how the processes involved might differ from learning mathematics, in which so many seem to struggle to learn.

A great deal has been written about the child's 'natural' capacity for language and communication. From the first days of life, the child's attention is *caught* and *held* by the human face and the voice. For the normal baby, human beings possess all the attributes needed to guarantee attraction and engagement. There is usually no 'problem of attention' to those aspects of the world that implicate the thing that is to be acquired – the ability to communicate. As children master their language, they 'hear' more and 'tune out' less. In mathematics attention has to be 'earned'. Those children who find the first stages of what they are taught difficult to master, may, as lessons move on to ever more difficult topics, perceive and memorize less than those who are doing relatively well. In a large group of mixed ability, those with least expertise are in danger of falling ever further behind.

The infant seems naturally tuned to pay attention to and to 'imitate' the sounds of language around him. The way in which the auditory system works guarantees that he soon and seemingly without effort learns how to produce specific features of what he hears, like patterns of intonation, word-like segments of sound and elements of speech that receive stress and convey meaning.

Language, from the very first sounds produced (and non-verbal communication before these occur), is *purposive*. There is no problem of 'motivation' because the act of speaking is itself a *manifestation* of personal and interpersonal needs, requests, demands and comments (invitations to *share* the world). The process of communication, as we have seen, is often *child-driven*. Looking for signs of competence in the pre-verbal baby, adults are likely to seize upon, respond to and interpret acts and vocalizations from the infant that might conceivably make sense or indicate an intention to communicate. Later, in the immediate pre-school years, children often dictate what is talked about and responded to. Even if the other person's reaction is one of refusal or denial, it is still *contingent* upon the child's attempts to control his world through speech. Only much later, when he enters school and, eventually learns how to read, do the demands of language *learning* begin to resemble those involved in learning mathematics.

In order to learn in school the child must often make his line of thought contingent upon that of the teacher. Teacher questions, for instance, constrain what is to be thought about. Whereas, for most young children, people at home often make what they say and do contingent upon their activities, in school this process is most likely to be *reversed* as the child has to make what he does contingent upon his teacher's demands. Children also have to solve problems set by the teacher, not those that arise as a natural consequence of their own intentional activities. If they do not grasp or understand the motivation behind the questions asked and problems set, they are unlikely to appreciate what goals they are supposed to be pursuing or why they are doing what they are doing. The communicative and intellectual problems involved in these 'special' types of social interaction have been explored in several chapters of the book.

The infant and child are surrounded by the sounds of human voices which suffuse their daily experience. Children often *recognize* sounds and linguistic structures before they are able to *produce* them. It is difficult, otherwise, to account for the many observations which reveal the child at work perfecting his own acts of speech. Self-correction, I have argued, is a sign of self-instruction. The child knows more than he can currently say and, in consequence, can solve his *own* language-learning problems. Many children do not self-correct their own answers to problems in mathematics. Any 'feedback' they receive in the form of 'ticks and crosses' is likely to be less than immediate. Consequently, the source of any difficulties or misconceptions that such feedback is supposed to feed back to is likely to be long gone from mind. Indeed, ticks and crosses alone may only reinforce 'buggy' procedures that yield some right answers but cause errors in other contexts. Without a well-founded *interpretation* of the nature of the child's problem, feedback is likely to result in noise and interference. I believe the observation that many children do not correct their own work signals the fact that they have little sense of what *looks and feels* right in mathematics. Whatever their goals are in producing answers, they are often incompatible with those underlying the problems set.

When the child is involved in everyday talk with another person, what he hears and says is, given the nature of discourse, naturally contingent. Because people take relatively short 'turns' in everyday talk, usually respond to what the other has just said, and continually display verbal and non-verbal signs of comprehension, or lack of it, the conditions for *learning* approach an optimum. Even if the consequences of speaking are not always positive, they usually occur as a reasonably direct and immediate consequence of what is said and done. The connections between acts of speech and what they entail occur close together in time and are, therefore, likely to be grasped and learned.

Adults seem to face few problems in diagnosing 'where the language learner is at' in his communicative development. For most of the time, they seem to understand and respond to what an infant or child tries to mean. Although our knowledge of language is not usually explicit, our intuitive knowledge is robust and extensive. We know a great deal about, and have expertise in using, what it is the child is seeking to learn. Indeed, we quite literally *embody* that knowledge. Adults are able to adjust the nature of their speech to guarantee, most of the time, that what they have to say can be assimilated by the child. This implies that our intuitive knowledge of how to adjust the content and complexity of what we say to fit the child's current level of comprehension is also well founded. Because children begin their life (usually) communicating with individuals who are familiar with and to them, conditions for mutual understanding are further strengthened. Knowing a child's life history, his likes, dislikes, fears, joys, interests and problems, our interpretation of what he is trying to say and do is likely to prove valid. So our 'theories' about what it is the child is seeking to master and our tacit understanding of the knowledge, needs and current level of ability that he brings to bear on his task are often reliable. These approach the optimum conditions for effective teaching.

Effective instruction, I argued in chapter 3, displays a number of features. It rests on a workable theory of *what it is* the learner is trying to learn. Bruner refers to such knowledge as the 'psychology of the subject matter'. He employs the term 'psychology' rather than, say, the 'logic of the subject matter', quite deliberately. As I have argued several times, creating a formal 'syntax' to describe the structure of a problem or subject is only one way of *representing* it. Formal, syntactic representations serve certain purposes for those who create them. However, they do not necessarily provide a useful or reliable guide to the 'representations' and mental processes of other people, whose purposes and knowledge may be different in kind. Hart (1981) makes a similar point: 'If a child can successfully deal with one aspect of mathematics the next stage may not be the one we as teachers see as a logical next step.' An expert mathematician may see commonality of structure 'underlying' very different problems. It may be tempting to conclude that these represent the 'basic structure' or 'logic' of the subject. Perhaps we then decide to *teach* these things; these 'basic concepts'. But learning mathematics, I suggest, does not usually proceed like this. Children, as we have seen, often 'invent' their own mathematical procedures. This is no accident, nor is it a trivial observation. Tackling a new and unfamiliar problem, the child quite naturally brings his own past *experiences* to bear on it and tries to make productive use of it. The first stages of seeking a solution to an unfamiliar problem involve drawing *analogies* between the present situation and previous ones. In learning through problem-solving, we seek to *generalize* what we already know. What else is there to do?

If we can already solve the problem, then we have no problem, only work to do. At this point, when our performance is 'stable', it may be possible to write a 'syntax' to describe our activities. But when we first begin problem-solving, the processes involved are far more idiosyncratic. Children who are mathematically gifted, for whatever reason, often invent ingenious and *workable* methods for solving problems – methods that their teachers never envisaged. Children who *struggle* sometimes do the same thing: the problem is, their methods do not work.

This process, though often idiosyncratic, is seldom 'random'. When we look at the mistakes that children make in mathematics, we can usually *infer* what they did and, perhaps, why they did it. On several occasions, I have talked to teachers about children's errors in maths. The teachers did not need me to 'interpret' what children meant by what they said about their errors. Rather, teachers came up with such interpretations themselves. If we are prepared to talk to and negotiate with children, they will usually tell us why they did what they did and, more often than not, as the CSMS study illustrated, we can make *sense* of what they mean. We then have some ideas as to 'where the learner is at' and, perhaps why and how he got there.

The CSMS team argue for a more verbally interactive, discursive and explanatory approach to mathematics teaching. This, I suggest, would yield both insights into the learner's knowledge and stimulate processes of self-instruction. 'Talking to individual children may soon clear up certain misconceptions which the child will not voice in public. It was noticeable during the interviews, carried out as part of this research, that children were learning simply by voicing their own thoughts' (Hart, 1981).

Many of the experiences that underlie the analogues that children draw upon when they tackle maths problems are, unsurprisingly, based on common, everyday experiences. Indeed, a desire to make maths 'relevant' and 'meaningful' might suggest that this is desirable. Recall, however, one child's views on 'sharing' and how this interfered with her mathematical thinking. It led her to an everyday *interpretation* of the problem that was at variance with a mathematical one, so she reacted to the 'wrong' problem. Similarly, the kinds of things that children think and say when they respond to mathematical problems that sound like 'real world' issues are based upon the parallels they suggest with experiences that they have in that world. They interpret the problem, rather like the Kpelle discussed in the last chapter, in terms of its common sense *plausibility* and may not 'see' the problem as a mathematical one.

A well-constructed ideal curriculum would, of course, offer a common base of mathematical experiences which, if genuinely shared by teacher and pupils, would provide a common point of reference and a source of analogies (though one would never expect all children to formulate the same hypotheses at the same time). 'If teachers do feel it worthwhile to teach pencil and paper algorithms, then either more time must be devoted to practising and recalling them, or they must be better related to children's knowledge to assist recall. Perhaps the present methods should be abandoned in favour of others, maybe less efficient, but more related to children's own informal methods, and hence easier to remember' (Hart, ibid., p. 47). Accepting the *personal* nature of ideas and hypotheses does not entail an abdication of *goal structures* in the curriculum. Nor does it represent a call for infinite plasticity or idiosyncratic aims. Rather, it invites a more *interactive* approach to teaching and learning.

Knowing where a learner is 'at' in mathematics is difficult. Unless we talk to a child we are unlikely to find out. And talking, as I said in chapter 5, demands more than the question–answer exchange if children are to contribute 'openly' to the topic at hand. If you do not know what a child thinks, you are unlikely to ask the right questions. And if you ask lots of questions, then children are unlikely to offer their own views, so we are not likely to discover what these are. Another technique is to offer the child our own *interpretation* of what we think he thinks or why he did what he did. Recall Hundeide's experiments discussed in chapter 2. Saying 'I think . . .' to children solicited more active, thoughtful and ultimately successful responses from children than a question beginning 'Why is there . . . ?'

Knowing what people mean by what they say, being able to interpret and act upon the symbols they employ, demands a basis in relevant, shared activities. The importance of activity with tasks, problems and materials is widely recognized and acknowledged. However, there is reason to believe that this wisdom is not *acted* upon as often as mathematics learning demands. The CSMS team, for example, report on the results of a survey in which teachers of ten-year-olds were asked how often they used apparatus in teaching their class mathematics. None of the schools surveyed used equipment every day. About a half employed it once or twice a week.

The study by Bruner and Kenney, which I discussed early on in this chapter, demonstrates how complex and 'abstract' mathematics can be *exemplified* and embodied. Children's understanding of what the mathematical symbols and problems *meant* was not left to chance. One hopes that the analogues that these children drew upon when they went on to learn more about variables and algebra were those founded in practical activity in the classroom. Children will continue to draw upon the 'closest' relevant experiences and interpretations when they construct their hypotheses about how they should tackle new and unfamiliar problems. If the *language* of these problems activates procedures that are based on past *classroom* experiences, and not, as often seems to happen, on the everyday, non-technical meanings of words and utterances, then perhaps children's interpretation of what they mean will prove more adaptive and generalizable.

The CSMS team, quite rightly to my mind, call for greater *individualized* instruction. They also discuss classroom management arrangements that might make this feasible, a topic about which I have little of relevance to say. But the notion of 'individualized instruction' needs careful thought. On the one hand, it destroys any learner if and when they are left to persist alone in trying to solve problems that make no sense to them. There is, I suggest, strong evidence from the CSMS investigations that this is happening to many children in mathematics. Given that such children are in secondary schools where, according to the CSMS team, there is often strong resistance to the use of practical activities to teach maths, what happens is that the same, basic mathematical procedures are taught to children several times. If the *meaning* of mathematical concepts are not 're-rooted' or renegotiated in shared practical activities, it seems unlikely that children will learn much more. Going over ground already covered and teaching 'more of the same' seems unlikely to succeed. The available evidence suggests that it does not. Persistent 'practice' of existing procedures that are founded on an inappropriate or non-existent intuitive conceptual base cannot work. Rather, the foundations must be rebuilt, and this calls for more practical activity. Far better, of course, is to construct firmer foundations the first time around. Similarly, more abstract concepts, like those involved in algebra, can be exemplified and their *uses* brought to life. 'Abstract' mathematics and the notion of variables might also, I suggest, benefit from greater attention to practical tasks that embody and exemplify their use.

Children who are relatively mathematically gifted, for whatever reason, present a different set of challenges in a discussion of individualized instruction. On the basis of a wide range of educational studies, Snow and Yallow (1982) conclude that the (continued) use of practical activities, illustration, concrete examples and small-step teaching benefits children who are *struggling* to learn. But the same processes slow down and may inhibit the performance of children who find learning relatively easy. Snow and Yallow too underline the fact that children invent their own procedures and reason analogically in mathematical problem-solving. The child who is inventing procedures that work and making good progress is best left to his own devices. A good indicator of effective progress is not only the number of correct answers generated, I suggest, but also evidence that self-correction is taking place. If we try to 'intrude' and provide 'help' or 'feedback' to such a child, we are more likely to generate noise and interference, since the learning processes involved are often idiosyncratic and rather inscrutable. If they work well, for that child, why should they not be left alone?

Of course, any child is likely to get into difficulties at some time or another. The able child's problems may be difficult to diagnose. Here too, one suspects that the best tactic is discussion; if the child feels free to ask and ready to talk, perhaps such problems will find their own solutions.

Concluding comment

Developing an effective theory of 'where the learner is at' and constructing a workable 'psychology of the subject' present formidable challenges in mathematics. Marrying these two theories to know what 'next steps' to take when working with a large class of children takes on the semblance of an impossible demand. I suggest that we not not possess a very detailed or extensive psychology of mathematics. Isolated studies, like that undertaken by Bruner and Kenney, shed new light on how we might conceptualize and teach specific concepts, like the notion of a variable and the quadratic function. But we do not possess this level of knowledge in relation to the vast majority of concepts taught in the classroom. If we did, perhaps we could build a curriculum based on mathematical meaning and not simply on its (assumed) formal syntax.

A sound psychology of mathematics would subsume a theory of the (common) conceptions that children bring to bear on mathematics problems. It would also offer a sense of direction as to how, where and when we respond to these. However, in my view, such knowledge would not provide a *map* of the learner's terrain, though it would improve our sense of direction.

The perspective I have adopted on the nature of knowledge and its relation to formal systems of thinking, if you share it, precludes an approach to teaching that is based on universal and invariant 'steps' and 'stages' (even if these are enshrined in a computer program). Rather, it invites interaction, negotiation and the *shared construction* of experiences which will enable the child to learn the 'language' of mathematics. This, of necessity, will always demand an element of contingency and serendipity. Indeed, in my experience, a measure of uncertainty, the possibility of finding surprises and the chance to discover and resolve new ambiguities is what *drives* and motivates both teaching and learning. It is when ambiguity rests on ambiguity and when uncertainty exceeds personal confidence that the two processes are destroyed. The only way to avoid the formation of entrenched misconceptions is through discussion and interaction. A trouble shared, in mathematical discourse, may become a problem solved.

Chapter 8

Education and educability

In this final, blessedly short, chapter, I intend to try to extend the analysis of teaching and learning that we have been exploring throughout this book to look at some aspects of individual differences in children's adjustment to schooling. No topic in the history of education has created more debate, argument and outright hostility between different schools of thought, than that which still rages about the origins of differences in the educational achievements of children from different social and ethnic backgrounds. Important debates about what should be taught, to whom, by whom, when, where and how are certain to continue and to involve more voices and tongues as societies discover how to come to terms with their multicultural and multilingual character. To my mind, no single discipline or interest group should expect to dictate or even to adjudicate what the outcomes of these issues should be or will be. I certainly do not intend to try to attempt anything of the sort here. Rather, I will look at some of the issues involved from the perspectives on learning, thinking and teaching that we have been exploring in earlier chapters.

Insights from Piaget, Vygotsky and Bruner

Throughout this book I have been exploring and emphasizing the importance of social interaction, communication and instruction in the intellectual development of children. In doing so, I have tried not to lose sight of the constructive, creative and generative abilities of the child. While disagreeing with some of the central features of Piaget's theory of stages and his views on the nature of logical thinking, I have attempted to preserve his basic 'image' of children as major architects of their own understanding. However, following Bruner and Vygotsky, I have also tried to etch out the role of instruction and communication in the transmission of cultural expertise. The activities of the child as she learns, solves problems and attempts to understand and master the demands of schooling are often enveloped within the constructive, interpretive and facilitative activities of the more mature and knowledgeable. Knowledge and expertise, I have argued, are often a product of *shared* constructions by teachers and children. It is not, of course, a process that always runs smoothly or ends in success, but I suggest that a view of children's thinking and learning which conceptualizes the activities involved as social and interactive affairs, helps us to understand some of the ways in which the process of education might sometimes prove less than fully successful.

Children usually attempt to make productive use of the lessons that they are taught. But sometimes, perhaps often, what they try to generalize *from* is poorly founded. As we saw in the last chapter, for instance, abstract symbols and procedures that are at the heart of mathematical thinking often create enormous problems of understanding for children. These problems are signalled by their (common) use of procedures and routines that are, at best, only partially correct. The reasons for this state of affairs lie not in some 'defect' or limitation located 'inside' children but in a breakdown in mutual understanding with those who (should) already embody the expertise they seek. Mathematical symbols and the procedures that these should evoke are often not rooted in shared practical activity and problem-solving. Lacking a jointly constructed fund of mathematical practices, a child's attempts to understand and use symbolic mathematical expressions are likely to fail. What these are supposed to be abstracted from does not exist. Criticisms of methods of mathematics instruction, or attempts to teach any other abstract system of knowledge, which proceed by teaching children how to manipulate symbols that are not grounded in personal experience and practical problem-solving do, of course, echo Piaget's views. Where the accounts of the processes involved differ, however, is in the view taken here that learning how to form concepts, symbolic representations and formal procedures is fundamentally a shared, social and communicative process.

Another theme that has surfaced in a number of chapters is a view of learning and thinking as more-or-less skilful attempts to process information in the course of problem-solving. Viewing the process of learning as the acquisition of expertise helps us to identify the many, often very specific processes, that are implicated in skilful thinking and problem-solving. In company with many present-day students of learning and cognition, I have argued that Piaget's account of rational thought couched in terms of logical operations does not provide an adequate description of what people do as they think, reason and solve problems. We need, I suggest, finer-grained and more task-specific analyses to help to understand what a particular child can and cannot do in a given learning situation.

What Vygotsky has offered to us is a historical and cultural sense of the nature and origins of mental processes. The procedures, practices and concepts that we attempt to inculcate in children, and these include expertise in certain ways of thinking and learning, are not simply 'natural' products of the mind or the sole creations of children. Rather, they are cultural *inventions* that have to be learned and perfected in interaction with those who already possess and practise them. From Bruner, we have taken more explicit, contemporary views on the nature of the instructional process. In relation to language development, we have discussed his theory about the role played, usually spontaneously, by the mature in establishing the conditions for communication and the emergence of language in infants. His theory about the principles and practices underlying formal instruction were discussed in relation to mathematics learning and problem-solving. I have attempted to relate and, in places, to synthesize the insights from these different 'traditions' in child study around the concept of 'expertise' and its development. I have also tried, where evidence exists, to show how the various images of childhood being considered have led to effective educational practices and to insights into the process of formal instruction.

Formal education faces children with many demands that are not a regular or frequent feature of their everyday experiences outside the classroom. The practice of education confronts all children with important and necessary *discontinuities* in their intellectual, social and linguistic experiences. While it is self-evident that children from some social backgrounds often find it easier than do others to accommodate to these novel demands and practices, I believe it is a mistake to think of schooling *simply* as a preserve of one social group. It is not, I suggest, profitably seen as a 'middle-class' institution, for example. It may well be populated by adults from such social backgrounds, but simply viewing school as a *continuation* of experiences that are typical of one social group is, I believe, a gross oversimplification. Such a view ignores and belies the many specific demands that are 'special' to schooling. Put another way, schools have a culture of their own.

Some barriers to educational achievement

The traditional role played by psychologists in long-standing arguments about the nature and origins of educability has revolved around questions about the nature of intelligence and its measurement. What do IQ tests 'really' measure? Why are the scores of children from some social backgrounds higher or lower, on average, than those achieved by children from other groups? How should we interpret the relations between IQ test scores and measures of academic achievement? To what extent are correlations between the scores achieved by children and their parents transmitted genetically or by means of differential opportunities and experiences? These are some of the issues that have traditionally shaped the psychologist's role in, and contributions to, debates about the origins of educability.

Questions about the relative 'importance' of genes and social experiences in determining educational performance will not loom large here. As I said in the last chapter, knowing that a child has a high or a low score on an IQ test, of itself, tells us nothing about how we should proceed to educate that child. Similarly, estimates of the supposed 'magnitude' of the genetic contribution to a child's measured intelligence are unlikely to help in the construction of a curriculum or in developing the educational means to realize it.

Throughout this book, I have been concerned with *processes* of learning and development and with issues about the importance of communication and instruction in fostering or impeding these. Tests of general ability, which provide predictions about the likely future achievements of different *groups* of children, can be used to contribute to discussions of these processes and issues in a number of ways. For example, several investigations and classroom experiments that I have discussed in this book have employed formal tests of 'general academic ability' to address questions like 'How does the perform-ance of a child with a high test score differ from that of a child with a low one?' or 'How might such differences be implicated in the relative difficulty a given child experiences in learning how to read or to solve specific types of learning problem?' Where we find, for example, that children with high scores are more expert in processes of *self-regulation*, we can go on to ask if other children can be taught how to develop these abilities. Such comparisons prove useful to the extent that they provide insights into the sorts of classroom activities we might use to help children become more effective in learning and self-instruction. The work of Brown, Ferrara and their colleagues, discussed in several chapters, illustrates this approach to curriculum development.

In each chapter, we have considered different abilities that underlie the capacity to learn in school. Problems in one or in any combination of these abilities will create learning problems for a child. They include a desire and ability to attend, concentrate and memorize; knowing how to apportion one's time and resources in order to study and learn; understanding what people mean by what they say and do; possessing the confidence and expertise to present and explain oneself and knowing how to make what one has to say or write accessible to one's audience; the ability to evaluate and redirect one's efforts, to self-correct and self-instruct; and knowing how to make one's attentions and actions contingent upon the requests, demands and needs of others. Difficulties in gaining expertise in any of these activities will generate problems for a child. To the extent that we are able to help a child to gain and perfect such expertise, that child is educable.

What I propose to do in these final pages is to re-examine, briefly, some aspects of the processes involved in learning how to think and learn in school that we have considered at greater length in the preceding chapters. I do not intend to present a summary, but instead will apply some of the ideas, findings and questions we have already discussed to ask what, if anything, we know about the nature and origins of individual differences in children's powers in these areas.

Attention and concentration

Picture a classroom in which all but one or two children are concentrating on the task at hand. Then imagine another in which the majority of children seem restless, talkative, fidgety and inattentive to the lesson in hand. If, observed over time, the same handful of children in the first class seem inattentive and distractable, then one would be led to ask what it is about those children that renders their concentration so poor. If the state of affairs persists in the second imaginary class, one might be led to ask questions about the teacher and what is being taught.

Common observation and experience suggest that some children find concentration and study easier than others. We may be tempted to conclude that some pupils lack 'powers' of concentration or are 'naturally' distractable. However, I have argued several times in different chapters that the ability to attend and concentrate is not simply a natural capacity that children 'possess' to a greater or lesser extent. When we examined what was involved in the development of powers of concentration, for example, we found that it implicates a number of *processes* of self-regulation, some aspects of which have to be learned. Further, what can be perceived and memorized depends upon a learner's existing knowledge and expertise. Where the gap between a child's current level of understanding and that demanded by what is being taught is too great, then we cannot expect to find the child concentrating on what is being said and done.

But common observation suggests that children differ in the extent to which they find easy or difficult such things as learning how to concentrate, learning how to buffer themselves from distraction, and developing the ability to study. A rather neglected feature of the recent literature on individual differences in learning is the topic of temperamental differences between children and how these emerge. There are signs that interest in this topic is being revived. There are several lines of evidence which suggest that some (and I emphasize the word) children do face problems of adjustment to school because they are temperamentally ill-suited to sitting still and concentrating. The relationships between 'inborn' temperamental characteristics and social experiences in the formation of personality are complex and controversial. A detailed consideration of the issues involved lies outside our immediate concerns. However, I think it is useful to look at some of the studies in this field since they illustrate how, for some children, learning *how* to pay attention and concentrate is difficult because of their temperaments. For a tiny minority of children, I think we must conclude that their problems of attention and concentration are not of their own, or anyone else's, making. Some of the evidence for this argument comes from what looks like an unlikely source – the study of anatomy.

Most of us are born with two or three 'minor physical abnormalities' (MPAs). For instance, one of our toes may be too long relative to the others, we may have no ear lobes or a slight palatal defect. Children with an unusually large number of such minor physical characteristics may display learning problems in school (Bell and Waldrop, 1982). For example, boys with five or more minor abnormalities are likely to appear restless, fidgety and inattentive in comparison to children with fewer than five, whereas girls with five or more are more often passive, shy and withdrawn.

Most of these minor defects are invisible to the non-clinical eye and careful inspection is needed to discover them. So it seems highly unlikely that other people's responses to the child cause such learning problems. Identifying precise causes is difficult. However, there is evidence of association between minor physical abnormalities at birth and both maternal *diet* during pregnancy, such as a high intake of refined foods, and maternal infection at crucial periods in the development of the foetus. Such evidence suggests that the causes of MPAs lie in damage to foetal chromosomes during gestation. Thus, social factors, like maternal diet, and socially-related experiences, such as the probability of exposure to infection during pregnancy, are known to damage the developing foetus. Children's bodies and aspects of their mental adjustment, like levels of activity and proneness to distraction, are affected by impaired biological processes. The divide between social and biological influences on development and that between physical and mental characteristics of an individual are not clear-cut. Similarly, malnutrition is a pretty good prescription for producing apathy in normally alert, active and attentive children.

There are other lines of evidence that point directly to the effects of a child's life-experiences on her ability to concentrate in class. For example, children from abusing homes are sometimes (though by no means invariably) overactive, distractable and disruptive in school (Kempe and Kempe, 1978). Similarly, the study of children with different histories of local authority, institutional care and adoption reveal differences in school behaviour, including fidgeting, restlessness and an inability to concentrate (Tizard and Hodges, 1978). Children who in their first years of life experience long periods of time being cared for outside their family may, when they are returned to the family, exhibit problems of concentration and attention. Interestingly, many of these problems are more evident at school (where children are in groups and usually have to make what they say and do contingent upon the teacher's demands) than they are at home.

If a particular child is characteristically restless and inattentive in class, and there is any reason to suspect poor diet or chronic stress and upset as causes for his or her problem, then, clearly, more than educational intervention is called for. I do not think we know how far and to what extent differences in children's powers of concentration are attributable to such factors. However, where a large proportion of children find concentration heavy going and the classroom admonition 'pay attention!' is heard frequently, it is probably a sign that the match between what children understand and what they are being required to attend to is too great for them to bridge. Other factors that may seem to make certain children inattentive or overly boisterous stem from the process of communication and styles of 'self-presentation', as we see in the next section.

Problems of communication

The view, put forward and explored in the 1960s and 1970s, that children from some social and ethnic backgrounds enter school with little or no speech has been rejected. What is not yet clear is whether and to what extent some dialects, accents and creoles create learning problems for children because they interfere with processes of communication in the classroom. Conceptualizing language-related learning problems as issues concerning *communication* rather than *language per se* is not simply a semantic quibble. The notion that a child has 'language problems' implies that her ability to speak, make herself understood and communicate are somehow defective. Viewing the problem as one of communication acknowledges the fact that the problem is *shared* by those who do the talking and those who are listening. Any problem, so to speak, lies *between* the two, not 'inside' the child or her home.

When children come to school they face several new species of communication demands and requirements. It is reasonable to suppose that a child who *shares* a dialect and way of speaking with her teacher is less likely to face problems of communication and, hence, learning, than is a child whose dialect is very different. This observation, of course, is compatible with the spirit of Bernstein's thesis. However, recognizing that children face problems of communication need not lead us to assume that the language of any group of children is in some way defective or deficient. In chapter 6 we examined features of language use and the structures and linguistic devices that are learned to realize those uses in relation to the development of literacy. The use of language to narrate, inform, explain and instruct involves a range of linguistic and intellectual skills in planning and self-monitoring that are *not* a 'natural' product of most everyday talk. We also examined evidence which showed that some children, probably a sizable minority, are far from expert in these uses of language as they approach the end of schooling. The fact that they can be helped to improve their ability to express, explain and give an account of themselves with relatively little specific help and instruction suggests that what such children lack is not 'language' as such but experiences in putting it to certain uses. What they are learning in such classroom experiments is not a different dialect but a range of intellectual, interpersonal and communicative abilities that, for some reason, they have not mastered during their years at school. The fact that they can be helped to do so late in their school careers demonstrates that they have the *competence* to learn.

The origins of these special forms of language use, like narration and giving verbal explanations, are still unclear. We do not fully understand how, why and when children master them in the course of schooling or why some children fail to do so. Those who find learning to read and write relatively easy may well discover and perfect such abilities as a by-product of becoming literate. As I argued in chapter 6, achieving fluency in reading and writing transforms aspects of the child's thinking and verbal communication. Children whose dialect involves sounds and structures that differ from Standard English and Received Pronunciation face special problems in learning to read and write. As Perera (1984, p. 213) concludes, 'although all children have to alter their language significantly as they move from casual speech to formal writing, those whose oral language differs markedly from Standard English will have a particularly demanding adjustment to make'. They may fail to reap the linguistic and communicative benefits that literacy may bestow. It is important to bear in mind, however, that the written word is not a direct 'encoding' or translation of *any* dialect. It exhibits special properties that may create problems for a child from any linguistic background.

Investigations into the home experiences of children who learn to read early in life, including those of children who can read before they start school (Clark, 1976), have revealed relationships between parental attitudes towards literacy, the frequency with which a child is exposed to books, stories and literary experiences, and children's rates of progress in learning to read. Indeed, Gordon Wells and his colleagues, in the Bristol longitudinal language study referred to in several chapters of this book, found that the extent to which parents displayed and encouraged an interest in reading and writing was more highly correlated with their children's progress in reading than factors like the facilities, resources and methods of instruction employed in the child's school (Wells and Raban, 1978). Although children from some social backgrounds are more likely, as a group, to have such experiences at home, what seems important is not socio-economic background as such, but early and frequent literary experience itself. The fact that such experiences vary from group to group, helps to explain the *statistical* association between socio-economic status and measures of reading progress. It seems unlikely, however, that differences in things like dialect are totally responsible for this association. More simply, children with most *relevant experience* with the written word tend to know more about it and make better progress in mastering it.

Research by Hewison and Tizard (1980) reinforces this interpretation. Working in twelve primary schools in Inner London, they compared the progress in learning to read made by three groups of children over a period of two years. One group acted as 'controls' and received no special help in learning to read, other than that normally given in school. A second group was allocated an additional teacher and given extra instruction in reading. A third group involved parental participation. Parents were asked to listen to their child read at home for ten minutes each day. This group of children (which included some from families with non-literate parents and some non-English-speaking ones) made significantly greater progress in reading than those in the other two groups. The researchers, it should be pointed out, ensured that the three groups were as comparable, in terms of those factors known to influence children's progress in literacy, as one can make them in such investigations. These results also imply that whilst it may be true that the language or dialect used in the home make learning to read more or less difficult, it does not, alone, explain why some children experience problems.

Although literary experiences at home exert an important influence on rates of progress in learning to read, it seems certain that some children face 'special' problems. These may or may not have their roots in early experience. For example, the research by Bryant and Bradley (see chapter 6 above) indicates that some children who find learning to read difficult have specific problems in perceiving or analysing the structure of speech sounds. Lacking a clear sense of the way in which spoken words are 'constructed' and can be 'decomposed', these children face problems in relating spoken and written words and make, at best, slow progress in reading and writing. The Bryant and Bradley intervention study, designed to sharpen children's awareness of speech sounds and to improve their ability to analyse speech, led to significant improvements in reading levels.

Not all children who achieve good 'encoding' and 'decoding' skills go on to write and read fluently. Studies by Wiener and his colleagues, for example, identified two groups of poor readers amongst American college students (Wiener et al., 1980). One group, when asked to read aloud, did so in a 'word by word' manner, reading connected text as though it was made up of a list of isolated words. Their 'reading voices' displayed few signs of intonation, rhythm or stress. These students did relatively well in a sight vocabulary test; they could read a normal range of words for their age. Yet although their 'word attack' skills were average, they found it difficult to read connected text for comprehension. The second group, asked to read aloud, did speak in phrases, showing some appreciation of the 'information units' in written language. These, however, had poor sight vocabularies. More interesting was the finding that the group with normal word attack skills could be helped to improve their reading comprehension. This was done using a technique that made textual organization more obvious and salient. When they were presented with specially constructed text in which the phrase structure was made explicit by writing each phrase on a separate line, their comprehension (under these conditions) reached age-normal levels. But this technique did not help students with poor word attack skills. It seems, then, that readers who do not or cannot 'impose' structure and organization read with understanding when normal conventions for 'justifying' text (i.e. organizing it arbitrarily into page-width layouts) are waived in favour of a structure that more closely mirrors that found in speech.

In a follow-up to these observations with fourth-graders (usually ten-year-old children), a similar group of children was identified. They had mastered the basic 'rules' for translating written into spoken words, but were finding reading difficult because they were not aware of or did not know how to exploit aspects of spoken language like stress, intonation and pauses to help to organize and interpret written text. When children who were experiencing these reading problems were asked to listen to speech that was electronically 'doctored' so that it lacked changes in intonation and pitch, they also found comprehension hard. However, children who were reading relatively well did not experience such problems with 'monotonic' speech. As I argued in chapter 6, an expert reader interacts with text to 'impose' prosodic organization in order to interpret what is being read. Good readers, it seems, are able to do the same thing when they listen to atonal speech, whereas at least one group of poor readers cannot.

Bryant and Bradley offer an approach to the teaching of reading to children who find encoding and decoding difficult. Wiener and his colleagues offer some practical suggestions about how we can identify children with other problems, and have shown how changes in text layout can facilitate the comprehension of children who have difficulty 'imposing' a phrasal organization on what they read. The fact that *different* aspects of the reading process present problems to different groups of children should not surprise the experienced teacher. Even so, one wonders, in view of the large numbers of children who leave school still facing reading problems, whether enough attention is paid to the nature and locus of such problems.

Communication and prejudice

As I have argued on many pages, interpersonal communication rests on a great deal more than words and grammar. Conversation, for instance, is deeply embedded in non-verbal communication. The movements of a speaker and her listener are usually in close temporal harmony. While a capacity to move in synchrony with another seems to be a part of our biological heritage, communicative movements, like the speech patterns with which they synchronize, vary from culture to culture and across different social groups within the same culture. A hearer who is in temporal 'tune' with her speaker is *anticipating* where vocal stress and new information are likely to come. What happens, say, when a speaker of Black American English interacts with a white person who speaks with a different dialect of American English? Judged in relation to the Black rhythm, white speakers of American English talk and move in a *syncopated* rhythm (or, if you choose to take the 'white beat' first, vice versa). What effects does this state of affairs have on feelings of mutual comfort and verbal understanding? Well, there is some evidence which suggests that problems of understanding which one might expect to occur when people are 'out of tune' – expecting to find movement, vocal stress and verbal information where they do not occur – do arise. Such interactions, compared with those between speakers of the same dialect, are disrupted (Condon, 1980).

Research into non-verbal dimensions of communication and their effects on teaching and learning is sparse and permits no ready generalizations. Although there have been studies which show, for instance, that children from different socio-economic backgrounds respond differently to a teacher's tone of voice in experimentally contrived situations (Wiener et al., 1980), no one, as far as I know, has looked at the effects of verbal and non-verbal aspects of communication in classroom teaching situations. We do not know, for instance, whether or not people from different social and ethnic groups achieve mutual adjustment and greater synchrony when they have known each other for some time. Or is it the case that an early history of disruptions creates a sense of unease which has a negative effect on developing relationships? We do not know.

Aspects of non-verbal communication and its role in comprehension might also help to explain why people who can quite happily read a second language may experience great problems when they try to use that language in conversation with native speakers. Written text, as we saw in chapter 6, leaves a reader free to proceed at her own pace and in her own way. The 'same' language when spoken, in which intonation, bodily movement and mutual synchronization are important bases for comprehension, is a very different affair. Some of the problems of mutual understanding that one experiences when talking to people from other linguistic communities may arise not only from differences in the sounds that they make but also from the timing of their movements.

Labov, recall, produced evidence to argue that black children, who appeared monosyllabic in interactions with white adults, had no problems of language or communication in interaction with their peers. Recall too, in passing, the result of Brown and her colleagues, concerning the differences between informal conversation and more demanding information-giving speech. Labov draws our attention to relatively 'high level' considerations like prejudice and mutual distrust to explain why black children do not talk to white adults. One wonders, however, how important much less obvious features of mutual adjustment and timing in communication might be in creating feelings of discomfort. Might it be the case that when black and white talk together, even if they have every intention of getting along, non-verbal features of communication undermine their best efforts? Consider the possible effects on meeting someone who talks to a different tune and moves to a different verbal rhythm if you are, say, five years of age. How might the comprehension of such a child be affected? How does she feel and respond to unfamiliar rhythms? She is, in a sense, being asked to dance, after all.

Problems of communication between black and white people that arise spontaneously and take place without being detected by the participants have also been illustrated by Kochman (1981). Briefly, he argues that the way in which (American) black college students present themselves in discourse differs from the self-presentation conventions adopted by white students. For example, a black student, when holding the conversational floor, intends that her listeners should be left in no doubt about the *stance* that she is taking on the issue under discussion. She *advocates* a point of view with zest and signs of personal commitment. She loses the floor when someone, with neat verbal footwork, scores a point or throws her off balance. Unless she can retaliate to regain the initiative, she yields the floor. The apparent emotion and commitment with which the black student argues her case disturb a white audience. Preferring not to show heat or emotion, expecting conversational turns to be shared equally, and looking for common ground on the issue involved, the white student feels uncomfortable and is likely to misinterpret the intentions of the black student, who may be seen as aggressive and uncompromising. The black student, meanwhile, is likely to interpret the relatively dispassionate, withdrawn and inscrutable approach to debate taken by the white student as evidence of secrecy and of a desire not to reveal what they 'really' think and feel about the issue at hand. She too misinterprets the significance of what the white student is trying to mean.

It would, of course, be naïve and unrealistic to suggest that racial prejudice stems from such subtle aspects of communication. A great deal of racial prejudice is anything but subtle and seems to be shared between people who seldom if ever communicate with each other. However, these observations might help us to understand why black and white people who have every desire to get along may find themselves experiencing discomfort and, perhaps, beginning to doubt if they really are as non-prejudiced as they might wish to be.

The importance of these observations is not simply that they raise issues about the origins of prejudice, though these alone are important enough. They are also intended to illustrate the depth and subtlety of the factors we have to bear in mind when we consider problems of communication. Attention only to differences in the sorts of sounds we make and the language structures we use may lead us to neglect what may prove to be equally important features of the process of communication and, by implication, teaching, that create obstacles for all concerned. If we accept this possibility then an understanding of, and discussions about, the very different ways in which members of various social groups go about the task of *presenting* themselves to each other may help to make communication more relaxed and productive. Looked at in this way, mutual understanding of life in different groups and cultures is not a luxury. If we genuinely want to ensure anything approaching educational equality, striving to achieve such an understanding may turn out to be a necessity.

Concluding comments

In a wise and scholarly book that I referred to at the very start of this book, E. B. Castle (1970) explores the historical influences that have acted upon and helped to shape our modern conceptions of what it is to be a teacher. He traces several perspectives on the teaching profession that arose and spread out from Greek, Roman and Judaic origins. At different times and in different parts of the world, teachers have been cast as disseminators of literacy, guardians of culture, vicars of morality, architects of the 'good citizen' and agents of the Gods. In more recent times, schools have been allocated the task of achieving social equality, overcoming material disadvantage and eradicating prejudice. Teachers are also expected to be capable of diagnosing the needs of the individual learner and to know how to meet these once discovered. In my less optimistic moments, I wonder whether such demands can possibly be considered realistic when one adult is asked to achieve all these ends in the service of twenty, thirty or perhaps forty children in a classroom.

This has not been a book about classroom management nor about 'teaching skills'. Instead we have explored several dimensions of development, and considered different views on how and why these come about and the influences that shape their course. Throughout, however, I have been aware of the fact that discussions about the needs and problems of children at different stages of development and learning hold out implications for teachers that are difficult if not impossible to meet given the current state of our knowledge and the circumstances that prevail in our schools. For example, being able to observe and interact with a child in order to discover what she knows, understands and can do, takes time, considerable knowledge and skill. Having sufficient knowledge not only about the development of children but also about the 'psychology of subject matter', say in mathematics and literacy, entails daunting and in some cases impossible demands. Even where, as a society, we know about these things, and there is clearly much yet to be discovered, putting such knowledge to work in the service of large groups of children is a formidable requirement.

Being aware of these somewhat unreasonable implications in what I have been discussing, I had intended, when I first began to write this book, to include a chapter discussing the issue of 'individualized instruction'. Such a chapter would have revolved around a consideration of what we have discovered from studies of co-operative learning and problem-solving in children. Time and space, however, precluded any lengthy treatment of such issues. Let me conclude with a brief overview of what I would have said at greater length had I had more space!

Among the many contributions that Piaget has made to our understanding of children, perhaps the most important legacy of his theory viewed in educational terms is the respect it inspires for children's capacities as learners and as architects of their own understanding. Throughout this book, I have emphasized phenomena like children's capacity for self-correction and self-instruction which lend credibility to a view of children as self-motivated and self-directing agents of their own development. Such insights make the task of education seem a little less daunting, to the extent that children individualize their *own* learning and self-instruction.

Similarly, Chomsky's revolutionary views on the nature of language and the processes involved in its acquisition have motivated new perspectives on children's ability to acquire language 'naturally'. His ideas and the research that they helped to stimulate have led us to question and, in some instances, to reject, explanations for the cause of differences in the educational achievements of children from different linguistic and socio-economic backgrounds.

However, we have also been led to question the implication often drawn from both Piagetian and neo-Chomskian theory that social interaction and communication with the more mature play a relatively minor role in shaping a child's knowledge, ability and understanding. Vygotsky and Bruner have drawn our attention to the historical and cultural relativity of knowledge and to the importance of social interaction, communication and instruction, both informal and formal, in the transmission of that knowledge. In discussions of the role of social interaction and communication in the development of learning and thinking, I have concentrated mainly on relations between children and adults. In so doing, I am aware of the fact that I have stressed the roles and responsibilities of teachers. For Piagetians, interactions between *children* themselves play a major role in facilitating the course of development. Children who occupy a similar stage of development and, in consequence, entertain similar views of the world may, according to Piaget, stimulate each other towards more objective and rational understanding. Vygotsky also emphasized the role of interactions between children as playing an important part in the transmission of knowledge. In his view, interactions benefit a child when she is helped by another who knows more about the task at hand than she herself does. The more knowledgeable child may also benefit, since the process of making her ideas more *explicit* and *external* renders her grasp of what she knows clearer and more objective.

There are now a number of studies which lend credibility to these views. For example, in a review of research in this area with the apt subtitle 'Can two wrongs make a right?', Glachan and Light (1982) discuss the results of various experiments which show that children working together are able, in some circumstances, to solve problems and construct explanations for phenomena that, alone, they have not been able to solve or explain. The study by Brown and her colleagues (see chapter 5) also demonstrates the importance of peer interaction in learning. They, recall, explored children's ability to talk informatively and demonstrated that their performance could be improved by using specially designed communication tasks for use in the classroom. They exploited the fact that children are more relaxed and less guarded when they communicate with each other than they are with their teachers. The researchers opted to use child–child communication as the basis for their intervention for this reason. Doise and Mugny (1984) in an extensive study of the conditions that underlie successful, co-operative learning and problem-solving adopt a theoretical perspective similar to that explored in this book. Basically, they attempt to synthesize insights from Piaget's theory and from the psychometric tradition to understand how and in what circumstances co-operation and communication lead to the shared construction of knowledge and understanding between children. They conclude, like Light and Glachen, that, under certain conditions, children are able to help each other to solve conservation problems and to achieve a better understanding of other people's perspectives and points of view. Where children share similar but 'erroneous' and egocentric views on the world, their perspectives and opinions (being egocentric) lead them naturally to conflicting ideas. Such conflicts, in true Piagetian style, motivate children to reformulate their ideas and may lead them to develop a deeper understanding of the phenomenon under consideration.

Such studies inspire confidence in the idea that teachers may be able to exploit child–child interactions to help facilitate learning. However, systematic observations of children working in groups in the classroom suggest that the payoffs often found in laboratory studies appear rarely in school. Rather, group work usually leads to little directed learning activity (Bennett et al., 1984). It is certainly theoretically possible that increased opportunities for learning can be achieved by co-operative problem-solving, but to be successful, this approach demands techniques for 'matching' children, for selecting tasks and assignments and managing group work. The available evidence suggests that we have yet to find reliable ways of achieving these goals. Perhaps future developments in education may show us the way to exploit a potentially invaluable learning and teaching resource in the classroom – children. To date I don't think we can be very confident that we know the way to proceed.

At a time when many new challenges and opportunities are emerging in education, thanks to the advent of new technology and computerized aids to learning and instruction, I think it is worth reminding ourselves about the social, interactive dimensions of human growth and development. My own view is that the most optimistic claims about the contribution that can and will be made by new technology in creating 'individualized aids' to instruction are grossly inflated. I hope that the ideas, theories and findings explored in this book provide a persuasive case for the central importance and the enormous complexity of the communicative process in teaching and learning. It may, some time in the future, prove possible to discover and make explicit the complex abilities that underlie skilful communication and teaching with children. If so, perhaps the processes involved can be programmed into mechanical teaching aids. However, both the current state of our knowledge about the nature of language and communication, and the existing powers of our computers are, to my mind, a long way away from such achievements. For some time to come, I suspect that the most valuable resources within the classroom will be found in human form.

Bibliography

Bartlett, F. C. (1932). *Remembering: A Study in Experimental and Social Psychology*. Cambridge University Press, Cambridge.
—— (1958). *Thinking*. Basic Books, New York.
Beer, S. (1977). Cybernetics. In *The Fontana Dictionary of Modern Thought* (ed. A. A. Bullock and O. Stallybrass). Fontana/Collins, London.
Bell, A. W., Costello, J. and Kuchemann, D. (1983). *A Review of Research in Mathematical Education. Part A: Research on Learning and Teaching*. NFER–Nelson, Windsor, Berks.
Bell, R. Q., and Waldrop, M. F. (1982). Temperament and minor physical abnormalities. In *Temperamental Differences in Infants and Young Children* (ed. R. Porter and G. Collins). Pitman, London.
Bennett, N., Desforges, C., Cockburn, A. and Wilkinson, B. (1984). *The Quality of Pupil Learning Experiences*. Lawrence Erlbaum, London.
Bereiter, C., and Englemann, S. (1966). *Teaching Disadvantaged Children in the Pre-school*. Prentice-Hall, Englewood Cliffs, New Jersey.
Bernstein, B. (1960). Language and social class. *British Journal of Sociology*, 11, 271–6.
—— (1961). Social class and linguistic development: a theory of social learning. In *Education, Economy and Society* (ed. A. H. Halsey, J. Floud and L. A. Anderson). Free Press, Glencoe.
—— (1970). A sociolinguistic approach to socialisation with some references to educability. In *Language and Poverty* (ed. D. Williams). Markham, Chicago.
Blank, M., Rose, S. A. and Berlin, L. J. (1978). *The Language of Learning: The Preschool Years*. Grune and Stratton, New York.
Boden, M. A. (1979). *Piaget*. Fontana Paperbacks, Glasgow.
Brown, A. L. and Ferrara, R. A. (1985). Diagnosing zones of proximal development. In *Culture, Communication and Cognition Vygotskian Perspectives* (ed. J. V. Wertsch). Cambridge University Press, Cambridge.
Brown, G., Anderson, A., Shillcock, R. and Yule, G. (1984). *Teaching Talk. Strategies for Production and Assessment*. Cambridge University Press, Cambridge.
Bruner, J. S. (1957). Going beyond the information given. Reprinted in *Beyond the Information Given* (ed. J. M. Anglin, 1973). W. W. Norton and Co., New York.

—— (1966a). *The Process of Education.* Harvard University Press, Cambridge, Mass.

—— (1966b). *Toward a Theory of Instruction.* Harvard University Press, Cambridge, Mass.

—— (1968). *Processes of Cognitive Growth: Infancy.* Clark University Press, USA.

—— (1971). *The Relevance of Education.* W. W. Norton and Co., New York.

—— (1983). *Child's Talk: Learning to Use Language.* Oxford University Press, Oxford.

——, Goodnow, J. J. and Austin, G. A. (1956). *A Study of Thinking.* Wiley, New York.

—— and Kenney, H. J. (1965). Representation and mathematics learning. *Monographs of the Society for Research in Child Development.* Serial 99, vol. 30, no. 1, 50–9.

——, Olver, R. R. and Greenfield, P. M. (1966). *Studies in Cognitive Growth.* Wiley, New York.

Bryant, P. (1974). *Perception and Understanding in Young Children.* Methuen and Co., London.

—— and Bradley, L. (1985). *Children's Reading Problems.* Basil Blackwell, Oxford.

Butterworth, G. and Cochran, E. (1980). What minds have in common in space: a perceptual mechanism for joint reference in infancy. *International Journal of Behavioral Development,* 3, 253–72.

Castle, E. B. (1970). *The Teacher.* Oxford University Press, Oxford.

Chase, W. G. and Simon, H. A. (1973). Perception in chess. *Cognitive Psychology,* 4, (1), 55–81.

Chomsky, N. (1957). *Syntactic Structures.* Mouton, The Hague.

—— (1959). Review of B. F. Skinner, *Verbal Behavior,* in *Language,* 35, 26–58.

—— (1965). *Aspects of the Theory of Syntax.* MIT Press, Cambridge, Mass.

—— (1980). *Rules and Representations.* Basil Blackwell, Oxford.

Clark, E. (1978). From gesture to word: on the natural history of deixis in language acquisition. In *Human Growth and Development. Wolfson College Lectures, 1976* (ed. J. S. Bruner and A. Garton). Oxford University Press, Oxford.

Clark, M. (1976). *Young Fluent Readers.* Heinemann, London.

Cole, M., Gay, J., Glick, J. A. and Sharp, D. W. (1971). *The Cultural Context of Learning and Thinking.* Methuen and Co., London.

—— and Scribner, S. (1974). *Culture and Thought. A Psychological Introduction.* Wiley, New York.

Condon, W. S. (1980). Interactional synchrony and cognitive and emotional processes. In *The Relationship of Verbal and Nonverbal Communication* (ed. M. Ritchie-Key). Mouton, The Hague.

Crystal, D. (1976). *Child Language, Learning and Linguistics.* Edward Arnold, London.

Department of Education and Science (1975). *A Language for Life* (The Bullock Report). HMSO, London.

—— (1980–2). *Mathematical Development.* Primary Survey Reports, nos 1–3 and Secondary Survey Reports, nos 1–3. (Assessment of Performance Unit). HMSO, London.

Dienes, Z. P. (1960). *Building up Mathematics.* Hutchinson, London.

—— and Jeeves, M. A. (1970). *The Effects of Structural Relations of Transfer.*

Routledge and Kegan Paul, London.

Doise, W. and Mugny, G. (1984). *The Social Development of the Intellect.* Pergamon Press, London.

Donaldson, M. (1978). *Children's Minds.* Fontana, London.

Dweck, C. S., Davidson, W., Nelson, S. and Enna, B. (1978). I: Sex differences in learned helplessness. II: The contingencies of evaluative feedback in the classroom. III: An experimental analysis. *Developmental Psychology*, 14, 268–76.

Elkind, D. (1974). *Children and Adolescents. Interpretive Essays on Jean Piaget.* Oxford University Press: Oxford.

Ghiselin, B. (ed.). (1952). *The Creative Process.* University of California Press, Berkeley.

Gibson, J. J. (1950). *The Perception of the Visual World.* Houghton and Mifflin, Boston, Mass.

Glachan, M. and Light, P. (1982). Peer interaction and learning: can two wrongs make a right? In *Social Cognition* (ed. G. Butterworth and P. Light). The Harvester Press, Brighton.

Gleitman, L. R. and Wanner, E. (1982). Language acquisition: the state of the state of the art. In *Language Acquisition: The State of the Art* (ed. E. Wanner and L. R. Gleitman). Cambridge University Press, Cambridge.

Goody, E. N. (ed.) (1978). Introduction to *Questions and Politeness: Strategies in Social Interaction.* Cambridge University Press, Cambridge.

Halliday, M. A. K. (1975). *Learning How to Mean – Explorations in the Development of Language.* Edward Arnold, London.

—— and Hassan, R. (1976). *Cohesion in English.* Longman, London.

Hargreaves, D. (1967). *Social Relations in a Secondary School.* Routledge and Kegan Paul, London.

Hart, K. M. (ed.) (1981). *Children's Understanding of Mathematics: 11–16.* John Murray, London.

Heckhausen, H. (1982). The development of achievement motivation. In *Review of Child Development Research* (ed. W. W. Hartup), 6, 600–68.

Hewison, J. and Tizard, J. (1980). Parental involvement in reading attainment. *British Journal of Educational Psychology*, 50, 209–15.

Hickman, M. E. (1985). The implications of discourse skills in Vygotsky's development theory. In *Culture, Communication and Cognition. Vygotskian Perspectives* (ed. J. V. Wertsch). Cambridge University Press, Cambridge.

Hilgard, E. R. (ed.) (1964). *Theories of Learning and Instruction.* University of Chicago Press, Chicago, Illinois.

Holt, J. (1967). *How Children Fail.* Pitman, New York.

Hundeide, K. (1985). The tacit background of children's judgements. In *Culture, Communication and Cognition. Vygotskian Perspectives* (ed. J. V. Wertsch). Cambridge University Press, Cambridge.

Isaacs, S. (1936). *Intellectual Growth in Young Children.* Routledge and Sons Ltd., London.

Johnson-Laird, P. N. (1983). *Mental Models.* Cambridge University Press, Cambridge.

Kail, R. (1979). *The Development of Memory in Children.* Freeman, San Francisco.

Kaplan, E. L. (1969). Cited in P. Menyuk, *The Acquisition and Development of Language*, p. 273. Prentice-Hall, Englewood Cliffs, NJ.

Karmiloff-Smith, A. (1979). *A Functional Approach to Child Language. A Study of Determiners and Reference.* Cambridge University Press, Cambridge.

Kempe, R. S. and Kempe, C. H. (1978). *Child Abuse.* Fontana/Open Books, London.

Kempton, W. (1980). The rhythmic basis of interactional micro-synchrony. In *The Relationship of Verbal and Nonverbal Communication* (ed. M. Ritchie-Key). Mouton, The Hague.

Keough, B. K. (1982). Children's temperament and teachers' decisions. In *Temperamental Differences in Infants and Young Children* (ed. R. Porter and G. M. Collins). Pitman, London.

Kochman (1981). In *Language in School and Community* (ed. N. Mercer). Edward Arnold, London.

Labov, W. (1969). The logic of nonstandard English. Reprinted in *Language and Social Context* (ed. P. Giglioli). Penguin, Harmondsworth.

Light, P., Buckingham, N. and Roberts, A. H. (1979). The conservation task as an interactional setting. *British Journal of Educational Psychology*, 49, 304–10.

—— and Gilmour, A. (1983). Conservation or conversation? Contextual facilitation of inappropriate conservation judgements. *Journal of Experimental Child Psychology*, 36, 356–63.

List, G. (1963). Cited in *The Relationship of Verbal and Nonverbal Communication* (ed. M. Ritchie-Key), p. 369. Mouton, The Hague.

Lunzer, E. A. (1973). Formal reasoning: a re-appraisal. Reprinted in *Cognitive Development in the School Years* (ed. A. Floyd), 1979. Croom-Helm, London.

McNeill, D. (1970). *The Acquisition of Language*, MIT Press, Cambridge, Mass.

Menyuk, P. (1971). *The Acquisition and Development of Language.* Prentice-Hall, Englewood Cliffs, NJ.

Mercer, N. and Edwards, D. (1981). Ground rules for mutual understanding. In *Language in School and Community* (ed. N. Mercer). Edward Arnold, London.

Miller, G. A. (1956). The magical number seven plus or minus two. Some limits on our capacity for processing information. *Psychological Review*, 63, 81–97.

Mohr, C. (1965). 'Head Start' plan for pupils begins. In *New York Times*, 19 May.

Murphy, C. M. and Wood, D. J. (1982). Learning through media: a comparison of 4- to 8-year-old children's responses to filmed and pictorial instruction. *International Journal of Behavioral Development*, 5 (2), 195–216.

Newson, J. and Newson, E. (1974). Cultural aspects of child-rearing in an English-speaking world. In *The Integration of a Child into a Social World.* Cambridge University Press, Cambridge.

Nuthall, G. and Church, J. (1973). Experimental studies of teaching behavior. In *Towards a Science of Teaching* (ed. G. Chanan). NFER, Slough.

Olson, D. R. (1977). Oral and written language and the cognitive processes of children. *Journal of Communication*, 27 (3), 10–26.

Opie, I. and Opie, P. (1959). *The Lore and Language of Schoolchildren.* Oxford University Press, London.

Palinscar, A. S. and Brown, A. L. (1984). Reciprocal teaching of comprehension-fostering and monitoring activities. *Cognition and Instruction*. Erlbaum, Hillsdale, NJ.

Pavlov, I. P. (1927). *Conditioned Reflexes*. (trans. S. V. Anrep). Oxford University Press, London.

Perera, K. (1984). *Children's Writing and Reading. Analysing Classroom Language*. Basil Blackwell, Oxford.

Piaget, J. (1967). *Six Psychological Studies*. London University Press, London.

—— (1971). *Structuralism*. Routledge and Kegan Paul, London.

—— and Inhelder, B. (1969). *The Psychology of the Child*. Routledge and Kegan Paul, London.

Pilling, D. and Pringle, M. K. (1978). *Controversial Issues in Child Development*. Paul Elek, London.

Redfield, D. L. and Rousseau, E. W. (1981). A meta-analysis of experimental research on teacher questioning behavior. *Review of Educational Research*, 51, 237–45.

Resnick, L. B. (ed.) (1976). *The Nature of Intelligence*. Erlbaum, Hillside, NJ.

Robinson, M. P. (1981). Language development in young children. In *Psychology for Teachers* (ed. D. Fontana). British Psychological Society and Macmillan Press, London.

—— (1986). Children's understanding of the distinction between messages and meanings: emergence and implications. In *Children of Social Worlds* (ed. M. Richards and P. Light). Polity Press in association with Basil Blackwell, Oxford.

Romaine, S. (1984). *The Language of Children and Adolescents. The Acquisition of Communicative Competence*. Basil Blackwell, Oxford.

Rose, S. and Blank, M. (1974). The potency of context in children's cognition. *Child Development*, 45, 499–502.

Rosenthal, R. and Jacobson, L. (1968). *Pygmalion in the Classroom*. Holt, Rinehart and Winston, London.

Rowe, M. B. (1974). Wait-time and rewards as instructional variables, their influence on language, logic and fate control. I: Wait time. *Journal of Research in Science Teaching*, 11, 81–94.

Schwartzman, H. B. (1978). *Transformations: The Anthropology of Children's Play*. Plenum Press, New York.

Schwebel, M. and Raph, T. (1974). *Piaget in the Classroom*. Routledge and Kegan Paul, London.

Serpell, R. (1976). *Culture's Influence on Behaviour*. Methuen, London.

Sigel, I. E. and McGillicuddy-Delisi, I. (in press). Parents as teachers of their children. In *The Development of Oral and Written Language: Readings in Developmental and Applied Linguistics*. Ablex, Norwood, NJ.

Skemp, R.R. (1971). *The Psychology of Learning Mathematics*. Penguin, Harmondsworth.

Skinner, B.F. (1938). *The Behavior of Organisms*. Appleton-Century-Crofts, New York.

—— (1968). *The Technology of Teaching*. Appleton-Century-Crofts, New York.

Snow, R. E. and Yallow, E. (1982). Education and intelligence. In *Handbook of Human Intelligence* (ed. R. J. Sternberg). Cambridge University Press, Cambridge.

Swift, J. N. and Gooding, C. T. (1983). Interaction of wait time, feedback and questioning instruction in middle school science teaching. *Journal of*

Research in Science Teaching, 20, 721–30.

Tizard, B. and Hodges, J. (1978). The effect of early institutional rearing on the development of eight-year-old children. *Journal of Child Psychology and Psychiatry*, 15, 99–118.

Underwood, G. (1979). Memory systems and the reading process. In *Applied Problems in Memory* (ed. M. M. Gruneberg and P. E. Morris). Academic Press, London.

Van De Groot, A. D. (1965). *Thought and Choice in Chess*. Mouton, The Hague.

Vurpillot, E. (1976). *The Visual World of the Child*. Allen and Unwin, London.

Vygotsky, L. S. (1962). *Thought and Language*. Wiley, New York.

Walkerdine, V. (1982). From context to text: a psychosemiotic approach to abstract thought. In *Children Thinking Through Language* (ed. M. Beveridge). Edward Arnold, London.

Wardhaugh, R. (1985). *How Conversation Works*. Basil Blackwell, Oxford.

Wason, P. C. and Johnson-Laird, P. N. (1972). *Psychology of Reasoning*. Batsford, London.

Wells, C. G. (1981). *Learning through Interaction: the Study of Language Development*. Cambridge University Press, Cambridge.

—— and Raben, B. (1978). *Children Learning to Read*. Final Report to SSRC, no. HR/3797/1.

Wertsch, J.V. (ed.) (1985). *Culture, Communication and Cognition. Vygotskian Perspectives*. Cambridge University Press, Cambridge.

Wiener, M., Shilkret, R. and Devoe, S. (1980). Acquisition of communication competence: is language enough? In *The Relationship of Verbal and Nonverbal Communication* (ed. M. Richie-Key). Mouton, The Hague.

Wolters, M. A. D. (1986). Rules in arithmetic. Learning the basic facts. In *Pragmatics and Education* (ed. F. Lowenthal and F. Vandamme). Plenum Press, New York.

Wood, D. J. (in press). Instruction, learning and deafness. In *Learning and Instruction* (ed. E. De Corte, J. G. L. C. Lodewijks, R. Parmentier and P. Span). Pergamon, Oxford, and Leuven University Press, Leuven.

——, Bruner, J. S. and Ross, G. (1976). The role of tutoring in problem solving. *Journal of Child Psychology and Psychiatry*, 17, 2, 89–100.

——, McMahon, L. and Cranstoun, Y. (1980). *Working with Under Fives*. Basil Blackwell, Oxford.

—— and Wood, H. A. (in press). Questioning versus student initiative. In *Questioning and Discussion* (ed. J. Dillon). Ablex, Norwood, NJ.

——, Wood, H., Griffiths, A. J., and Howarth, I. (1986). *Teaching and Talking with Deaf Children*. Wiley, London.

——, Wood, H. A. and Middleton, D. J. (1978). An experimental evaluation of four face-to-face teaching strategies. *International Journal of Behavioral Development*, 1 (2), 131–47.

Wood, H. A. and Wood, D. J. (1983). Questioning the preschool child. *Educational Review*, 35, Special Issue (15), 149–62.

——, Wood, D. J., Kingsmill, M. C., French, J. R. and Howarth, S. P. (1984). The mathematical achievements of deaf children from different educational environments. *British Journal of Educational Psychology*, 54, 254–64.

Author index

Subject index

reading 177ff, 219ff
see also instruction, scaffolding,
    questions
teaching 'styles'/strategies 75ff
thinking
    abstract 183ff
    adolescent 150ff
    egocentric *see* egocentrism
    non-verbal 27ff
    verbal 26ff

see also logic, reasoning, stages of
    development

writing
    self-correction in 163ff
    self-regulation in 161ff
    see also talking

zone of proximal development 24ff,
    78, 196ff

666003